THE BRANCACCI CHAPEL

UMBERTO BALDINI | ORNELLA CASAZZA

THE BRANCACCI CHAPEL

HARRY N. ABRAMS, INC. | PUBLISHERS | NEW YORK

Translated from the Italian by Lysa Hochroth, with Marion L. Grayson

Editor, English-language edition: Marion L. Grayson
Designer, English-language edition: Judith Michael
Photographs by Antonio Quattrone

LIBRARY OF CONGRESS CATALOGING-IN-PUBLICATION DATA

Baldini, Umberto.
[Cappella Brancacci. English]
The Brancacci Chapel/Umberto Baldini, Ornella Casazza.
p. cm.
Translation of: La Cappella Brancacci.
Includes bibliographical references and index.
ISBN 0-8109-3120-6
1. Mural painting and decoration, Italian—Italy—Florence.
2. Mural painting and decoration, Renaissance—Italy—Florence.
3. Cappella Brancacci (Santa Maria del Carmine, Church: Florence, Italy) I. Casazza, Ornella. II. Title.
ND2757.F5B313 1992
751.6′2′094551—dc20 91-44033
CIP

Published in 1992 by Harry N. Abrams, Incorporated, New York
A Times Mirror Company

Printed and bound in Italy

CONTENTS

The Frescoes of the Brancacci Chapel

The History of the Brancacci Chapel and Its Restoration

Appendixes

This book, to which will be added a second publication containing the documentation of the analyses, studies and technical and scientific operational interventions in preparation for and during the course of the work, constitutes the final act of a project—that of the restoration of the Brancacci Chapel in the Church of the Madonna del Carmine in Florence—in which Olivetti has been interested since the beginning of the 1980s and has directly participated from the first moment of the operation.

We had already been involved for several years in the problems of restoration of great pictorial works of art needing intervention, dedicating to them one track of our activity in the field of art, the other being that of exhibitions of particular historical and scientific significance based on studies that explore new ground in research or formulate new critical theories. It seems in fact proper, as a large company engaged in an area of advanced technology, to give our attention to and assume some direct responsibility on behalf of the artistic patrimony of our country, so threatened, particularly in the last ten years, by an increasingly degraded atmospheric environment and by a perhaps too disorderly approach. Besides, the Brancacci Chapel presented a particularly urgent problem; the monument, nearly miraculous in coming down to us, is of the highest importance to the art of the Renaissance. It has either inspired or contributed to the formation of all the great artists of the epoch, from Raphael to Michelangelo. As Vasari wrote: "All the most celebrated sculptors and painters who worked and studied in that Chapel became excellent and illustrious."

The group of technicians organized to undertake the restoration was the best for the circumstances that could possibly be imagined. They came in fact from the miracle of perseverance that was the rescue and restoration of the frescoes following the flood of Florence in 1966. The group was also involved in another rescue, that of the painted wood *Crucifix* by Cimabue (Florence, Museo dell'Opera di Santa Croce), so badly damaged yet still so grand and overwhelmingly vital. Olivetti obtained some of these salvaged masterpieces to send to the great museums around the world in a memorable exhibition illustrating the work of recuperation in progress with new technologies of intervention on the part of the Florentine team led by Professor Umberto Baldini. The exhibit was also a recognition by Italy of the generosity, promptness and abundance of assistance manifested the day after the flood by the whole civilized world, which was so liberal with its help.

The enlightened administration of the Florentine Superintendency of Artistic and Historical Properties, the interested management of the Director of the Central Institute for Restoration and the support of the Ministry quickly made it clear that it would be possible to conduct the Brancacci Chapel project in a completely new way, on the basis of studies and examinations, using the most up-to-date methodologies of intervention and providing computerized analysis and documentation of every moment of the operation. Therefore, the convergence of these circumstances led to our participation in an enterprise that—even taking into account the possibility of so many unforeseen difficulties and the long duration of an initiative on a work of such complexity and quality, with so many problems—still merited being confronted.

The frescoes, on first examination, offered many pressing reasons for concern: diffuse and tenacious darkening, thickened surface areas with marks and swellings that indicated the precarious condition of the supporting walls. There were areas of obvious loss, poorly restored, and layers of organic substances over the frescoes impregnated by candle soot, as well as damage from the fire of 1771, not only from smoke but also from the superheating of the walls and the opening up of the destroyed church to the weather. Other damages had been caused by the crowds of devoted believers in the celebration of their rituals and by the many interventions carried out over the centuries, including structural. All were troublesome signs, and even more serious damages would be found.

The project did not go forward blindly, however. There were accounts from the recent past of examinations made in the chapel by Superintendent Ugo Procacci (1932), as well as his report to the Superior Council of the Ministry (1969). This report indicated the main directions to proceed, before beginning the actual restoration, in order to ascertain what possibly remained of the original parts that were damaged or presumably destroyed. In the first issue (1984) of our *Quaderni del restauro* (*Notebooks on Restoration*), accompanying and illustrating Olivetti initiatives in this field, we presented the program, laid out by Professor Baldini and given unanimous approval, which outlined the essential questions to be probed and resolved. Also reported there was news of important discoveries brought to light before the start of the restoration by the removal of the oversized eighteenth-century altar. Installed in the chapel before the fire, the altar had preserved behind it some areas of the original fresco painting on the back wall. Recovered were the jamb decorations of the original Gothic window including two beautiful heads with the colors nearly intact, as well as fragments of a fresco scene for which the lower part of the original window had been sacrificed. The intervention therefore presented not just a simple cleaning of the painted areas and a conservative restoration of the rest, but rather the possiblity of renewing, even if not completely, a complex work done at different times by different artists under dramatically changed circumstances with respect to the initial conditions. Moreover, this work had suffered irretrievable losses and grave mishandling over the centuries in which Masaccio's star was dimmed by critical opinion, up until his historical "resurrection."

For all these reasons, on this probably never-to-be-repeated occasion of general consensus about the necessity for intervention, together with the philological, technical and historical implications, and also for the possibility of conducting an intervention at the highest level of conditions that science and technology could now allow, Olivetti, in offering its collaboration and its support, decided to shirk nothing in its responsibilities for the operation in the way of studies, research and experience, and of precise documentation for every moment of the project in each of its successive passages. In this way, the fresco cycle could reemerge from its mortifying conditions with the stupendous force of its original artistic language. It did not seem possible, in fact, not to allow our generation, after centuries of errors and obscuration, to be able to see it finally restored to its original state and its true grandeur.

This book, the work of the two individuals most responsible for the restoration, is the first element of the documentation developed. In it, many details from each of the fresco scenes are reproduced in their actual size, on a scale of one-to-one, so they may be viewed without the constraints their reduction in size would impose. A film made for us in the course of the restoration work by Folco Quilici will be a second element showing the succession of progress from the first moment to its conclusion. The third element is the collection of the operational data from the computer to make it available for future research. Finally, the fourth element will be a volume of technical and scientific studies, to which I referred at the beginning and in which we will give account of all the requests made for collaboration, of the involvement that was instituted and of the large numbers of people who responded.

In taking leave of this project, I am able to say that Olivetti has done its duty as the supporter and the coordinator of the research projects. Art historians, the worldwide press and other professional people have witnessed the excellent results and given them unanimous approval. But I wish to add that, with this restoration project, we have also wanted to indicate a path, leaving aside old and new disputes, public and private, that the grave condition of the artistic patrimony of Italy cannot allow. Only by working together, without complexes, without arrogance and subjection, giving everyone his due, and forming integrated groups that had homogeneity, competence and dedication to the work, were we able to think of approaching a masterpiece that demanded—in this case with desperate urgency—the attention of a country, a culture and a technology sometimes too distracted and in pursuit of often insignificant objectives.

CARLO DE BENEDETTI
President of the Olivetti Corporation

When a restoration project is begun or an exhibition is opened, an introduction by the superintendent in charge is customary. In the specific case of the Brancacci Chapel, restored to world culture after an intervention lasting seven years, to introduce the volume that—edited with admirable diligence by the director of works, Ornella Casazza—officially illustrates the restoration, presenting its history and giving account of the technical difficulties overcome, the scientific innovations introduced and the philological augmentations produced, is not easy.

What else can be said, really, in addition to what has already been stated on so many public occasions? How can one comment on an undertaking that everyone knows to be one of the most important in our time? We would want to put forth some laudatory hyperbole, the customary *tabula gratulatoria*, the underlining—opportunely emphatic—of the importance for the city of Florence of such a clamorous and so long-awaited restoration. To avoid trite phrases and routine formulas, I shall limit myself to three considerations, all absolutely clear and, in my opinion, all appropriate.

The first concerns the paintings on which the restoration of the Brancacci Chapel was focused. In Italy at this time, there are a great many masterpieces of mural painting being worked on, some nearly finished and others still in progress, that are basically a summary of the history of art. It is sufficient to mention specifically *The Last Supper* by Leonardo, the Sistine Chapel frescoes by Michelangelo, the Camera degli Sposi frescoes by Mantegna and the Brancacci Chapel frescoes by Masaccio and Masolino. We can add to the list the restoration—at this writing not yet begun—of *The Legend of the True Cross* by Piero della Francesca in the Church of San Francesco at Arezzo, for which exhaustive and detailed examinations, never before today demanded in a situation of this kind, have already been produced and committed to a monumental catalogue.

Facing the challenges of these pictorial giants of Western civilization, our generation has assumed a very clear responsibility. Historians will one day debate the quality and appropriateness of the interventions recorded above, but, for now, we are limited to taking action on the phenomenon. The culture of our time has seen the necessity for recovering and preserving, in the best condition for the longest possible time, a more exact reading of the basic documentation—the genetic codes, one might say—of a pictorial history that involves everyone and also affects everyone. Perhaps the increased numbers of restorations of great pictorial cycles at the troubled end of this century are meant as an epochal inventory, as attempts to preserve (through safeguarding the greatest symbols of art history) a patrimony that we have never known to be in such a fragile and threatened condition as now. This could be one way—although not the only one—to explain the crowding of so many large restoration projects into these years.

The second consideration is of a more pragmatic kind. Of the interventions already carried out, half were financed by the Olivetti Corporation — those of the Brancacci Chapel, *The Last Supper* by Leonardo and the Camera degli Sposi decoration by Mantegna. This confirms a "strategic" patronage that for years has seen Olivetti in the vanguard of the important politics of the cultural heritage, actually on the "cutting edge" of that alliance between the public and the private sectors for the protection and improvement of the historical patrimony of the nation that is, well considered, one of the most significant innovations of our time.

A third and final consideration is in order—a consideration that I wish to emphasize with proper force by virtue of my role as Superintendent for the Artistic and Historical Properties of Florence. The intervention on the Brancacci Chapel represents a high point in the Florentine history of the restoration of frescoes. Moreover it is the synthesis of an ancient tradition developed in our city through an uninterrupted chain of experience and research. While it is true that the restoration of the Life of Saint Peter frescoes by Masaccio and Masolino bears in the epigraph the stamp of the Central Institute for Restoration in Rome (because Umberto Baldini, the initiator and supervisor of the intervention, was in those years the director of that glorious Institute which he involved in a scientific capacity), it is also true that Florentines, deeply rooted in the culture and in the practice of Florentine restoration, are protagonists in the Brancacci Chapel story: from Baldini himself and Ornella Casazza, the director of works, to the restorers Sabino Giovannoni and Marcello Chemeri; from Paolo Parrini, who now directs the Syremont, to the scientific experts of the University of Florence, Enzo Ferroni, Mario Fondelli, Vito Cappellini, Tito Arecchi, Lamberto Ippolito and Giuseppe Molesini; and from the experts of the Opificio, Mauro Matteini and Arcangelo Moles, to the many others who dedicated the best of their professionalism to this masterpiece by Masaccio and Masolino.

Above all, behind the restoration of the Brancacci, is the store of technical knowledge and theoretical development that increased greatly in this city during the second half of the century: from the experimental stage of the laboratory founded by Superintendent Ugo Procacci in the early 1930s; to the exhibitions after the War; to the superhuman interventions after the flood; to *Florence Restored* (1972) and *Scientific Method* (1982), the memorable exhibitions organized by Umberto Baldini at the time he was Superintendent of the Opificio and of the Fortezza da Basso; to the essays on method also published by Baldini (*Teoria del restauro e unità di metodologia*, 2 vols. Florence, 1978 and 1981).

In a certain sense the reopening of the Brancacci Chapel to the public is the crowning of a great epoch in the history of Italian restoration. My satisfaction as a historian of art, as a Florentine and as Superintendent lies in the knowledge that the "culture" which produced the intervention in the Brancacci Chapel lives on in the public civic structure of the restoration and lives, above all, in the young "company" of workers coming out of the school of the Opificio, that today constitutes the operative arm of the Superintendency.

ANTONIO PAOLUCCI
Superintendent of Artistic and Historical Properties of Florence and Pistoia

ACKNOWLEDGMENTS

At the end of the project the authors would like to remember and thank the many who have worked in various ways and at different times on, and made precious contributions to, the restoration of the Brancacci Chapel.

The Ministry of Cultural Properties: ministers A. Gullotti, C. Vizzini, V. Bono-Parrino, F. Facchiano, and directors-general: G. Triches and F. Sisinni; R. Zorzi, P. Viti, M. Broggi of the Office of Cultural Relations of Olivetti; the Carmelite Fathers of the Church of the Madonna del Carmine; the restorers M. Chemeri and S. Giovannoni; G. Botticelli, F. Bandini and A. Pandolfo of the Opificio delle Pietre Dure (O.P.D.), Florence; G. Germani, B. Poggio, P. Mariotti, L. Cinelli and F. Sereni; A. Quattrone, P. Rossin and C. Rocca; G. Accardo, P. Baldi, M. Caldonato, M. Bottoni, G. Fabretti, C. Giacobini, V. Santini, F. Talarico and G. Vigliano of the Central Institute for Restoration (I.C.R.), Rome; M. Matteini and G. Mores; C. Biliotti of the Opificio delle Pietre Dure, Florence; U. Procacci, Florence; D. Gioseffi, G. Bassani, M. Calvesi, M. D'Elia, M. Rosci and B. Toscano of the Regional Committee for the Artistic and Historic Properties of the National Council for Cultural and Environmental Properties; L. Berti, A. Paolucci, B. Santi of the Office of the Superintendency for Artistic and Historical Properties of Florence and Pistoia; A. Calvani, P. Mazzoni, R. Pentrella and B. Pacciani of the Office of the Superintendent of Environmental and Architectural Properties of Florence; F. Puccinelli and F. Scalia of the Office of Fine Arts of the Commune of Florence; P. Parrini, G. Pizzigoni, E. Mello, G. Perucca and V. Massa of the Syremont, Milan; E. Ferroni, P. Baglioni, G. Sarti of the Department of Chemistry, University of Florence; V. Cappellini and A. Nozzoli of the Department of Engineering, University of Florence; M. Fondelli, L. Ippolito, I. Chiaverini, W. Ferri and M. Quattrone of the Department of Civil Engineering, University of Florence; P. A. Rossi of the Conservation Department of Architectural and Environmental Resources, Polytechnic Institute of Turin; M. Bacci, F. Baldini and R. Carlà of the Institute of Research on Electromagnetic Waves of the National Center for Restoration (C.N.R.), Florence; T. Arecchi, G. Molesini and F. Quercioli of the National Institute of Optics, Florence; L. Masotti of the University of Florence; R. Innocenti, Florence, G. P. Mancini, Florence; F. Merlo and G. M. Garbasso of the Donegani Institute, Novara; C. Sorlini and G. Ranalli of the Department of Nutritional and Microbiological Science and Technology of the University of Milan; S. Sfrecola of Larac, Genoa; V. Magnelli, A. Cabrucci, P. Aminti of Galileo Siscam, Florence; V. Alinari of Editech, Florence; F. Quilici of Moana, Rome; The Carlo Erba Corporation, Milan; The Sollazzini Company, Florence; Dalmine Scaffolding, Florence; C. Caselli of Decoart, Florence; A. Zecchi of Florence; B. Rabatti of the S.A.R.I. of Florence; R. Ruggeri of Ruggeri Upholstery, Florence; G. Scheggi of the Scheggi Construction Firm, Florence; and the Gino Poggi Company, Florence.

NOTE ON TEXT FORMAT

This book, which documents analytically the pictorial decoration of the Brancacci Chapel on the occasion of its restoration, has been organized to create the most immediate relationship possible with the frescoes, allowing them to unfold sequentially with the same "surprise" that always fascinates visitors to the Chapel.

Each individual scene is illustrated according to the same procedure. First, the complete image appears at the beginning of the commentary on technique, iconography, state of preservation, alterations and critical hypotheses concerning the painting. From the complete image one moves to close-ups of parts of the scene and finally to a number of enlarged details grouped together, at which point the rhythm of the sequence changes abruptly. The details are reproduced in the same dimensions as in the fresco (1:1) and isolated from each other by black interleafing. They explore the painting analytically, moving from left to right and from top to bottom, focusing on various parts of the figures and especially on the heads.

Following this systematic presentation of the individual scenes are two essays by the authors that analyze the many problems relative to the restoration and document the general elements of art-historical interpretation.

The texts of the commentaries
for the fresco scenes in the Brancacci Chapel
are by Ornella Casazza.

THE FRESCOES OF THE BRANCACCI CHAPEL

The Brancacci Chapel, pictorial decoration of the left wall

The Brancacci Chapel, pictorial decoration of the right wall

MASOLINO

Adam and Eve: The Fall

Pilaster on the right side of the chapel's entrance arch, upper register, 2.14 × 0.89 meters

Two trees function as wings and backdrop for the episode related in Genesis:[1]

Then the Lord God planted a garden in Eden, in the east, and he placed there the man whom he had formed. Out of the ground the Lord God made various trees grow that were delightful to look at and good for food, with the tree of life in the middle of the garden and the tree of the knowledge of good and bad (2:8–9). . . . The woman saw that the tree was good for food, pleasing to the eyes, and desirable for gaining wisdom. So she took some of its fruit and ate it; then she also gave some to her husband, who was with her, and he ate it (3:6).

The tree around which the Serpent of Temptation twines, and from which Eve has picked the fruit in her right hand, is a fig tree with characteristic lobed leaves. The fruit she holds and others visible among the leafy branches directly above her retain only traces of their original reddish-brown color.

According to a nineteenth-century description of the scene by G. B. Cavalcaselle (1864), there was once a wealth of foliage and grass that has now completely disappeared. This can also be seen in the illustrations for his text, which reproduce original engravings of the chapel decorations by Carlo Lasinio (1757–1839) and his son Giovanni Paolo (1796–1855).[2] Cavalcaselle wrote: "The flowering branches laden with fruit extend into the blue of the sky. A small expanse of rolling hills, a verdant field and a few trees punctuating the blue sky form the Garden of Eden, whose background and figures have lost part of the freshness of their color."

The condition of the fresco in Cavalcaselle's time would not have been very good, because it had already been reduced in height by thirty-three centimeters, and additions and corrections made to embellish and complete the scene, in the eighteenth-century renovation of the chapel's entrance arch (1746–48). After its recent cleaning, however, imprints of leaves and grass, superficially worn away over time, reappeared in the ground area. These had been executed probably *a secco* (painted on the dry fresco surface) over the black monochrome background.

Not only is the Biblical text faithfully interpreted, but also the traditional pictorial and sculptural iconography for this event is perpetuated in the placement of the two figures in a garden. The identification of the Tree of Knowledge as a fig tree was probably Mediterranean or Eastern, while the "apple" came out of a more northern tradition that spread during the International Gothic period.[3]

Masolino thus relied on the most current and traditional iconography of his time, and the two figures of Adam and Eve exhibit in their gestures and poses the genteel, courtly ambiance which has always contrasted this scene with the one opposite, painted by Masaccio. The latter is valued as a unique and extraordinary manifestation of new cultural and formal constraints of spiritual "harmony" and technical ability. "It is at this point that the 'naturalism' of Masolino and that of Masaccio seem to be two 'idealisms' as opposing and noncommunicating as they are different in the way belief in 'nature' was conceived of in each artist's mind."[4]

Nevertheless, this did not prevent Masolino from clothing his figures of Adam and Eve in a "classicism" of pure beauty. Adam has features somewhat reminiscent of Tiberius: a pointed oval face framed with short tufts of hair adhering to the skull and falling over the neck and forehead to form a notched effect at the temple, a decisive nose, a small mouth with sinuous lips, and a bold chin. Similarly, the body of Eve already exhibits a plasticity and pearly light that evoke a Classical statue.[5]

The traditional attribution of this scene to Masolino in the commentaries on Vasari, as well as in various other treatises and guides (L. Lanzi, 1795; C.F. Rumohr, 1827; J. Burckhardt, 1855; and G. Milanesi, 1906), was overturned in favor of Masaccio and the painting seen as an early work still influenced by the "master's" style by a number of scholars, beginning with A.H. Springer (1855) and G.B. Cavalcaselle (1864), followed by W. Lübke (1887), W.J. Stillmann (1889), A. Schmarsow (1895 and 1928), Brockhaus (1930), F.X. Kraus (1908), K. Escher (1922), W. Bode (1923), and finally by R. van Marle (1928) and Oertel (1933).

Nevertheless it was returned to Masolino by A. Zahn (1869), H. Delaborde (1876), A. Woltmann and K. Woermann (1882), B. Marrai (1891), A. Philippi (1897), F. Knudtzon (1900), M.K. Kreutz (1902), and then, decisively, by B. Berenson (1902), A.H. Layard (1902), P. Toesca (1908) and A. Venturi (1911). They were then followed by other scholars, who took the scene as a representative example by which to define the difference in Masaccio's artistic language.

The scene, painted on the face of the entrance pilaster of the chapel, does not have a white frame as in the scene facing it of *The Expulsion*. Rather, the gray-black color of the background extends onto the left side of the projecting architectural pilaster to meet in the corner juncture with the painted pilaster that delimits the adjacent *Raising of Tabitha* scene.

In the installation of the new entrance arch, the upper portion of the fresco, comprised of tree foliage and the sky which presumably appeared above it, was destroyed. Also lost was a considerable patch in the upper right-hand corner below the base of the pilaster capital, which had been immediately redone by copying onto new intonaco. During our work, this was eliminated when signs of the red underdrawing (*sinopia*) were discovered below it on the rough plaster (*arriccio*). In restoring this lost area, we were therefore able to make a formal restitution of colors more respectful of and closer to the original design.

Masolino created the flesh tones with an underlayer of very light green mixed with yellow ocher, which can be seen showing through on the figure of Eve.[6] A similar preparation of deeper and darker intensity was used for the figure of Adam, as it was for Adam in Masaccio's *Expulsion*, according to the custom of the time for distinguishing masculine bodies from the more delicate, pale female ones.

Leaves superimposed over the figures, which had rendered them more "modest" prior to the current restoration, were not original but, most assuredly, were added in tempera sometime after 1652.[7] Eve, however, despite her leafy branch, was visibly nude, whereas Adam was better "covered" by a greater quantity of foliage.[8]

The black color of the background, which

chemical analysis proved to be *nero vite*, has suffered much over time from abrasions and fading, owing not only to its application in an impalpably thin layer but also to a diffuse whitening following superficial abrasions undoubtedly caused by previous cleanings.

The scene was created in six work sessions or *giornate* in the following sequence, starting at the top: (1) the sky, the leafy branches and fruits of the two trees, (2) the serpent in a *giornata* including Eve's face, (3) Adam's head, (4) Eve's body, (5) Adam's body, and (6) part of Adam's left hand (the fingers) with its corresponding background area.

With regard to the black background, already mentioned as extending around the left side of the pilaster projection, it was found to be overlaying the painted pilaster to the right of the Tabitha scene at the juncture of the intonaco for the fifth *giornata*. This gives important testimony proving that *The Raising of Tabitha* preceded in execution the scene under examination, which was therefore the last to be painted in the second register.[9]

[1] Biblical citations were taken from *The New American Bible* (Confraternity of Christian Doctrine), The Catholic Press and World Publishing Company, Cleveland and New York, 1971.

[2] The Lasinio engravings were copied in reduced size by other engravers. See G. P. Lasinio and C. Lasinio, *Pitture a fresco esistenti in alcune chiese fiorentine, 1818–1832*, and *Peintures de Masaccio, Masolino*, Florence, 1812.

[3] As in the case, for example, of the pilaster decorations on the facade of Orvieto Cathedral by Lorenzo Maitani (begun 1310), where *The Fall* takes place under a large fig tree around which the serpent is entwined (R. Wittkower, *Dall'antichità al Novecento*, Turin, 1977, p. 45). This is true even earlier, in the thirteenth-century *Genesis* mosaics in the dome of the narthex of San Marco, Venice, where the Creation scenes are surrounded by many different varieties of leafy trees, while in the scenes of the Temptation and Fall, the fig tree's presence is dominant. Only much later did the tradition change, with the fig tree replaced by an apple or orange tree. There is a pomegranate bush amid a row of orange trees in *The Expulsion from Paradise* (1445) by Giovanni di Paolo (predella fragment. The Metropolitan Museum of Art, New York, Robert Lehman Collection).

[4] R. Longhi, "Fatti di Masolino e di Masaccio," *La Critica d'Arte*, 3–4, 1940, pp. 145ff.

[5] P. Bocci Pacini, "Umanesimo in Masolino," *Gli Uffizi, Studi e Ricerche*, no. 5, 1988, p. 22.

[6] See C. Cennini, *The Craftsman's Handbook* (*Il libro dell'arte*, late 14th c.), trans. D. V. Thompson, Jr., New York, 1933, pp. 45–47 and 93–95.

[7] For further discussion of this, see entry following for *The Expulsion*, as well as pp. 307–9.

[8] See p. 31, note 5.

[9] See pp. 293–96 for the sequence of execution for the scenes.

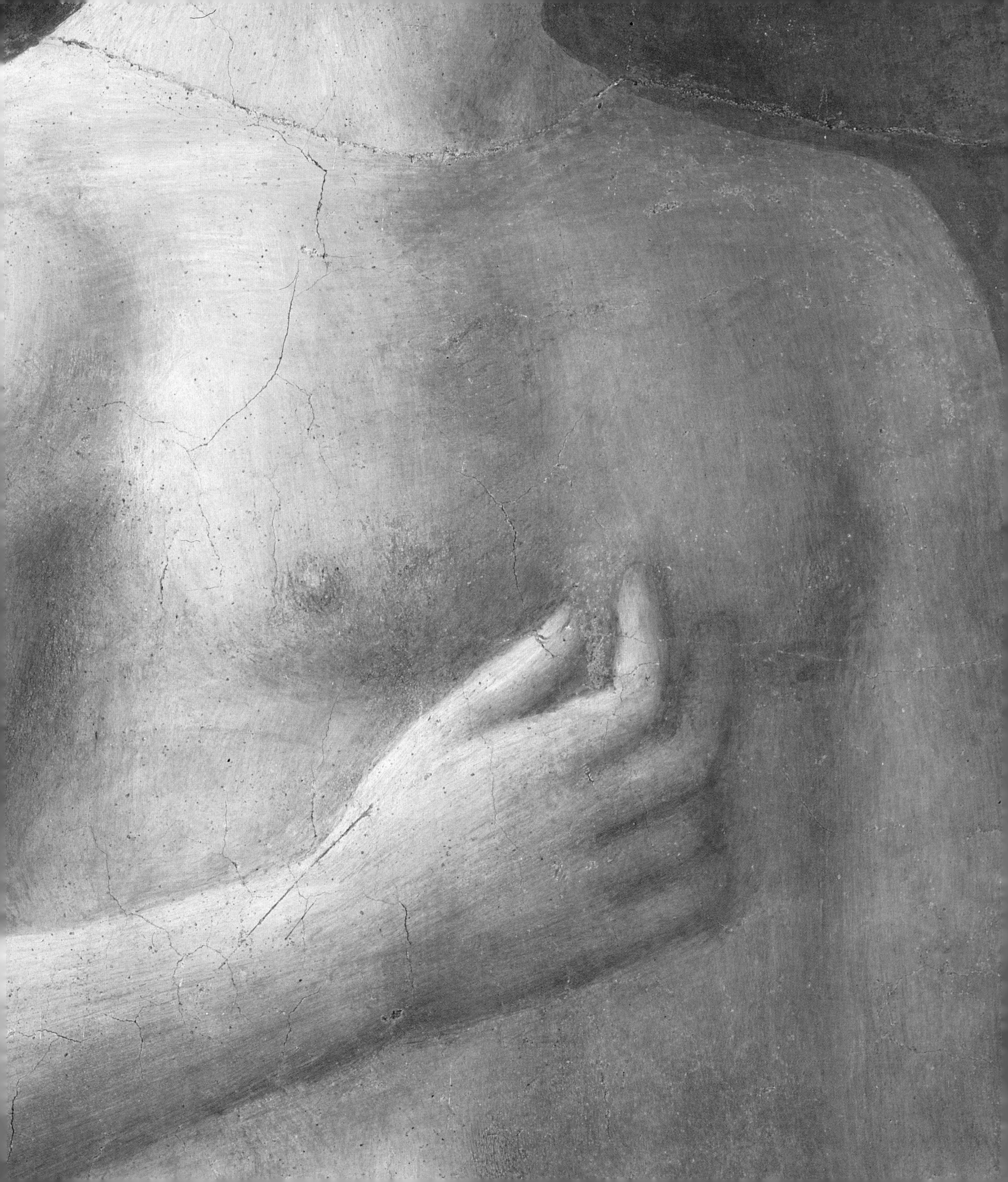

MASACCIO

Adam and Eve: The Expulsion

Pilaster on the left side of the chapel's entrance arch, second register, 2.14 × 0.90 meters

As in Masolino's *The Fall* opposite it, the upper part of this fresco was reduced by a good thirty-three centimeters where the base of the new round arch of the entrance was installed in an architectural renovation of the chapel in the eighteenth century (1746–48). The amount of the reduction can be deduced from comparing the height of the adjacent *Tribute Money* and that of *The Expulsion*, which should match up in the corner with the top of the painted pilaster, as it does in the register below between *Saint Peter in Prison* and *The Raising of the Son of Theophilus*. A significant portion of the sky was lost, as well as a good part of the angel's head, wings and sword, which, at the time, were partially mended and repainted in a crude attempt at pictorial restoration.

The scene is surrounded by a narrow white frame that is present also on the right side of the pilaster projection. This frame is repeated in the scene painted below it, *Saint Peter Visited in Prison by Saint Paul* by Filippino Lippi, but is missing from Masolino's pendant of *The Fall* on the opposite pilaster and, consequently, from *The Liberation from Prison* by Lippi below it.[1]

The Expulsion, along with Masolino's *The Fall*, relates to the rest of the cycle as a historical antecedent for the *historia salutis* or "salvation history."[2] In terms of the original appearance, this fresco is seriously affected by the loss of the final application of azurite, an expensive blue pigment made from copper ore, for the sky. Recording in the nineteenth century how the fresco stood out "on a blue background formed by the sky," Cavalcaselle expressed regret that the color had already "lost a great deal of its initial vigor." Yet even the blue seen by Cavalcaselle was not the original pigment. Rather, it was a dull monochrome owing to the varnish concoction (*beverone*) used in the restoration after the fire of 1771. This treatment had particularly affected the image of the angel, which was darkened in color more than the other figures.

When this varnish was removed, only the gray-blue undercoat came to light, with the azurite blue of the sky rendered *a secco* having been lost, as in the pendant by Masolino. Thus, while it may appear that the *giornata* including the figure of Adam, which shows a background aura of more intense color, is a deficiency or an error of execution of the gray-blue color of the sky (as if the hue could not be matched in the succeeding *giornata*), it is instead only testimony to the entire loss of the original color. This loss is highly visible and affirmable by examining the appearance of the rays of light coming from the entrance gate to Eden. Originally done in gold leaf, they are today chromatically altered: on the wall inside the door opening, they have lost their surface of gold leaf and show only oxidized traces of the preparatory undercoat (*preparazione a stagno*), and where they extend out into the sky behind Adam's back, the gilding has also been almost completely lost due to flaking. But in the latter area, the glue used in applying the gold leaf to the fresco surface increased the holding power of the medium that had been used to apply the azurite pigment to the intonaco. This reinforcement of cohesion allowed narrow bands of the original sky color to be preserved, thereby leaving us with a precious sample of how intense the blue background once was.

The flesh color of the figures was underpainted with a very pale green color mixed with yellow ocher,[3] which shows through on Eve's face in the area from her neck to her blond hair. With black added, it was used in a darker tone on the body of Adam according to the contemporary custom of distinguishing the male body from that of the female, whose skin was more delicate and paler.

As it was in *The Fall*, the foliage over the figures that could be seen prior to the current restoration was not original, but was added after 1652 in Verona green tempera.[4] Consequently, it was removed during restoration, after the necessary analyses and documentation were done.[5] In addition to interventions by numerous cleanings, "beautifications" and alterations over time, the fire of 1771 also left indelible marks on this scene. A wood cornice, which had been placed over the painted border running between the first and second registers, burned and caused serious damage not only to the color of the border but also to that of the ground on which the figures stand. Here, the ferrous *terra verde* pigments underwent a real "cooking" due to the high temperature, consequently turning an irreversible brick red.

Otherwise it can be said that the scene is in a good state of preservation, still completely legible despite the unfortunate loss of the original azurite blue of the sky, leaving the color of the preparatory undercoat exposed. This pale background tone, which varies according to the *giornata*, should in fact be considered a "fake" color, since the original color in its final rendering was raised to a high intensity, as seen in the light rays.

Accepted by scholars as entirely the work of Masaccio, this scene has been compared emblematically to the *The Fall* by Masolino. Masaccio's bodies express a concrete, synthesized dramaticity exemplifying "Renaissance" originality, which is in contrast to the lack of psychological depth in the "Late Gothic" work of Masolino. In effect, this example ratifies Masaccio's art as a break with the past and the Gothic mainstream still much appreciated in Florence at the time.

In Masaccio's depiction, Man, although an utter sinner, is not devoid of dignity. He is not degraded or brutalized; the beauty conveyed in his body, more than just an innovative expression, refers back to archetypes of ideal Classical beauty. Revivals and references from Classical Antiquity have been noted in the representation of the two characters. For the figure of Eve, the source is in the Greco-Roman "chaste" Venus (*Venere pudica*), but filtered through fourteenth-century models, such as *Temperance*, a caryatid figure on Giovanni Pisano's pulpit (1302–10) in the Pisa Cathedral. Also on a relief panel for this pulpit, two of the Damned in the *Last Judgment* who clutch their heads in their hands are probably the source for Adam's appearance in the Masaccio fresco. A comparison has also been made with *The Expulsion* (marble relief, c. 1280) on the Fonte Maggiore in Perugia by Nicola and Giovanni Pisano.[6] With regard to fifteenth-century models, a resemblance can be proposed between Eve's facial expression and that of the young Isaac in Brunelleschi's bronze relief panel, *The Sacrifice of Isaac* (Bargello, Florence), for the 1401–2 competition to execute the North Doors of the Florence Baptistry.

Concerning the supposed existence in Florence of a Venus *pudica* statue in the manner of the antique, there is proof in the comment made by B. Rambaldo da Imola to Dante: "In Florence and in a private home [there was] a marvelously beautiful statue of Venus decorated as in ancient times. Nude, she cupped her left hand to cover her private parts, and with the other hand held higher, she covered her breast. It was even said that this statue was the work of Polyclitus."[7] In his *Fourth Commentary*, Lorenzo Ghiberti wrote of a Venus statue found in Florence, during "underground excavations at the house of the Brunelleschi family," and transported to Padua, where he saw it. Masaccio's Eve, however, with her heavy, misshapen body and all the world's suffering in her face and dramatic posture, has only the arm gestures of a Venus *pudica*. In Adam, the magnificent *Belvedere Torso* (c. 50 B.C.) acquires flesh and blood,[8] and connections have been made as well with the *Laocoön* (A.D.79–81) and the *Marsyas* (Roman copy, 2nd c.).[9] Also mentioned as a close contemporary precedent is the anatomical posture of the figure of Christ in the *Crucifixion* by Donatello (Church of Santa Croce, Florence).[10]

The reelaborations from Classical Antiquity, and from the preceding and contemporaneous cultures, helped Masaccio to compose an absolutely original product that would have been most impressive. Consider, for example, the invention of the angel, foreshortened and hovering in flight, caught in the act of landing on a cloud of fire almost as red as its costume. With the nudes, he distanced the figures from the sphere of everyday life, immersing them in an ideal world that was then treated in a realistic way.[11] The nudity of the figures as a means of characterizing Antiquity was, thus, a profoundly ethical characterization —in a word, "ideal nudity."[12] The nudity of Adam and Eve in the Biblical sense can symbolize either the innocence of the Garden of Eden (Masolino) or the precariousness of life (Masaccio).[13] In actuality, these representations and themes are often united.

From the tall, narrow Gate of Eden marked in shadow and defined in perspective, (once) golden rays emanate, symbolizing Divine Will expelling Man after the Fall. The command is reiterated by the angel, whose left hand points the way to the world. In the bleak and barren environment outside Eden, two small hills seem to accompany the movement of the two figures.[14] That on the left descends sharply, reiterating the forward stride of Adam's left leg, while the more rounded one on the right extends the path of the light rays to reinforce the dynamics of the physical expulsion willed by the peremptory Divine Force.

The shadows cast by the figures clearly follow and point out the hard path ahead to the difficult life of the earthly world. The gravity of the event does not allow for superficial acts; the intensity of the drama extends to each and every form. All is essential and concentrated in an atmosphere saturated by the will of God. The rhythm, which we have noted as corresponding with the strides common to the two figures, heightens the expressivity that, through the gestures of the arms, culminates in their heads. Bending forward and clasping his head in his hands, Adam appears immersed in the conscious pain of repentance, while Eve, leaning backward, cries out her anguish to the world.

During the recent restoration, a new reading of the painted surface confirmed the number of working sessions (*giornate*) discovered by Tintori (published in 1958 by Procacci[15] and reaffirmed in 1968 by Berti[16]) but not the order these scholars indicate. The execution began from the top and proceeded as follows: (1) the sky and the angel, (2) the door of Eden and the sky immediately behind Adam, (3) the figure of Adam, and (4) the figure of Eve. These "four" *giornate* can possibly be reduced to only three days of actual work, because, as Procacci thought, "presumably the door of the Garden of Eden did not take up a full day's work." This assumption can be sup-

Masaccio, Adam and Eve: The Expulsion, *detail*

ported by the evidence that the base color for the sky in this portion is so perfectly reproduced and equal to that of the preceding *giornata* that it truly supposes one was executed immediately after the other.

1 O. Casazza, "La grande gabbia architettonica di Masaccio," *Critica d'Arte*, 53, no. 16, 1988, pp. 83ff.

2 See final chapter; and O. Casazza, "Il ciclo delle Storie di San Pietro e la 'Historia Salutis': Nuova lettura della Cappella Brancacci," *Critica d'Arte*, 51, no. 9, 1986, pp. 69ff.

3 This was also used mixed with equal parts of ocher, black and San Giovanni white. See C. Cennini, *The Craftsman's Handbook* (*Il Libro dell'arte*, late 14th c.), trans. D. V. Thompson, Jr., New York, 1933, pp. 45–47 and 93–95.

4 See discussion of this on pp. 307–9. Berti dates it after 1652, from the time of Cosimo III, Grand Duke of Tuscany from 1670 to 1723 (L. Berti and R. Foggi, *Masaccio*, Florence, 1989). See also U. Baldini, "Le figure di Adamo e Eva formate affatto ignude in una cappella di una principale chiesa di Fiorenza," *Critica d'Arte*, 53, no. 16, 1988, pp. 73ff; and O. Casazza and P. Cassinelli Lazzeri, *La Cappela Brancacci: conservazione e restauro nei documenti della grafica antica*, Modena, 1989.

5 An infrared telethermo-reflectographic examinination, penetrating the paint levels, gave evidence for the complete anatomy of the nude bodies and assured the total recovery of the original painting underneath. The fact that the foliage was added after centuries of aging of the original surface texture was confirmed and reaffirmed by the investigations and verifications we accomplished. Even with the naked eye, in fact, it was possible to see clearly how abrasions and cracks in the original color surface below—signs of natural aging and the passage of time—were clogged up by the repainting of the foliage.

6 M. Salmi, *Masaccio*, Milan, 1947, p. 187.

7 Cited in P. Bocci Pacini, "Nota archeologica sulla nascita di Venere," *Gli Uffizi, Studi e Ricerche*, no. 4, 1987, p. 22.

8 Bocci Pacini, "Nota archeologica," pp. 22ff.

9 W. Kurt, *Die Darstellung des nachten Menschen in dem Quattrocento von Florenz*, Berlin, 1912; J. Mesnil, *L'art du Nord et au Sud des alpes à l'époque de la Renaissance,* Brussels, 1911, and "Masaccio and the Antique," *Burlington Magazine*, 48, 1926, pp. 91–98; M. Dvořák, *Geschichte der Italienischen Kunst in Zeitalter der Renaissance,* Munich, 1927, 1, p. 60; and P. Murray, *Apollo,* 1965.

Editor's note: The *Belvedere Torso,* the *Laocoön* and the *Marsyas* are now preserved in the Vatican Museums, but none had yet been rediscovered in Masaccio's time.

10 L. Berti, *Masaccio*, Milan, 1964, p. 94.

11 N. Himmelmann, "Nudità ideale," *Memorie dell'Antico*, 2, 1985, pp. 191–278.

12 S. Settis, in *La colonna Traiana*, Turin, 1988, 3, p. 464.

13 Himmelmann, "Nudità ideale," p. 223.

14 Berti, *Masaccio*, 1964, p. 93.

15 U. Procacci, *La tecnica degli antichi affreschi e il loro distacco e restauro*, Florence, 1958, p. 26, Plate IX.

16 L. Berti, *L'opera completa di Masaccio*, Milan, 1968, p. 93.

MASACCIO

The Tribute Money

Left wall, second register, 2.47 × 5.97 meters

The scene refers to the Gospel passage in Matthew 17:24–27 telling of the arrival of Jesus and his apostles in Capernaum:

> When they entered Capernaum, the collectors of the temple tax approached Peter and said, "Does your master not pay the temple tax?" "Of course he does," Peter replied. Then Jesus on entering the house asked, without giving him time to speak: "What is your opinion, Simon? Do the kings of the world take tax or toll from their sons, or from foreigners?" When he replied, "From foreigners," Jesus observed: "Then their sons are exempt. But for fear of disedifying them go to the lake, throw in a line, and take out the first fish you catch. Open its mouth and you will discover there a coin worth twice the temple tax. Take it and give it to them for you and me."

Masaccio has illustrated the three-part episode in one scenic space. At the center is the demand from the temple tax collector and Jesus's immediate response telling Peter how to procure the necessary money. At the far left, Peter is extracting the coin from the mouth of a fish on the lakeshore (Lake Gennesaret). At the far right, Peter is paying the tax collector in front of the house (the *domus* and *oikia* in the Latin and Greek Gospel texts).

The Capernaum episode is linked to another in Matthew 22:15–22 (also mentioned in Mark 12:13–17 and Luke 20:20–26) that records Jesus's view on the legitimacy of paying taxes to political authorities:

> Then the Pharisees went off and began to plot how they might trap Jesus in speech. They sent their disciples to him, accompanied by Herodian sympathizers, who said: "Teacher, we know you are a truthful man and teach God's ways sincerely. You court no one's favor and do not act out of human respect. Give us your opinion, then, in this case. Is it lawful to pay tax to the emperor or not?" Jesus recognized their bad faith and said to them, "Why are you trying to trip me up, you hypocrites? Show me the coin used for the tax." When they handed him a small Roman coin he asked them, "Whose head is this and whose inscription?" "Caesar's," they replied. At that time he said to them, "Then give to Caesar what is Caesar's, but give to God what is God's." Taken aback by this reply, they went off and left him.

Christ's affirmation of the lawfulness of the tribute request has been interpreted as an allusion to the tax reform debate underway in Florence at the time, which concluded in 1427 with the Catasto, instituting the practice of declaring financial resources in order that a more equitable levy of taxes could be made (U. Procacci, 1953; M. Meiss, 1963; and L. Berti, 1964).

Other possible connotations have been proposed along the way by scholars. Peter's act of paying the tax requested by the temple could be considered in relation to the active efforts on the part of Pope Martin V (reign 1417–1431) to reaffirm the supremacy of the Church. Also, the episode of finding the money in the lake or sea could be a symbolic reference to Florence's new maritime interests promoted by none other than Felice Brancacci, a member of the Board of Maritime Consuls (K. Steinbart, 1948). The Capernaum text could also be taken as evidence for the principle according to which the Church ought not to raise money by means of taxes on its own properties but should derive it from external sources (P. Meller, 1961).

This episode is an elemental part of the *historia salutis* or "salvation history,"[1] and it may be recalled that M. Meiss (1963), following Saint Augustine's interpretation of the Gospel passage, had already upheld the religious significance of the story as one of redemption through the Church. First of all, Peter recognized that Jesus was not obliged to pay the tax because, as he had already solemnly professed to believe, Christ was the son of God (Matthew 16:16–20). Moreover, the words of Jesus to Peter, "Give it to them for me and you," not only convey affection for the man he chose as his vicar on earth but also express a declaration of Peter's special mission.

The "tribute" signifies how closely the salvation plan is tied into historical reality. The Church's mission is not of a political, economic and social order, but even though the Church transcends temporal realities, it respects their autonomy. Without doubt, the grace of salvation elevates human reality, since reconciliation with Christ embraces the whole temporal order. Whether the "tribute" is paid to the Temple or to the Romans [to the Church or to the State], one is obliged to "give to Caesar what is Caesar's, but give to God what is God's" (Luke 20:25), and to "pay each one his due: taxes to whom taxes are due; toll to whom toll is due; respect and honor to everyone who deserves them" (Romans 13:7).

Obviously, it is possible to entertain other interpretations and references. For example, it could be seen as a reaffirmation of the principles of political and ecclesiastical order, for which the stimulus to depict such an episode may have been the heresy of the Hussites (followers of Jan Huss) and the ensuing reaction against it by Pope Martin V and Cardinal Branda Castiglione (H. von Einem, 1967). Prior to the recent restoration, a symbolic connection was even drawn between *The Tribute Money* and *The Expulsion* adjacent to it, in that Christ's gesture points to the way of the Kingdom of God (represented in *The Expulsion* by the gate to the Garden of Eden), while the gesture of the tax collector points toward a "broken" stake in the foreground at the right, a symbol for the corrupted world (Eidko M. L. Wakayama, 1978). It is now known, however, that the stake is not broken, but rather the splintered appearance was caused by a lacuna in the fresco surface.

Among the apostles, the only ones who can be definitively identified are (1) Peter, recognizable as he receives Jesus's command, extracts the money from the mouth of the fish and gives the coin to the tax official, and (2) John, recognizable by his proximity to Christ, his youth and his blond hair. The identification of the other ten apostles is more problematic, since none has the attributes or symbols necessary to being recognized (i.e., those elements that became iconographically attached to them as references to their martyrdom and the codification of their apostolate). Nevertheless, credible hypotheses can be put forward on the basis of certain affinities and observations with regard to their identities. Starting from the left, the apostle in the green robe may be (3) Andrew, since he shows clear physiognomic similarities (nose, orbital arches, straight hair and beard and green cloak) to the Saint Andrew from the now dismantled polyptych painted by Masaccio in 1426 for the Carmelite Church in Pisa (panel now in The J. Paul Getty Museum, Malibu). The next apostle, in profile with a black beard, may be (4) Paul, since a black beard is also found on Saint Paul in *The Raising of the Son of Theophilus*. Moreover, he resembles the apostle as depicted in the scene on the pilaster on the left of the entrance to the chapel of *Saint Peter Visited in Prison by Saint Paul* by Filippino Lippi.

The next two apostles have no truly distinguishing marks, but, because of their youth, they may be (5) Mark and (6) Thaddeus. By tradition, Mark the Evangelist was identified with the young man cited in the Gospel of Saint John as being present at the multiplication of the loaves and fishes. Thaddeus is portrayed as a young man in *The Last Supper* (1445–50) by Andrea del Castagno (Convent of Sant'Apollonia, Florence).

Considering the ranking of Peter, John and Mark in the group around Christ, it would be possible to think of a "hierarchy" with honorable placement given then to the two other future Evangelists, Luke and Matthew. In this case, (7) Luke may be identified with the bearded figure between Saint John and Christ, and (8) Matthew, called "the apostle closest to the people," with the balding man between Christ and the tax collector. To the right of the tax man, the blond apostle in profile is probably (9) James, the brother of John, since his head is a near replica of John's. Parronchi's identification (1975) may be accepted for the figure to the right of James as (10) Judas, for his "perverse grimace" and malevolent, Nero-like visage.[2] The next apostle could be (11) Bartholomew, who is always represented with a long, full beard.

A long tradition exists, following Vasari, for the identification of the last apostle on the right as a self-portrait of Masaccio, and, in fact, the features were used for the portrait of Masaccio that precedes his biography in the 1568 edition of *Le vite*.[3] From this, a convincing case can be made for seeing in this apostle the one whose name Masaccio bears—Tommaso or (12) Thomas. Apart from the self-portrait hypothesis, reasons for calling this figure Thomas have been well-documented otherwise and the identification could still be correct.[4]

The Tribute Money is the most celebrated scene in the chapel fresco cycle. Vasari described it in detail as follows:

> The most notable among the scenes [of the Life of Saint Peter], however, is the painting in which Saint Peter, in order to pay the tribute, at Christ's command is taking the money from the belly of the fish; for as well as being able to see in one apostle, the last in the group, a self-portrait of Masaccio executed so skillfully by him with the help of a mirror that it seems to be alive, we recognize the boldness of Saint Peter in his questioning and the attentiveness of the apostles as they stand in various attitudes around Christ, waiting for his decision with such animated gestures that they seem truly to be living; and Saint Peter, especially, whose face flushes with the effort he makes in bending down to retrieve the money from out of the belly of the fish; and more so when he pays the tribute [to the tax collector], where his emotion can be seen as he counts out the money, as well as the greed of the man who is receiving it, who looks at the money in his hand with great pleasure.[5]

Up to now, a great deal of attention to the fresco has centered around the recognition of exceptionally realistic details, detectable in spite of the chromatic obscuration from the black smoke of candles and the congealed *beveroni* or varnish solutions applied after past cleanings. Today, of course, the reading of the painting is facilitated by the reemergence of the formal elements in great objective definition, from the cane used by Peter as a fishing rod to the large mouth of the fish, rendered in every detail, to the effect of the clear water of the lake rippling in circles as it moves toward the shore. This kind of attention to mirroring the natural environment suggests that a new and ample "reality" was an important element of the story of "earthly salvation."

The awareness of the characters in the scene of the great event—this extraordinary happening which they are about to witness—creates a state of tension. It is as if they are suspended between a pronounced and solemn focus of attention, in pausing to listen to the word of Christ, and an

eager searching with their eyes for the actual miraculous act of the discovery of the money. Everything occurs as a dynamic emphasis on the moment, causing the figures to brace, as it were, for quick and immediate movement.[6] Behind the figures is a mountain landscape that assumes a variety of colorations as it recedes into the distance—from a somber green at the nearest level to shimmering snow-white farther away, ending in a stark white luminosity below the sky, which is rendered in tones of blue and white and dotted with clouds "measured in perspective" (U. Baldini, 1989). The hills and mountains rising from the plain assume a new earthly scale in the scattering of cottages, trees and hedges through the use of perspective foreshortening. This will serve as an example for Paolo Uccello, Domenico Veneziano and, later, Piero della Francesca.

More importantly, in the grave and solemn individualization of the figures and their arrangement, the distinctive character of the new classicism appears. This new style has previously been recognized as a reelaboration upon Greco-Roman models,[7] either through actual examples Masaccio had seen, or mediated through Giotto and Nicola, Giovanni and Andrea Pisano, or found in the classical revivals of Nanni di Banco[8] and Donatello.[9]

A Classical model exists in the Roman Column of Trajan (A.D. 106–13) for the optical correction made in the two registers of the fresco cycle, for viewing from the chapel floor.[10] On the Column, the spiral band of figural scenes widens as it ascends toward the top to counter the effect of distance and make the spiral appear of consistent width when viewed from the ground. In the fresco cycle, the height of the paintings on the second register has been increased by fifteen centimeters (nearly six inches), and the figures are larger and more spread out.

Rather than being arranged horizontally, in the manner of a Classical frieze, the figures in *The Tribute Money* are arranged in semicircular fashion following a "hemicycle" pattern of Classical origin derived from such depictions as Socrates among his disciples. This arrangment came into Early Christian art in the depiction of Christ among his apostles. It was later grafted onto the geometric-symbolic concept of the "perfect circle" favored in the early Renaissance, beginning with Brunelleschi (Meiss, 1963), but also present earlier in the work of Giotto (*Pentecost*, Arena Chapel frescoes, Padua, after 1305) and Andrea Pisano (*Funeral of John the Baptist*, bronze relief, South Doors, 1336, Florence Baptistry and, at Orvieto, figures of the risen). This spatial ordering by means of an elliptical line, derived from Classical sources and verifiable in the design plan of the scene, unifies the space and acts as the great fulcrum of the whole perspective and architectural arrangement with the central "vanishing point" on the head of Christ.[11]

In this plan, it is as if the spectator were part of the ellipse, situated immediately behind the shoulders of the tax collector so that "the viewer and the painted view are on the same level." The figure of the tax collector, in his posture and placement with his back to the viewer, is an important pivotal point for the composition. He is the intermediary for the spectator and the distancer from the perspective planes; between his legs, spread in a wide stance, the shadows cast by the bodies of the apostles are like steps on a stair by which to enter and become a part of the scene.

The figures are freely borrowed from the Classical world and are dressed "in the Greek manner," with tunics cinched at the waist and robes thrown over the left shoulder, wrapped around the figure and gathered up on the left forearm. Some of the physiognomic models, such as the young Saint John and his twin (Saint James) to the right of Christ, who have square jaws and large blond curls, are reminiscent of the angular heads of Muses represented on Late Roman sarcophagi. To give another example, these traits can also be seen in the angular heads portrayed on a Roman altar in the Uffizi Gallery, where the following salient features appear: strong jaw, profile of the nose in line with the forehead and hair in curls framing the face and falling on the shoulders. This treatment with large volumetric planes is typical of ornamental heads from the Imperial Roman period, which are characterized by pronounced expressivity, well-defined eyes rendered by hollows for pupils and furrows for the irises, and partially open mouths.

If such representations from Classical sar-

Masaccio, The Tribute Money, *detail*

cophagi and altars are fundamental to the plastic vigor of some of the heads, other heads of a more spiritual cast are derived from the facial prototype of the "philosopher" deep in thought, one of the most ancient of which is the portrayal of Plato. In effect, a characteristic of these faces framed with hair and a full beard are the wrinkles that furrow the forehead and emphasize the bridge of the nose, producing the thinker's "knotted brow." The mouth, set off with a full moustache, is enclosed with similar furrows on either side that descend from the nares. Even the pose of Saint Peter in the act of taking the money from the fish's mouth, with the right leg deeply bent and the left extended, is somewhat reminiscent of a statuary pose common in Greek sculpture, on Etruscan urns and in Roman reliefs.

The authorship of *The Tribute* has been debated because of the appearance of the head of Christ, which closely resembles that of Adam in *The Fall* by Masolino. Longhi (1940), for example, attributed the execution of the head to Masolino.[12] He was followed in this belief by Meiss (1963), Berti (1964 and 1968), Parronchi (1966) and Bologna (1966). The rereading of the *giornate* has made it impossible, however, to accept the procedure hypothesized by Longhi, in which Masolino began *The Tribute* by painting the head of Christ, and then Masaccio later painted the rest of the fresco alone.[13] The cleaning has freed the picture surface from all the heavy obscuration and allowed for a more accurate determination of the exact executional technique.

From the point of view of technique and the actual manner in which Masolino worked and handled the brush, there is no similarity whatsoever between the head of Christ in *The Tribute* and the one with which it has most often been compared—that of Christ in the *Pietà* by Masolino at Empoli, also recently emerged from a very important restoration that has revealed its technique more clearly. Nor is there any similarity of technique between the head of Christ in *The Tribute* and the head of Adam in *The Fall*, and it is in just such a comparison that one determines the authorship of each head, according to U. Baldini (1988).

Since the two physiognomies are indisputably similar in outward appearance, those who have formally identified Christ's head in *The Tribute* as being by Masolino have judged correctly on this basis. But until now, because of the thick layer of dirt and the darkening produced by the numerous "nutriments" applied to the frescoes, it was impossible to judge anything beyond the form, the light and the contours of plastic definition. Today everything can be seen and followed in a store of new and irrefutable technical data regarding composition, painting style and method of execution.

Even if, in the head of Christ, the delineation of the face, eyes, nose, and mouth corresponds faithfully to work done by Masolino, and even if the head of Adam corresponds with that of Christ nearly point to point when superimposed, it must be recognized that neither the Adam nor any other figure painted on the walls of the Brancacci Chapel or elsewhere by Masolino has the pictorial definition, composition and executional technique of volumes, constructed through the use of light, as in Christ's head in *The Tribute Money*. It would be enough to see the newly revealed pictorial intensity of the head which, more than ever before, unites it with the other heads and figures, or to note the sinew of Christ's neck muscles expressing the potential for movement with a force surpassed in confidence only by Michelangelo's *Brutus* (marble bust, c. 1542, Bargello, Florence). It would be sufficient, too, to recognize the harsh flow of light over the sharp planes of the face, as opposed to that typically soft embrace of the light on rounded surfaces that Masolino's figures never lose, even when he has sought dramatic effects.

We have no doubt, therefore, that Masaccio executed this head. To better define the significance and value of the "collaboration" of the two artists working side by side, however, we may go so far as to hypothesize that the head was based on a drawing by Masolino,[14] but this does not detract from Masaccio's authorship. It is not even too farfetched to suppose that, for his head of Christ, Masaccio used the same drawing made by Masolino for Adam in *The Fall*. (Even if the pendant frescoes of *The Fall* and *The Expulsion* on the pilasters of the entrance arch had not yet been painted, the drawings must already have been completed.) In realizing that Christ's face could not, with impunity, be altered or treated in the same manner as those of the working-class apostles, perhaps Masaccio decided, as a bow to conventional typology, that the best way to retain that perfection of ideal beauty, long standardized iconographically in a recognized and recognizable face, would be to imitate the "ideal beauty" of Adam, made in the image and likeness of God in the Creation. Quite possibly, in the pictorial realization of the head of Christ, Masaccio remembered and reflected on the fact that his friend Filippo Brunelleschi had branded the Christ figure of Donatello's *Crucifix* in the Church of Santa Croce as a "peasant."

In *The Tribute Money*, there are thirty-two *giornate*, as opposed to the previous count of twenty-eight in the Tintori survey published by Berti.[15] Included in the additional *giornate* are those for the construction of the architectural framing comprised of the corner pilasters and their horizontal "entablature," no longer extant but similar to the dentiled dividing strip that acts as the entablature for the scene below it. Being able to read the surface better has also permitted us to deduce a different succession for the *giornate* and thereby to propose more securely an alternative overall procedure for the execution.

In treating the heads, Masaccio had applied the intonaco in variously sized portions capable of holding three, two or just one head at a time. In enlarging the surface to include more than one head, he followed exactly and precisely the limitations of the underdrawings of the figures already completed in *sinopia*. In a similar way, in the other *giornate*, the borders of the intonaco application match up precisely with the formal delineations of underdrawing. This is true for the clothing, the architecture, and the mountainous background as well, where the application follows the contours of the figures silhouetted against it.

The only exception to this is the *giornata* with the head of Saint John, where it seems quite likely that there was another head drawn in *sinopia* in the space between his head and the apostle's to the right. The fact that it was never translated into the final fresco could mean a modification during the execution, motivated by the opportunity and desire to make the figure of Christ stand out in greater relief. For that same reason, the head of Christ was painted after those of the apostles flanking him to create a balance whereby the accompanying heads exalted his. In the overall procedure, Christ's head was neither the first nor the last to be executed, as demonstrated positively in a precise reading of the overlapping pattern of the intonaco for the *giornate*.[16]

The apostle originally placed next to Saint John would then have had to be repositioned. This was accomplished, without changes to the already completed work, by the insertion of a new *giornata* situated between the head of the third apostle from the left and the head of Saint Peter. This intonaco overlays that of the *giornate* for the heads and the bordering landscape, therefore the head in question was painted afterwards.[17] One can also propose that another change occurred in the execution of the head of Judas, although within the course of the same *giornata*. This head appears to be painted on a "troubled" surface, unlike the smooth, polished one adjacent to it with the blond apostle in profile. This suggests that an erasure was made while the intonaco surface was still damp and could accommodate a new incorporation, uniting it with the rest without signs of seams or superimpositions of material.[18]

The succession of the *giornate*, compared to previous findings, now defines a new operative procedure in the following order: (1–3) the architectural "cage" of corner pilasters on either side and an "entablature" across the top (obliterated in the eighteenth-century renovation), (4) the upper part of the house, (5) the wall adjacent to the house, (6–7) in the scene of the payment of the tribute, the head of Saint Peter and the head of the tax official, (8) the rest of the house behind them, (9) Peter's body, (10) the tax official's tunic, (11) and the legs and the ground around them, (12–13) all the mountainous landscape, (14) the scene with Saint Peter by the lake at the far left, followed by a succession of heads in the central group of (15) Andrew, Paul and Mark, (16) Peter, (17) Luke, (18) Matthew, (19) Christ, (20) John, (21) Thaddeus, (22) Bartholomew and Thomas, (23) the tax official, James and Judas (24) the body of Thomas, (25) the tax official's back and (26) the rest of his body, (27) Christ's tunic; (28) the mantles of Christ and John; (29) Peter's mantle, (30) Christ's right hand, (31) Andrew's mantle, and (32) the central area of the ground on which the figures stand.

So far as the state of preservation of the whole scene is concerned, it is certainly among those that suffered the greatest damage in the fire of 1771, to the point that the overall chromatic effect is very different from what it must have been originally. Nearly all of the left side of the scene has turned toward reddish brown tones. This negates the perspectival definition originally created with *terra verde* pigments varied here and there with accents of bright yellow ocher, as seen in the areas unchanged by the heat of the fire. Also, the effect of the apostles' cast shadows on the ground must have been much more incisive in measuring the space and giving it more realistic dimensions. The materials used to restore the surface after the fire previously prevented this kind of analysis. Cavalcaselle, not noticing that there were large losses of intonaco, declared in fact that, "except for some areas of the color missing here and there from the clothing, [the whole] is fairly well preserved. . . . The background has suffered and some trees lack color. Also, the sky, instead of blue, shows a very dark and heavy lead-colored tone. In some of the clothing, especially Saint Peter's, the original liveliness of the color has been lost."

The clothing described is that of Saint Peter standing in the central scene, which was once deeper in tone and more luminous from yellow ocher highlights now turned reddish from the fire. Moreover, the effects of the heat reddened the flesh colors, such as the hands, feet and face of Saint Peter in the scene at the far left. Perhaps the fire was also responsible for the almost total loss of the original gold leaf decoration, as well as the loss of the "changeable color" shading with red of the folds on Saint Andrew's green mantle, traces of which can still be seen in the areas to the right of his beard and just below Saint Peter's hand. The original color of the ground is preserved in a lighter-colored strip that runs horizontally just above the painted dividing cornice at the bottom of the picture, where it had been protected by the previously installed eighteenth-century wood cornice from the heat of the 1771 fire.

The haloes that were visible at the start of the restoration work turned out not to be the original ones. Moreover, in the preceding restoration, neither the still-existing traces of gold nor signs of the outlines of the haloes had been detected for the four apostles at the far right of the group, therefore they had been left without them. The repainted haloes were removed in the cleaning process, and traces of the original haloes and their precise outlines for Christ and all of the apostles were discovered underneath. These permitted a reconstruction of the chromatic effect, via the method of chromatic selection, as well as the "rediscovery" of the meaning of the "foreshortened" perspective of the haloes, essential to the precise marking of the location of the figures in the ellipsis around Christ.

At the far right of the picture, after the removal of the repainting done after the fire, the underdrawing for the schematic architectural construction of the low wall and short flight of steps was found on the underlying *arriccio*. This was the basis for the recovery and reintegration of this area with the correct perspective construction for the steps and especially for the wall that had been lost in the cleaning.

Being able to see the picture surface without the opaque screen of dirt and overpainting that obscured all of the painterly texture allowed for the rediscovery of the impressions of the measuring strings and the incised lines executed on the wet intonaco for the perspective construction and modular division of the spaces. In a recent analysis made by P. A. Rossi on the spatial meaning and purpose of this scene,[19] it emerged that Masaccio conceived the perspective arrangement as a function of its visual relationship to the observer, who would enter into the chapel in such a way that the scene was presented as a veritable continuation of real space.

[1] See final chapter; and O. Casazza, "Il ciclo delle Storie di San Pietro e la 'Historia Salutis': Nuova lettura della Cappella Brancacci," *Critica d'Arte*, 51, no. 9, 1986, pp. 65–84.
[2] Parronchi believes, however, that this head might be a sixteenth-century modification of a Masaccio-like but less orthodox version.
[3] Vasari says there is "in one apostle, the last in the group, a self-portrait of Masaccio executed so skillfully by him with the help of a mirror that it seems to be alive" (*Le vite de' più*

eccellenti pittori, scultori ed architettori (Florence 1568), ed. G. Milanesi, Florence, 1878–81, reprint Florence, 1971, p. 130).

M. Salmi (*Rivista Storica Carmelitana*, 1929, pp. 99ff.), rejected the figure as self-portraiture, citing the impossibility of capturing a full profile view in a mirror. Such a self-portrayal could only have been done with a series of mirrors.

[4] A fascinating hypothesis, for all the implications that could be read in it, is that this apostle is a portrait of Felice Brancacci, a proposal made by P. Meller (1961), L. Berti (1968) and Foggi (1989). This is not very probable, however, not so much due to the defacing of the Brancacci portraits in the *damnatio memoriae* following Felice's exile, but rather owing to the lack of crediblity in having the patron's features converge with those of an apostle. Moreover, these suppositions regarding Felice's portrait were based on the fact that, before the recent restoration, this figure and others near him did not have haloes. The recovery of the haloes of these four apostles from under a thick layer of varnish excludes, in our opinion, any and all temporal references to the patron or to real portraits. As Salmi noted, Vasari had already pointed out Felice's portrait in the *Consecration of the Church* painted by Masaccio in the cloister (now destroyed), and he wouldn't have made the glaring error of not recognizing him here, if this was another instance of his likeness (*Civiltà fiorentina del primo Rinascimento*, Florence, 1967, pp. 50ff.).

If Felice's image is to be found in the cycle, a more probable hypothesis is that he is among the witnesses in *The Raising of the Son of Theophilus*, where portraits of merchants, benefactors and the illustrious have been inserted by Filippino to convey a contemporaneity already expressed in other ways.

[5] Vasari, *Vite*, 1971, pp. 130–31.

[6] See R. Fremantle, "Masaccio e l'antico," *Critica d'Arte*, 103, 1969, pp. 39–56. Worth mentioning here is the difference in Masolino's bystanders listening to Saint Peter in the *Preaching*.

[7] L. Berti, "Masaccio 1422," *Commentari*, 1961, pp. 84–107; and M. Meiss, "Masaccio and the Early Renaissance: The Circular Plan," *Studies in Western Art* (Acts of the 20th International Art History Congress), Princeton, 1963, 2, pp. 123–45.

[8] For the central nucleus of the *Tribute* ellipse, a model exists in the sculpture of *The Four Crowned Martyrs* (c. 1413) by Nanni di Banco in the niche of the Stonemasons and Carpenters, Orsanmichele, Florence.

[9] The full robe on the figure of Thomas clearly refers to Donatello's *Saint Louis of Toulouse* (1425, gilded bronze, Museo del Opera di Santa Croce, Florence), until 1460 in the exterior niche of Orsanmichele owned by the Guelph Party.

[10] S. Settis, A. La Regina and B. Agosti Farinella, *La colonna Traiana*, Turin, 1988.

[11] See P. Rossi, "Lettura del *Tributo* di Masaccio," *Critica d'Arte*, 54, no. 20, 1989, pp. 39–42; and M. Lorber, "Una rilettura del sistema prospettico proposto nel *De Pictura* (1436) di Leon Battista Alberti," *Critica d'Arte*, 54, no. 20, 1989, p. 43.

A prime Classical example is the "carrousel" of horses and riders, *Ceremonial Circular Gallop of the Cavalry*, from the base of the Column of Antoninus Pius (c. 161, marble relief,

Masaccio, The Tribute Money, *detail*

Vatican Museums, Rome). Describing the Trajan Column, R. Bianchi Bandinelli used terms that equally apply to *The Tribute Money*: "The spectator becomes a participant in the same space in which the painted figures move, on the first level where they are seen from the back as they look into the composition. Thus the spectator feels situated in the second row immediately behind the shoulders of these figures."

[12] After the recent cleaning, A. Parronchi (*Arte e Vacanze*, 2, Florence, 1989, p. 16, n. 8) added Christ's left hand to the Masolino attribution. Also, among other things, he attributed to Masolino the head of Saint Peter, at the far right in the act of paying the tax collector, and noted that the dark blue color of Peter's tunic exists nowhere else in the chapel.

[13] Christ's head, inscribed in a single *giornata*, turned out to have been executed after the heads of the apostles on either side of him, as well as after the mountainous background had been completed. The *giornata* for his clothing overlays that for his head, and it therefore was painted afterward. This latter finding excludes the hypothesis made by F. Bologna (*Masaccio*, Milan, 1966, p. 11) that "Masolino, upon Masaccio's death, was called in to restore sweetness to Christ's face, substituting his mitigated realism for who knows what kind of intolerable ugliness."

[14] U. Baldini, "Del *Tributo* e altro di Masaccio," *Critica d'Arte*, 54, no. 20, 1989, pp. 29–38.

[15] L. Berti, *Masaccio*, Milan, 1964, p. 99.

[16] See Note 13 above.

[17] This fact did not emerge in the Tintori survey where the heads were judged to have been executed in succession from left to right, up to and including the head of Christ (Berti, *Masaccio*, 1964, p. 99).

[18] This proves that the alteration was contemporary with the fresco and not ascribable to the sixteenth century as Parronchi suggested.

[19] Rossi, "Lettura," pp. 39–42. Found here are analyses based on new evidence of the *giornate* along with the incised lines and measuring string impressions on their surfaces for *The Tribute Money*, *The Healing of the Crippled Man and the Raising of Tabitha*, *The Expulsion* and *The Baptizing of the Neophytes*.

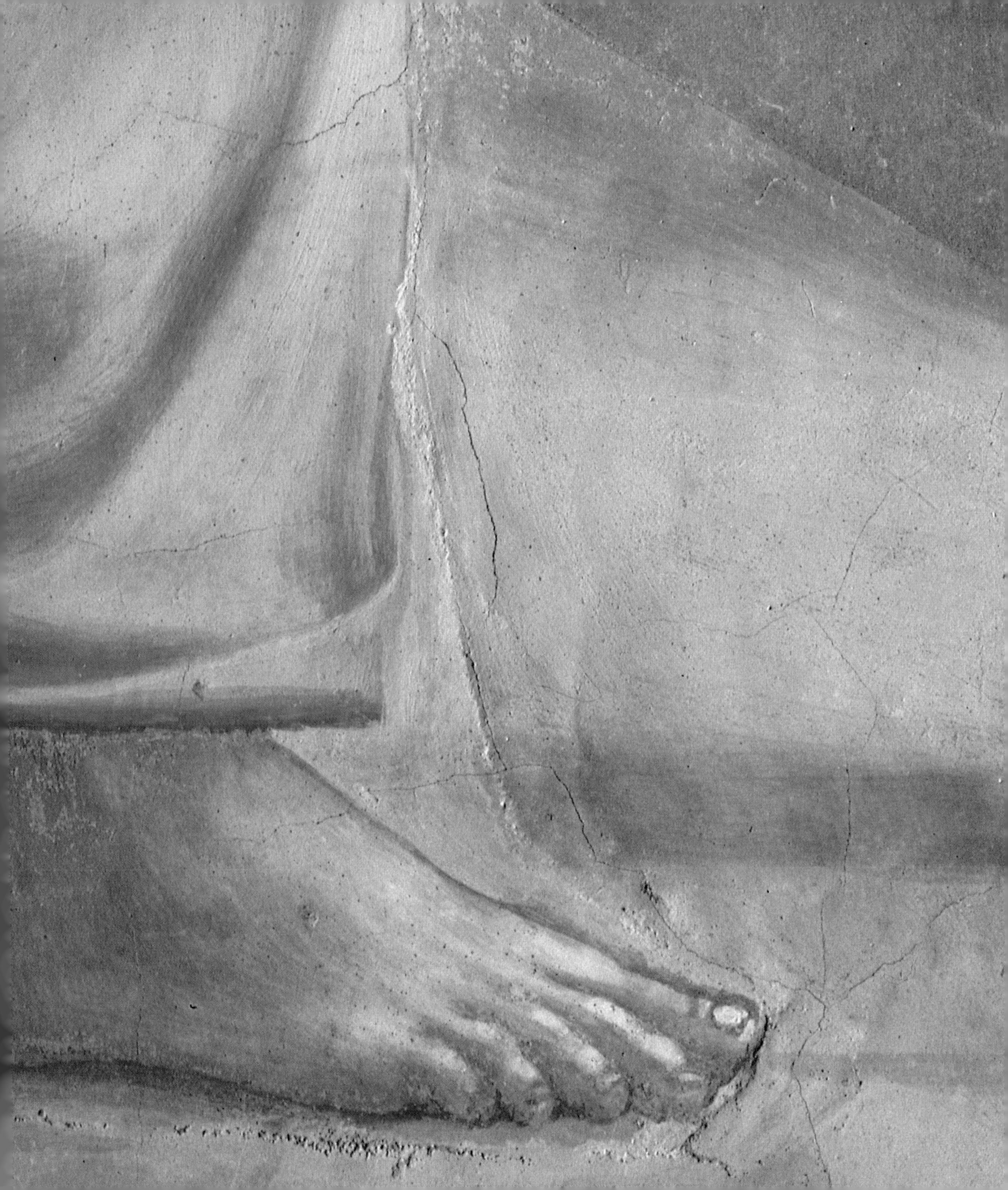

MASOLINO

Saint Peter Preaching

Back wall to the left of the window, second register, 2.47 × 1.66 meters

This scene depicts Saint Peter's great sermon delivered after the Descent of the Holy Spirit on Pentecost in Jerusalem, which begins: "You who are Jews, indeed all of you staying in Jerusalem! Listen to what I have to say" (Acts 2:14). Represented in this scene is the conclusive moment when Peter proclaims:

> You must reform and be baptized, each one of you, in the name of Jesus Christ, that your sins may be forgiven; then you will receive the gift of the Holy Spirit. It was to you and your children that the promise was made, and to all those still far off whom the Lord our God calls. In support of his testimony he used many other arguments, and kept urging, "Save yourselves from this generation which has gone astray." Those who accepted his message were baptized; some three thousand were added that day (Acts 2:38–41).

This scene, in being transferred by Masolino from the city to the country, in a sense prepares the way for *The Baptizing of the Neophytes* painted by Masaccio in the same location to the right of the window. There is an evident equivalence between the two scenes in plan and arrangement. In both, Peter is placed to the left in the performance of his action, standing in profile with his arm outstretched in a gesture accompanying his words. Behind him in both are two bystander-witnesses, and the landscape backgrounds also share a similar tone.

The fresco, due to its location on the chapel wall toward the exterior of the building, has suffered considerably from negative climatic effects in being subjected to drastic changes of temperature and to water seepage through the wall. Already in the second half of the nineteenth century, Father Santi Mattei[1] described the scenes on this window wall as severely whitened by the dampness. The surface also showed large cracks caused by mildew formation which, interestingly, appear in the Lasinio engraving (1825) of the scene but interpreted in the drawing as if they were arboreal forms of rounded shrubs.

A century later, Salmi (1932 and 1947) described both this scene and that of *The Baptizing of the Neophytes* as the most damaged of the entire cycle, noting that efflorescence from salt crystals invading the upper section had heavily clouded the figures. Brandi too (1957) reported that the precarious conditions of preservation had given the painting a hazy appearance. In any event, as with the *Baptizing* also, all of the documentation gathered before the recent restoration testified to the enormous degradation of the scene, which made it almost impossible to "recognize" repainting, original texture or different hands at work.

Today, the painting techniques of the two artists are far more "exposed" for inspection, nevertheless there are those who still believe that this scene is another of their collaborations. After the decline of widespread belief, led by Cavalcaselle, that Masaccio alone was responsible for the extant frescoes (panmasaccism), Longhi (1940) was the first to reattribute this scene to Masolino. He brought Masaccio's name back into play, nevertheless, in crediting him with the "insertion" later on of the three bystanders on the left ("of a grim and modern look") and of the figure of Saint Peter ("except for the ridiculous head"). Longhi's view was followed by Bologna (1966) and Parronchi (1966), who shared this judgment even though Berti (1964) had already put the "insertion" hypothesis in doubt, based on the determination of the *giornate* which showed the heads of the three bystanders to be in the same *giornata* with Saint Peter's head. Berti pointed out, however, that "this kind of alternation, even during the same *giornata*, is perfectly comprehensible, given the hypothesis of the two painters working side by side."

Berti had earlier rejected the idea of reciprocal insertions by the artists in the pendant frescoes, holding that the *Preaching* was completely Masolino's and the *Baptizing* completely Masaccio's, but he changed his mind when he saw the works after the 1988–89 cleaning. He now believes that the *Preaching* was begun by Masaccio, who executed only the mountainous landscape, while the *Baptizing* was begun by Masolino, who also only painted the landscape. At that point there was an actual exchange between the two artists in the course of the work, with Masolino completing the *Preaching* and Masaccio completing the *Baptizing*. With regard to the three bystanders in

Masolino, Saint Peter Preaching, *detail*

the *Preaching*, Parronchi's opinion (1989) is that they are undoubtedly by Masaccio, whereas Berti has confirmed the hand of Masolino by comparing them to the "dandies" in *The Raising of Tabitha*.

Quite to the contrary, Baldini (1989) has been led by the clearer reading afforded after the cleaning to give the *Preaching* to Masolino as a totally autonomous work, which the artist has harmonized in arrangement and space with Masaccio's *Baptizing* through a balance of rhythms that had been fixed in one form in the overall plan of the collaborative project.

As with its pendant, the restoration of this scene has revealed an appearance completely unknown up to now, due to the exceptional recoveries. For example, the wooded landscape, in its profile on the horizon, continues the mountainous background of *The Tribute Money* across the dividing corner pilaster in an intentionally sought spatial and temporal unity. As others have previously noted,[2] there is a seamless relationship between these two pictures that is neither fortuitous nor accidental, but rather studied and defined on the drawing table in the common working out of the scenic development of the whole cycle.

In this scene, the crowd of listeners is packed together, as in Masolino's fresco, *Saint Ivo Among His Pupils* at Empoli, and the spatial depth for this dense grouping has not been defined by the oblique method used by Masaccio. The mountains do not recede to infinity, as in the *Tribute Money* and the *Baptizing*, and they fail to create space (Salmi, 1947), weighing instead rather heavily on the figures. The mountains do continue the line of those in the *Tribute*, but they have a nearly frontal orientation without articulation of the space. Also, the trees seem too large in relation to their location in the distance.

There are ten *giornate* discernible on the picture surface, beginning at the top: (1) the top half of the pilaster and the mountains with the sky, (2) the rest of the pilaster, (3) the heads of the three standing figures and the head of Saint Peter, (4) in the same location on the right, the heads of the four standing figures, (5) the body and the clothing of one of the standing figures on the left and of Saint Peter in the act of speaking with his arm raised, (6) the four heads of kneeling figures at the back of the group, (7) to the right of those, three more heads of kneeling figures and the clothing of the tonsured monk, (8) the robes of the standing monk at the right, (9) the heads of the rest of the kneeling figures, and (10) the robes of the kneeling woman and old man at the front of the group, along with the ground.

The scene was executed entirely in fresco except for the blue areas, such as the sky and the robes of Saint Peter, which were painted *a secco*—the robes with pure azurite and the sky with a mix of azurite and lead white. Alterations in color occurred in some areas because of the fire, which also caused the detachment of the intonaco on the base of the painted pilaster. On the pilaster up to about half its height the color has reddened, and on the yellow robe of Saint Peter it has turned toward a brownish color, as it has also on the feet and the ground around them.

[1] P. Santi Mattei, *Ragionamento intorno alla antica chiesa del Carmine di Firenze*, Florence, 1869.
[2] O. Casazza, "La grande gabbia architettonica di Masaccio," *Critica d'Arte*, 53, no. 16, 1988, pp. 78–97.

MASACCIO

The Baptizing of the Neophytes

Back wall to the right of the window, second register, 2.47 × 1.72 meters

This scene illustrates the episode in Acts 2:37–41, which concludes: "Those who accepted [Saint Peter's] message were baptized; some three thousand were added that day" (2:41). In the unfolding of the Life of Saint Peter cycle, this event precedes those depicted in the scene immediately below, *The Distribution of Goods and The Death of Ananias*. Continuing the Biblical passage, one reads that the baptized faithfully heeded the teachings of the Apostles: "A reverent fear overtook them all, for many wonders and signs were performed by the apostles. Those who believed shared all things in common; they would sell their property and goods, dividing everything on the basis of each one's need" (Acts 2:42–45).

This fresco has suffered greatly over time, and its pigments show signs of very serious deterioration. Cavalcaselle had noticed (1897) the appearance of sizable whitish spots here and there, caused by salt formation: "Besides the damage to the painting in the various areas mutilated by the installation of the marble decoration on the window, the two figures behind the Saint and those standing opposite were ruined by nitrous salts in the wall." Cavalcaselle continues his description of the scene as having "a few mountains and some small trees standing out against the blue sky to complete the painting," which repeats the interpretation given in the Lasinio engraving of the scene, where the outlines of areas invaded by nitrous salts and stained by humidity were drawn in as arboreal forms.

Transformations made in the church and the convent before and especially after the 1771 fire included the creation of an atrium or open courtyard on the outside of the chapel wall. Subsequently, stairs and galleries were built in the atrium as well, with some set directly against the wall above the window level, and the whole was enclosed with a glass roof, but this did not prevent deterioration of the color pigments on the surface of the frescoes inside the chapel. In many areas, deterioration continued due to the attacks from salts leached through the wall by water seepage and constant, severe thermo-hygrometric fluctuations. Added to this problem was the whitening caused by the degradation of protein substances and the complete debasement of chromatic values due to repainting and the deposits of fixatives and varnishes applied in earlier restorations.

Compared to its prior appearance, this fresco, more than any other, appears richly renewed by the recent restoration work. The extraordinary recuperation of colors, scenic illumination and painterly calligraphy fully justify early descriptions regarding its remarkable beauty. According to Anonimo Magliabechiano, "Among the other figures, there is one who is trembling, something wonderful to see." Vasari, too, mentions this figure: "Very highly praised is a nude man, who trembles, among the others being baptized, chilled by the cold; he is executed in beautiful relief and in a charming manner, which has always been revered and admired by artists both in the past and today."[1]

Behind this standing nude youth is another figure, handled with mastery and rapidity, of a man about to be baptized but still dressed in a robe of changeable red-green color [i.e., his light green robe is "shaded" with red instead of the expected darker green]. This new painting technique of juxtaposing bands of complementary colors looks forward to that of Michelangelo for the Sistine, while the Mannerist style is prefigured in the red and violet robes in the scene.

The cold running water of the river flows around the legs of the kneeling neophyte, as Peter pours baptismal water from a bowl with a gesture like that of a sower of grain.[2] As it falls over the youth's head, the water creates many little bubbles and soaks his hair, the strands of which drip as if from a tap onto the surface of the river, producing more ripples and bubbles. There are in fact many such details that cannot be seen by spectators from the chapel floor below, for example, the way the beard grows on the man watching the baptism from behind Peter, or the way his ear is bent over by his turban.

Whereas in *The Tribute Money* the Apostles form a circular "colosseum of men," in this scene the twelve figures, plus Saint Peter, form an infinite procession that seems to continue downstream beyond the painted corner pilaster.

Returning to the kneeling neophyte, in spite of

the alteration of his skin tone to a reddish color from the heat of the fire, an almost summary painting technique can be seen in the modeling with rapid touches of light and shadow. This technique achieves an anatomical synthesis of forms of great plastic strength, recalling Classical statuary and glyptics.[3] Here in this figure is exemplified a revival of Classical Antiquity and its historical concept of beauty, yet reinvented and reelaborated. If the pose of humility refers to canons of Christian iconography, the powerful back and ample muscularity, as in the Adam of *The Expulsion*, evoke the *Belvedere Torso* (c. 50 B.C., Vatican Museums) and certain cameos showing Hercules at His Labors in all the robustness of nudity.[4] The "implacable" profile of the neophyte calls to mind the Classical heads on the Gnaios cameos, whose monumental solidity has been discussed as an extrapolation of statuary composition.[5] The Apollo-like youth's strong, straight nose, full-lipped mouth and sturdy chin seem to retrace the forms of the head of a Maenad now in the National Museum of Naples,[6] or of the Apollo of Myllos in Leningrad,[7] both of which are recorded in the inventories of Lorenzo de' Medici. The standing nude figure shivering from the cold has another possible Classical source mentioned by Fremantle, who compared it to a bronze now in The Metropolitan Museum of Art in New York.[8] Other specific Classical sources are brought to mind by the paired busts of the two onlookers behind Saint Peter, which suggest those on coins, seals and cameos, for example the double portrait of Tiberius and Livia on a white onyx cameo.[9]

The marvelous bearded man in blue at the center yields a totally new reading now that he has been freed from overpainting and retouching. Previously described as a "neophyte to be baptized" in the act of undressing, he is now revealed to be in the process of getting dressed, finishing the buttoning of his costume with his head and hair still wet.

The summary painting technique is again encountered, even more graphically, in the heads of the people standing between the man in blue and the shivering nude. There the linear definition by quick strokes, creating rapidly and decisively the outlines of the features—mouth, eyebrows, nose—had been previously misunderstood, due to retouching in an earlier restoration.[10]

A great revelation also came regarding the light that penetrates the scene in a nearly "raking" manner, coming from the direction of the actual chapel window and creating an extraordinary play of shadows on the bodies and clothing. In particular, the light functions, apart from the excellent drawing technique, as a means of "constructing" the head of Peter, which was thought by some to be by Masolino, or even redone by Filippino.[11] Also, the light creates definite cast shadows[12]—that of Saint Peter projected onto the riverbank, as well as other traces, although altered by the heat of the fire, on the other bank behind the kneeling nude. Moreover, the shadows resolve sculpturally the spatial definition of the mountains. As these fade in intensity, they create a sense, not of circumscription, but of a continuous spatial recession extending far beyond the limits of the bordering pilaster.

Whereas the relationship between the contiguous scenes of *The Tribute Money* and *Saint Peter Preaching* perpendicular to it was developed by linking up of the profiles of the mountains in each scene, the reinforcement of the visual connection between the similarly placed *Baptizing of the Neophytes* and *The Healing of the Crippled Man and the Raising of Tabitha* was achieved via chromatic assonance. The barren mountains of the *Baptizing* are treated in shades of green that tie up with the green used on the temple portico at the left in *The Healing of the Crippled Man*. In both instances, the painted corner pilasters act as structural articulation, standing out from the background and establishing the foreground plane.

In the past, some scholars believed that they could distinguish the different hands in the fresco, variously mentioning Masolino and Filippino, in addition to Masaccio to whom is obviously owed the concept of the scene. Longhi (1940), for example, supported the idea that Filippino had intervened in the "paired-bust" figures of the onlookers at the left.[13] Accepted by Bologna (1966), this attribution was not shared by Salmi (1947), who called the *Baptizing* "extremely damaged, but still possible to judge." Maintaining that Peter's head was redone by Filippino, Salmi affirmed Masaccio's authorship of the rest of the figures, in spite of their disfigurement by repainting. Procacci (1951), followed by Parronchi (1966), originally assigned the head of Peter and the two onlookers to Masolino, but subsequent to the cleaning, he now no longer doubts Masaccio's authorship of the entire scene. Parronchi now maintains (1989) that the heads of the two onlookers were done by an anonymous follower after Masaccio, and that the head of Peter is also very weak and certainly not by either Masolino or Masaccio.

Berti (1964 and 1968) was the first to speak out decisively, contrary to the hypotheses of earlier scholars, for Masaccio's complete authorship of both the landscape setting and the figures. He dismissed the idea of any reciprocal insertions in the two pendant frescoes and compared the "barren hills in perspective forshortening in the background, the bearded onlooker and the pair of contemporary portraits" in the *Baptizing* with a similar pattern in Masaccio's *Adoration of the Magi* on the predella from his polyptych for the Carmine of Pisa, done in 1426 (panel now in the Berlin Painting Gallery). Nevertheless, now that the cleaning has rendered these perspectively foreshortened "bare hills" more legible, he and other scholars have begun to suspect an equal collaboration between Masaccio and Masolino, to be considered as well for *Saint Peter Preaching*.

As for the heads of the figures on the left, Berti was again the first to emphasize the impossibility of a later insertion, having determined from Tintori's descriptions of the *giornate* that these heads had been painted prior to that of Saint Peter. Crediting a verbal hypothesis proposed by Luciano Bellosi, contrary to one in which an "alternating" division of the work had been set up in the original design phase for the chapel (O. Casazza, 1988), Berti opted for assigning the landscape to Masolino. This supposed an initial agreement to split up the work quite simply with "the right side all for Masolino and the left for Masaccio."

Once the landscape in this scene had been executed, this plan was changed only because Masolino, "realizing the difficult test of the anatomy" called for in the *Baptizing*, may have acquiesced to a request from Masaccio, "who hoped to show off his bravura, proposing and enacting an exchange which brought about an alternative execution of the respective figural groupings in the pendant frescoes below the landscape backgrounds," in a deviation from the original plan.[14] According to Berti, this would explain "the absence of cast shadows in the scene."[15]

Apart from the technical artificiality of such an operation,[16] it would appear, since the cleaning, that it is far more difficult to point out "generic Masolino-like characteristics" in the landscape, which is now clearly seen to be in perspectival foreshortening in the drawing and the rigorous placement of light and shadow to define the exact spatial location.

The *giornate* have been recounted and now number ten, instead of the nine reported in Tintori's survey first published by Berti (1964).[17] The working sequence is as follows: (1–2) the sky, the mountains and the righthand pilaster, (3–4) the two figures on the left, (5) the head of Saint Peter, (6) the center of the group of neophytes, (7) the three figures standing at the extreme right, (8) Peter's robe and gesturing arm, (9) Peter's feet, the ground and part of the river immediately around them, plus the lower part of the clothing of the already-baptized neophyte and (10) the kneeling neophyte receiving the baptismal waters and the immediate environment around him.

A variation on this sequence can be deduced by considering a type of execution not strictly tied to the work levels (i.e., high-low) but rather handled by groups. Beginning in the same way with the mountains and the pilaster (1–2), it might be hypothesized that the entire left section was completed next, from the sixth *giornata* through the eighth and ninth, using the above designations. These would then be followed by the section with the shivering nude and that for the kneeling neophyte (*giornate* 7 and 10 above respectively).

[1] G. Vasari, *Le vite de' più eccellenti pittori, scultori ed archittetori*, (1568), ed. G. Milanesi, Florence, 1878–1881, 2, p. 131.

[2] Because of this gesture and particularly due to the "tubular" working of the sleeve, Brandi expressed doubts regarding Masaccio's authorship and thought that this area had been repainted later ("Masaccio," unpublished course handout, University of Palermo, 1961–62). Berti hypothesized that the area had probably been repainted by Filippino (*Masaccio*, Milan, 1964).

[3] R. Fremantle, "Masaccio e l'antico, *Critica d'Arte*, 103, 1969, pp. 39ff.; *Il tesoro di Lorenzo il Magnifico*, exhibition catalog, Florence, 1972, p. 51, entry nos. 17 and 18; and A. Giuliano, *I cammei, dalla Collezione Medicea del Museo Archeologico di Firenze*, Rome, 1989.

[4] Giuliano, *I cammei*, p. 188, no. 80, which illustrates a *pietra stellara* cameo showing Hercules wrestling the Nemean lion with his back almost completely turned. Note: The *Torso* had not yet been rediscovered at the time.

[5] Giuliano, *I cammei*, pp. 30–38.

[6] *Tesoro*, p. 51, entry nos. 17 and 18.

[7] Giuliano, *I cammei*, p. 50.

[8] Fremantle, p. 46, fig. 48.

[9] Fremantle, p. 51; and, more recently, Giuliano, *I cammei*, p. 159, which includes a vast amount of documentation. The onyx of Tiberius and Livia (Medici Collection, Museo Archaeologico, Florence) is cat. no. 159, pp. 234–35.

[10] M. Salmi, *Masaccio*, Milan, 1947, p. 190.

[11] For Masolino's hand: U. Procacci, *Masaccio*, Milan, 1951, but who, after the cleaning, now attributes it to Masaccio; and A. Parronchi, 1966, who now believes neither Masolino nor Masaccio did it. For Filippino: Salmi, *Masaccio*, 1947, p. 190; and Berti, *Masaccio*, 1947, who then believed it to be a repainting by Filippino but now (1988 and 1989) gives the whole composition to Masaccio, except for the mountain landscape done by Masolino.

[12] Berti still claims that the cast shadows do not exist: "There are no shadow projections in the *Baptizing*, for the reason that it followed the Tabitha scene which had no such shadows, and as its homologue also would not have them" (*Masaccio*, 1989, p. 19).

Of course, shadows do appear in *The Raising of Tabitha*, not only cast by the figures but also by the individual stones of the piazza's pavement.

[13] "In the inefficient repetition of almost three-quarters which look identical, the two youths on the left lead us to suspect that they were also a deft insertion by Filippino in an area that Masaccio had inadvertently left unfinished or barely traced in *sinopia* on the *arriccio*" (R. Longhi, "Fatti di Masolino e di Masaccio," *Critica d'Arte*, 3–4, 1940, p. 170).

[14] Berti, *Masaccio*, 1989, p. 19.

[15] The fact that shadows are indeed present can be seen in the photographic reproductions illustrating this book, and this is discussed in the text wherever relevant.

[16] Considering that the *sinopia* was already presumably delineated in its entirety, would Masolino really have stopped after painting the mountain landscape because he wasn't able to execute successfully the nudes and other figures already designed for the scene? And how would Masaccio have reacted to this? If both had already drawn the complete *sinopie* for their scenes, would not the makeup of these have been taken into consideration?

[17] Berti, *Masaccio*, 1964, p. 147.

MASOLINO

The Healing of the Crippled Man and the Raising of Tabitha

Right wall, second register, 2.47 × 5.88 meters

Prior to the recent restoration, the lower part of this wall showed considerable disruption in the form of two large cracks caused by the installation of new church structures on the exterior of the wall in the eighteenth century. These were significantly reduced by the removal of the coarse refacing of intonaco that was meant to suture the gaps and its replacement with a chromatically selected new intonaco applied wherever necessary to reconstitute the surface. During this work, it was possible to observe and document the underdrawing (*sinopia*) on the rough plaster beneath (*arriccio*).

Here as in *The Tribute Money*, Saint Peter is shown in two different testimonies of faith. In the same scene are depicted two miracles performed by him—the healing of a crippled man and the raising of the dead woman Tabitha, as told in Acts. The healing episode should not be confused, however, with that of the healing of the paralytic Aeneas, even though this event is found immediately preceding that of the raising of Tabitha told in Acts 9:36–43. (The healing of Aeneas, which has no connection with the fresco, took place in Lydda and is described, without specifying its exact location, in Acts 9: 33–35: "There he [Peter] found a man named Aeneas, a paralytic who had been bedridden for eight years. Peter said to him, 'Aeneas, Jesus Christ cures you! Get up and make your bed.' The man got up at once.")

This fresco is closely tied to the narrative of the healing of the crippled man in Jersualem, recounted in Acts 3:1–10:

Once when Peter and John were going up to the temple for prayer at the three o'clock hour, a man crippled from birth was being carried in. They would bring him every day and put him at the temple gate called "the Beautiful" to beg from the people as they entered. When he saw Peter and John on their way in, he begged them for alms. Peter fixed his gaze on the man; so did John. "Look at us!" Peter said. The cripple gave them his whole attention, hoping to get something. Then Peter said: "I have neither silver nor gold, but what I have I give you. In the name of Jesus Christ the Nazorean, walk!" Then Peter took him by the right hand and pulled him up. Immediately the beggar's feet and ankles became strong; he jumped up, stood for a moment, then began to walk around. He went into the temple with them—walking, jumping about and praising God. When the people saw him moving and giving praise to God, they recognized him as that beggar who used to sit at the Beautiful Gate of the temple. They were struck with astonishment—utterly stupefied at what had happened to him.

The episode of the raising of the dead woman Tabitha is related in Acts 9:36–41:

Now in Joppa there was a certain woman convert named Tabitha (in Greek Dorcas, meaning a gazelle). Her life was marked by constant good deeds and acts of charity. At about that time she fell ill and died. They washed her body and laid it out in an upstairs room. Since Lydda was near Joppa, the disciples, who had heard that Peter was there, sent two men to him with the urgent request, "Please come over to us without delay." Peter set out with them as they asked. Upon his arrival they took him upstairs to the room. All the widows came to him in tears and showed him the various garments that Dorcas had made when she was still with them. Peter first made everyone go outside; then he knelt down and prayed. Turning to the dead body, he said, "Tabitha, stand up." She opened her eyes, then looked at Peter and sat up. He gave her his hand and helped her to her feet. The next thing he did was to call in those who were believers and the widows to show them that she was still alive.

Masolino set the two episodes in a single location in the same city, even though historically they occurred in different places at different times. The healing of the crippled man is represented at the left and the raising of Tabitha at the right. In the piazza at the center of the picture, two elegantly dressed young men both divide and connect the scenes of the miraculous events. Their presence and that of the figures near the houses give the feeling of a normal civic event taking place, and the setting appears to represent an actual Florentine piazza. For example, it could

Masolino, The Healing of the Crippled Man and the Raising of Tabitha, *detail*

Masolino, The Healing of the Crippled Man and the Raising of Tabitha, *detail*

be a reproduction of the Piazza della Signoria, if one thinks of the temple portico on the left as a recollection or synthesis of the Loggia dei Lanzi (dell'Orcagna). Or, more simply, it may be a derivation of the traditional patrician Florentine loggia designed for religious celebrations. Similar recollections and syntheses are to be seen in the houses in the background that, in spite of modifications made in the facades, have the typical pattern of dimensions still preserved in Florence still today. The authentic representation extends even to the pavement that is differentiated between the main thoroughfare and the ground of the piazza, where the stones of varying sizes increase the effect of spatial depth with their cast shadows. Additional elements enhance an everyday reality—flowerpots on the sills, linens hung out to air, birdcages, two chained monkeys on a ledge, people chatting with each other from window to window, and the typical horizontal poles attached across the facades with iron brackets (*erri*).

The portico on the left, although described in the past as weak and shaky, now has an emphatic architectural stability coming from the original colors recovered in the cleaning that define the structural elements from the plain capitals to the red intonaco of the groin vaulting. Also, in the loggia on the right where the miracle of the raising of Tabitha takes place, the Albertian (and therefore classical) coloration of the wall-facing and entablature successfully gives substance and dimension to an architecture that is no longer an "unnailed box" (*cassone schiodato*), as it was wittily characterized in comparison with Masaccio's more solid structures.[1]

The entire scene was once attributed to Masaccio, beginning with Cavalcaselle (1865) and followed by Schmarsow (1895–1899), Kern (1913), Van Marle (1928), Trenkler (1932) and Oertel (1934). Only Mesnil (1929) claimed the contrary, that Masolino was the author. The concordance of opinion among the majority of historians and critics had already been contested in an unnoticed article of 1891 by B. Marrai, in which acute observations were made on the differences in the way that Masaccio and Masolino each formed haloes.[2] Masaccio's were foreshortened, according to how the head was positioned and turned in the space, and Masolino's were done in the Trecento manner. For this author, all doubts were erased as to attribution, and *The Healing of the Crippled Man and the Raising of Tabitha* was confirmed as the work of Masolino. In the same article, Marrai also affirmed the attribution to Masolino of *Saint Peter Preaching*, not on the basis of haloes, which do not appear there, but because of "characteristics in the painting also found in the scene with Adam and Eve under the tree of knowledge."

Although in agreement with the attribution of *Tabitha* to Masolino, Gamba was the first (1928) to propose the identification in it of some collaborations by Masaccio. Others following this were Giglioli (1930), who suggested that the genuflecting nun at the back nearest Tabitha was by Masaccio, and Toesca (1937), who believed the crippled man to be his. In 1932 and 1947, Salmi maintained that Masaccio had participated in this fresco as Masolino's assistant, and he attributed to him the drawing of the crippled man which was then finished by Masolino. Also, in 1947, Salmi specified that Masolino had done the houses and small background figures. The assignment by Longhi (1940) of the houses and all the small figures to Masaccio was accepted by Steinbart (1948), Procacci in part (1951 and 1965), Micheletti (1959), Parronchi (1966), Bologna (1966) and Berti (1964 and 1968).

Berti revised his opinion (1988 and 1989) after certain details of technique were brought out after the cleaning (O. Casazza, 1988), and he now believes in the total and exclusive execution of the whole scene by Masolino. Parronchi (1989) disagrees and maintains that the blocks of houses, the insertions on the horizon line, the figures and even the cobblestones with cast shadows are all the work of Masaccio. Baldini (1989) specifies his position on the new technical evaluations as follows:

> Regarding the execution, from a technical viewpoint, there are absolutely no differences in the original painting level between the background and the rest of the scene; and as for its connections to Masaccio, the absolute difference in approach has already been emphasized, for example, in what we could gather in the restitutions of the tiled roofs in *The Distribution of Goods* and *The Raising of the Son of Theophilus*.
>
> The background consists of a single *giornata*, nota-

ble for its unusually large surface. Usually in fresco technique, the area of the *giornata* is extended or restricted according to the amount of time needed for the execution of its painting. A single-color background with little drawing can be executed quickly over a large surface, whereas the head of a figure, requiring the perfecting of numerous drawn details and variations in color, needs more work time and therefore has an intonaco application of rather reduced size. Yet the large background *giornata* of this scene is in truth rich in details and shows a very large number of geometric measuring lines that were incised on the wet plaster to assist in the drawing. These marks give evidence for the very elaborate, complex structural "cage" all measured out and recorded with exact relationships onto the surface, serving as both rule and compass.

To allow for this kind of necessarily slow and extended development in a single work session or *giornata*, or to avoid risks where harmonious continuity might be affected by rests or breaks in the work session, the preparation of the intonaco should not be 'tirata a mestola' or troweled until completely smooth, but rather it should be left in a porous condition. Rendering a smooth surface acts to extract nearly all the water in the plaster mix. This accelerates the drying or setting time, which should be kept within the proper limits to allow for an extended work period by maintaining the damp plaster and retarding the carbonization process. And it was on a large surface prepared in just this way that the carefully articulated and previously worked-out drawing was transferred by incising. In such an operation, Masaccio's innovative perspective vision certainly must have been a determining factor. Masaccio himself could even have participated in the transfer by incising, working alongside Masolino, but the pictorial execution, definitive painting and coloration are all totally and uniquely related to the chromatic and working techniques employed by Masolino. And while this may elucidate materially the authorship of the background, it should be added that there is a variation in rhythm and proportions in the perspective view of the narrow alleyway seen on the right. This view is included in another *giornata* with the architecture of the loggia of the Tabitha scene, and the pattern of the scenic perspective has changed. Comparing it to the more realistic treatment of the houses included in the *giornata* extending from the right vertical edge of the temple portico to the right edge of the facade of the last house to the left of the alley, there is an intuitive perspective with a different "measurement," in that the houses along the right side are of a different height—five floors instead of three. They have no formal relationship in "reality" with the rest of the architecture, and they were not given the precise incised outlines like those seen for the alley on the left.

All of the small figures in front of the houses should be attributed to Masolino; their pictorial approach has—other than formal similarities—chromatic developments typical of him. This is justified not only by the woman holding a child by the hand, that we find again exactly repeated by Masolino at Castiglione Olona, [1435, ceiling fresco, *Marriage of the Virgin*, Collegiate Church], but especially by the painting technique, which is identical in color and light to that of the prophet figures in the tondi on the *Pietà* at Empoli.[3]

The cleaning has provided evidence of the value that Masolino placed on the lighting of this scene, with the real chapel window as the unique source of illumination. The light creates strong cast shadows on the ground, including those from the pavement stones. As Vasari wrote of Masolino: "And because he began to understand light and shadows well, because he had worked in relief, he made so many difficult foreshortenings very well; as it can be seen in the poor man who is begging for alms from Saint Peter, who has a leg extending into the background, agreeing so closely in the contour lines of the drawing and the shading of colors that it seems actually to be puncturing a hole in the [chapel] wall."[4]

These shadows that once again became clearly visible after the restoration (O. Casazza, 1988)[5] were never brought up by Berti (1989), who also did not notice those in Masaccio's *Baptizing of the Neophytes*. Berti in fact denied their existence to support and advocate a "homological consequence" on the side of Masaccio in relation to Masolino, and to guarantee his hypothesis that Masolino actually began the execution of the *Baptizing*.

Thirty *giornate* were found in the fresco's surface, as opposed to twenty-eight accounted for in Tintori's survey. Proceeding from the left across the picture above the contours of the figure groups, they are: (1–4) the corner pilaster, temple portico, background houses and the upper part of Tabitha's loggia, (5–6) the small figures sitting in front of the house on the left, (7–12) the left group of the crippled man, Saint Peter and Saint John and the piazza pavement around them, (13–15) the two young men in turbans at the center, (16) the tiny figure appearing in the right distance past the back of the companion of Saint Peter in the Tabitha scene, (17) the head of Peter and (18) the head of his companion in the Tabitha scene, (19) the robes of Peter and his companion, (20) the lower part of the right-hand loggia and the ground directly in front of it, (21–23) the heads of the three bearded figures behind Tabitha, (24–25) their bodies and gestures, (26) the heads of the two kneeling nuns, (27) the clothing of the nun at the right, (28) Tabitha's upper body, (29) Tabitha's lower body and bed, and (30) the body of the nun next to her.

An alternative sequence might be that the fourth *giornata* was followed by the execution of all of the heads of the standing figures in the same order as above (5–14), and then all the seated and kneeling figures in the same succession (15–30).

In this fresco, there are few serious or extensive chromatic alterations primarily linked to the fire. These appear limited to the dividing cornice at the bottom, the crippled man's stool, foot and a small area of ground below him at the left, and the flooring of the loggia along the extreme edges at the right. Color changes can be observed in the pictorial surface, however, that relate to the execution technique and alterations occurring over time. The light gray-blue of the sky is produced by the underglazing used prior to the application of the final blue azurite finish. It reappeared due to the complete loss of the blue pigment on the surface. Applied *a secco* (on the dry intonaco), the azurite failed to resist the effects of time, loosening and flaking off, either due to the medium used to apply it to the undercoat or as a result of abrasions or removal during "washings" in the previous old restoration work. As in *The Expulsion*, where traces of the original blue pigment were found preserved in the once-gilded light rays emanating from the door of Eden, it has been possible here too to recover a small trace of the original sky color. The azurite pigment penetrated a depression made in the wet intonaco by a measuring string, where it remained protected from the subsequent surface cleanings.

The young man on the left wearing a turban lacks volume due to the loss of definition by

Masolino, The Healing of the Crippled Man and the Raising of Tabitha, *detail*

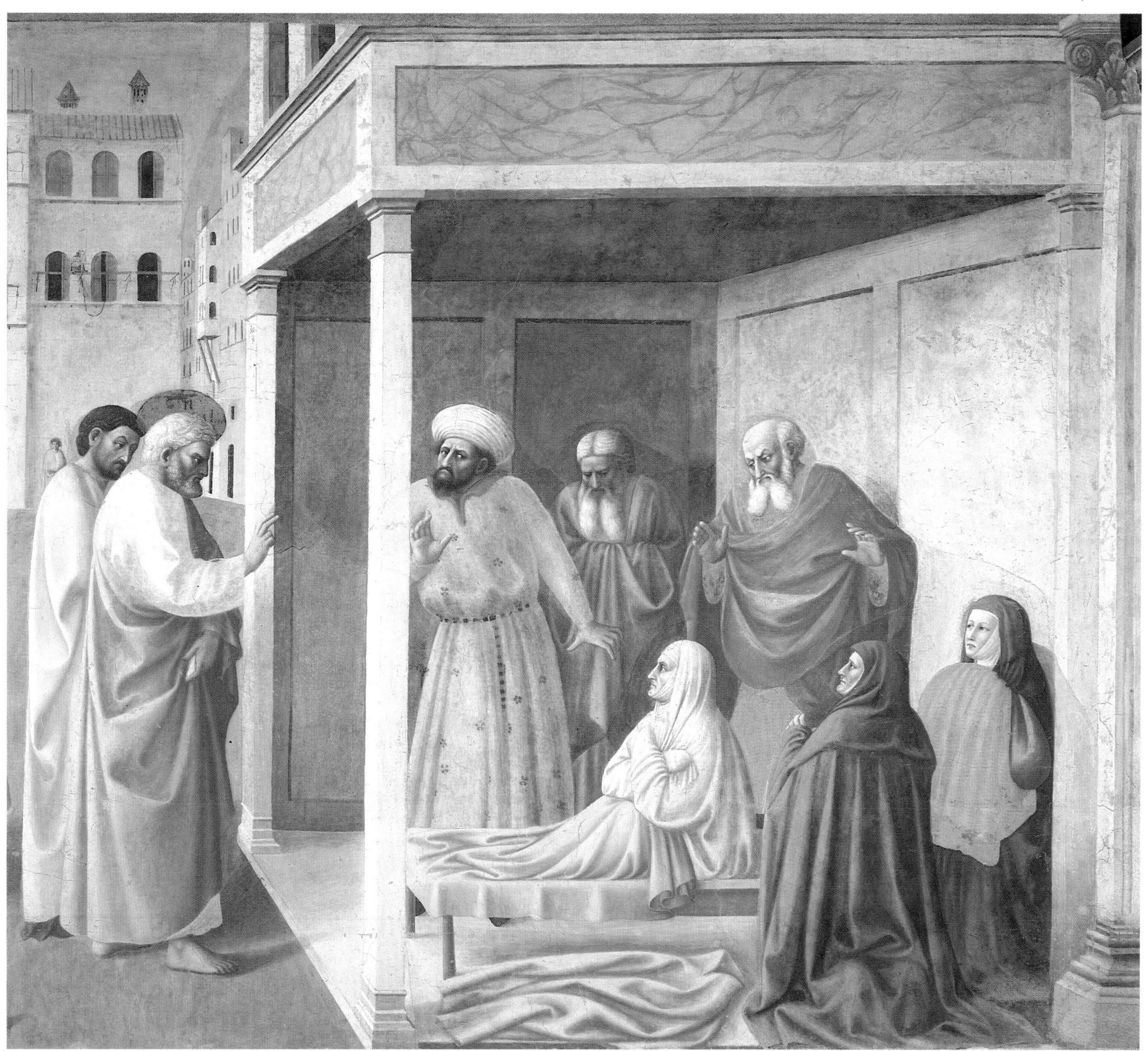

Masolino, The Healing of the Crippled Man and the Raising of Tabitha, *detail*

shading on his green damask costume. Either the shadow color was executed *a secco* or on a completely overworked intonaco.

Barely noticeable in the space to the left of the two young men, from the piazza back to the street near the houses, there are slight variations of color that can be ascribed to differences in the behavior of the intonaco during the hardening phase. The chimneys on the house roofs have lost a good deal of their original paint due to their nearly *a secco* execution, as is the case for some of the animals painted in the windows and on the ledges of the houses. Also, the figure in blue facing Saint Peter in the Tabitha scene once had a costume decorated in cut velvet like that of the young man in the piazza wearing the green cloak. The original floral design became visible again in the infrared reflectographic examination that revealed the remnants of pigment. Executed probably *a secco*, it quickly disappeared and was substituted by the present decoration of red flowers interspersed with little "tiles" in gold leaf.

[1] R. Longhi, "Fatti di Masolino e di Masaccio," *Critica d'Arte* 3–4, 1940, p. 158.
[2] B. Marrai, "Gli affreschi della Cappella Brancacci al Carmine," *Arte e Storia*, April 10, 1891, pp. 59–60.
[3] U. Baldini, "Del *Tributo* e altro di Masaccio," *Critica d'Arte*, 54, no. 20, pp. 30–32. For the Empoli *Pietà* and its 1987 restoration, see R. Proto Pisani, *Masolino a Empoli*, Empoli, 1987, pp. 113ff.; and A. Paolucci, *Il Museo della Collegiata di S. Andrea in Empoli*, Florence, 1985, pp. 92ff.
[4] G. Vasari, *Le vite de' più eccellenti pittori, scultori ed architettori* (1568), ed. G. Milanesi, Florence, 1878–81, 2, pp. 266–67.
[5] O. Casazza, "La grande gabbia architettonica de Masaccio," *Critic d'Arte*, 53, no. 16, 1988, p. 90 and p. 80, fig. 14.

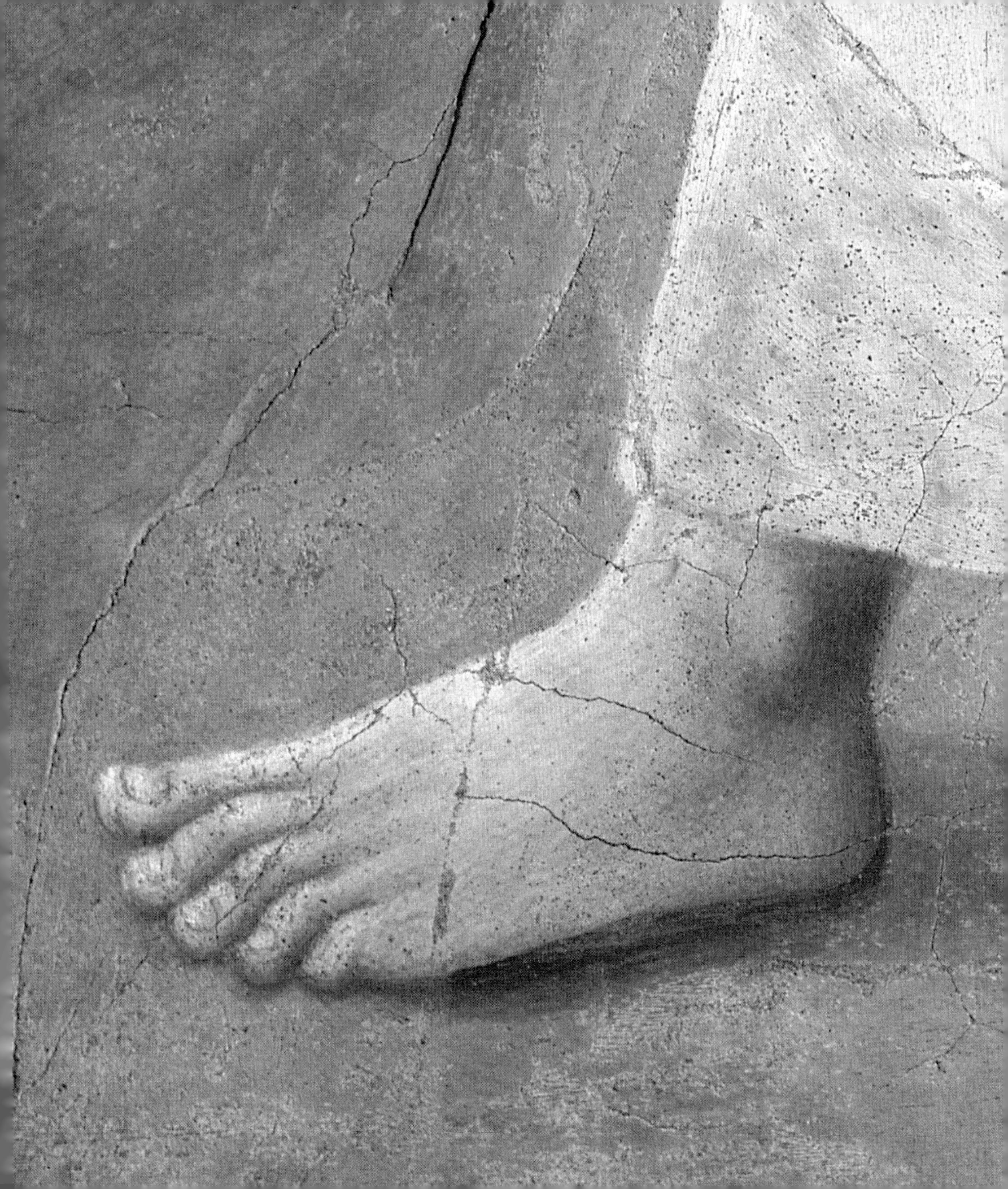

MASACCIO

The Distribution of Goods and the Death of Ananias

Back wall to the right of the altar, first register, 2.32 × 1.57 meters

These subjects are taken from related passages in Acts, one following the other. The story of the communal sharing of goods is told as follows:

The community of believers were of one heart and one mind. None of them ever claimed anything as his own; rather, everything was held in common. With power the apostles bore witness to the resurrection of the Lord Jesus, and great respect was paid to them all; nor was there anyone needy among them, for all who owned property or houses sold them and donated the proceeds. They used to lay them at the feet of the apostles to be distributed to everyone according to his need. There was a certain Levite from Cyprus named Joseph, to whom the apostles gave the name Barnabas (meaning "son of encouragement"). He sold a farm that he owned and made a donation of the money, laying it at the apostles' feet. (Acts 4:32–37).

The story continues, telling of the death of Ananias, depicted here, and the death of his wife as well:

Another man named Ananias and his wife Sapphira likewise sold a piece of property. With the connivance of his wife he put aside a part of the proceeds for himself; the rest he took and laid at the feet of the apostles. Peter exclaimed: "Ananias, why have you let Satan fill your heart so as to make you lie to the Holy Spirit and keep for yourself some of the proceeds from that field? Was it not yours as long as it remained unsold? Even when you sold it, was not the money still yours? How could you ever concoct such a scheme? You have lied not to men but to God!" At the sound of these words, Ananias fell dead. Great fear came upon all who later heard of it. Some of the young men came forward, wrapped up the body, and carried it out for burial. Three hours later Ananias' wife came in, unaware of what had happened. Peter said to her, "Tell me, did you sell that piece of property for such and such an amount?" She answered, "Yes, that was the sum." Peter replied, "How could you two scheme to put the Spirit of the Lord to the test? The footsteps of the men who have just buried your husband can be heard at the door. They stand ready to carry you out too." With that, she fell dead at his feet. The young men came in, found her dead, and carried her out for burial beside her husband. Great fear came on the whole church and on all who heard of it (Acts 5:1–11).

Masaccio summarized the two Biblical episodes—that of the distributing of the goods of the church by Saint Peter and that of the death of Ananias, whose body lies on the ground at Peter's feet—by depicting them as simultaneous events. The story unfolds with typical classical solemnity in a composition of opposed and graduated masses. The scene is set with a background view of the countryside beyond the houses, no doubt as a stylistic opportunity for a variation on the composition of the pendant on the other side of the altar, *Saint Peter Healing with His Shadow*. It may also have been done (Berti, 1964) because the text in Acts speaks of selling both "property (land) and houses."[1]

No one has ever doubted Masaccio's authorship of the whole picture, apart from a few indications (M. Salmi, 1947) of repainting and restoring on the body of Ananias in some extremely abraded areas at the left and on the figure of Saint Peter. In the nineteenth century, Cavalcaselle had already described and analyzed the scene as having "some houses far off on a hill that, as usual, stand out against the blue of the sky," adding only that "the painting has darkened a bit over the years, and the figure believed to be Ananias and the lower part of the woman with the baby were restored with new colors." Cavalcaselle pointed out here, as elsewhere, the deep blue of the sky against which the figures and landscapes were silhouetted. Yet the only blues that reappeared after cleaning in all of the scenes are the dull preparatory undercoats. There is no trace of the original blue finish applied *a secco* on the surface in this scene either. On the woman holding the baby, the considerable "retouching" of her clothing turned out in fact to be an actual restoration of the fresco done after the 1771 fire. In Cavalcaselle's drawing of this scene from his Notebook, he not only labeled all the characters—young woman, kneeling man, men, dead man, old crippled man, crippled man, Saint Peter, the young apostle—but also inserted the word "ground" to define the space immediately above the body of Ananias. There is even a sketch in this space of the leg of the woman holding the baby, which is no longer visible and did not reappear in the recent restoration. This may have been done from a reconstructive pastiche, or it

Masaccio, The Distribution of Goods and the Death of Ananias, *detail*

might be an interpretive transcribing of the fresco's appearance from the Lasinio engraving, where there was a total "reinvention" of the ground in the areas particularly damaged by the fire.[2]

The removal of the dirt and overpainting during the restoration did not bring forth changes in the sections repaired after the fire. Yet, rather than handle these nonoriginal, reconstructed areas in a neutral way, we preferred to readjust them in our restoration with a chromatic selection in harmony with the newly discovered color hues. These sections thus were treated, not as a purely arbitrary or invented adaptation, but as documents that could be assumed to be a recollection or reproposal of what had been legible and extant before the fire.

Among the important data which emerged was the fact that Saint John's cloak, tunic and feet, and the superimposed hands of Ananias were not by Masaccio but rather were products of a "restorative" intervention by Filippino (U. Baldini, 1986), since they were included in a *giornata* which overlays the original Masaccio surface.[3]

The presence of painting foreign to Masaccio's also appeared on the body of Ananias, thereby reinforcing the belief that Filippino's interventions in Masaccio's work were not limited to what had been left unfinished. In addition, he had performed actual restoration work on the damages incurred by the frescos due to deterioration, and also, very probably, to the ruination that happened during the *damnatio memoriae* in the expunging of the portraits of the Brancacci family and friends.[4] (Obviously excluded from such restoration was *The Dispute with Simon Magus and the Crucifixion of Saint Peter* left unpainted on the right wall, which had to be executed by Filippino in its entirety.) It should be noted that, just as in *The Raising of the Son of Theophilus* with the Masaccio head of a Carmelite brother in the group at the extreme left, Filippino's intervention here also respected Masaccio's original work. The faces of the individuals were neither destroyed nor redone, even when they had deteriorated and suffered from abrasions.

This fresco has been seen not only as a message of "salvation"[5] but also as a further secular reference and exhortation for compliance with the declaration of income under the new Florentine Catasto,[6] by way of the example of radical Early Christian communitarianism and divine punishment for false declarations of goods. Another contemporary reference—to the patron family of the chapel—was hypothesized by P. Meller, who identified the kneeling figure behind Saint Peter's right arm as the portrait of either Cardinal Rainaldo or Cardinal Tommaso Brancacci.[7]

Mentioned but not emphasized by Mesnil (1912)[8] was the fact, especially clear once the marble altar and balustrade installed in the mid-eighteenth century were out of the way, that the two impeccably constructed scenes on either side of the window could have ideally been merged in a single composition. They were created to be viewed from two different vantage points, however—*The Distribution of Goods* from the entrance, on the right side of the chapel on axis with the corner of the building in the center of the scene, and *Saint Peter Healing with His Shadow* from close up in the center of the chapel (A. Parronchi, 1966).[9] The visual linking of the scenes is fully confirmed by the recovery of the painted jamb on the left side of the window from behind the altar, and equally confirmed by the cleaning of the surface that, without the altar, allowed for a rereading of all of the incised lines and string impressions still visible on the intonaco. From this, the following facts can be confirmed: (a) an equivalence of horizon lines in the two scenes, (b) for the *Healing* scene, the confluence of the architectural perspective lines at a vanishing point on the horizon line at the center of the back wall of the chapel and, (c) in the *Distribution*, the confluence of the architectural perspective lines slightly above the horizon line at a vanishing point that coincides with the perpendicular frame on the right side of the *Healing* scene.

The open and connected relationship between the two frescoes is further evidenced by the fact that neither has a painted pilaster closing off the scene on the side of the window inset. The original light, slender form of the lancet would not have seriously interrupted the visual continuity between the wall surfaces. To the contrary, by means of its concavity a delicate relationship with real external space was established, not as another vista but only as an effective source of light to illuminate the scene and provide three-dimensional solidity to the figures controlled by light and shadow (Rossi, 1989).[10]

The twelve *giornate* follow this sequence:[11] (1) entablature and capital of the corner pilaster, (2) the rest of the pilaster, (3) part of the scenery and the background, with all the architecture up to the height of the heads of the figures, (4) the woman with the baby in her arms, (5) the head of Saint Peter, (6) the four heads to the right of Saint Peter, (7) the group of poor people to the left, (8) the body of the woman with her arm outstretched to receive the donation, Peter's arm extending toward her, and the kneeling figure between them, (9) Saint Peter's body, ruined but redone by Filippino, (10) the body of the figure on the extreme right originally with Saint John, also redone by Filippino, (11) the figure of Ananias and (12) Saint John's clothing, part of his hands and feet, and the hands of Ananias redone by Filippino.

[1] L. Berti, *Masaccio*, Milan, 1964; and L. Berti and R. Foggi, *Masaccio*, Florence, 1989, p. 120.

[2] O. Casazza and P. Cassinelli Lazzeri, *La Cappella Brancacci, conservazione e restauro nei documenti della grafica antica*, Modena, 1989, pp. 32 and 87ff.

[3] U. Baldini, "Restauro della Cappella Brancacci, primi risultati," *Critica d'Arte*, 9, 1986, p. 67.

[4] O. Casazza, "La grande gabbia architettonica di Masaccio," *Critica d'Arte*, 53, no. 16, 1988, p. 15.

[5] O. Casazza, "Il ciclo delle Storie de San Pietro e la 'Historia Salutis.' Nuova lettura della Cappella Brancacci," *Critica d'Arte*, 51, no. 9, 1986, pp. 69ff.

[6] L. Berti, *Masaccio*, 1964, p. 102.

[7] P. Meller, "La Cappella Brancacci, problemi ritrattistici e iconografici," *Acropoli*, 4, 1961, pp. 273ff.

[8] J. Mesnil, "Per la storia della Cappella Brancacci," *Rivista d'Arte*, 8, 1912, pp. 34ff.

[9] A. Parronchi, *Masaccio*, Florence, 1966, pp. 28ff. A diagram of this is reproduced here.

[10] P. A. Rossi, "Cappella Brancacci, una proposta: facciamola vedere 'vuota,'" *La Nazione*, Nov. 23, 1989.

[11] Berti, *Masaccio*, 1964, p. 148. The Tintori survey showed ten *giornate*, but their enumeration was not exact wherever there were serious losses of the original intonaco which had been repaired and redone several times, beginning with Filippino's intervention.

MASACCIO

Saint Peter Healing with His Shadow

Back wall to the left of the altar, first register, 2.32 × 1.62 meters

The scene is derived from Acts 5:12–14 and, as in the chronology of the New Testament narrative, it follows the stories of the distribution of goods and the death of Ananias depicted in the same location to the right of the altar:

> Through the hands of the apostles, many signs and wonders occurred among the people. By mutual agreement they used to meet in Solomon's Portico. No one else dared join them, despite the fact that the people held them in great esteem. Nevertheless more and more believers, men and women in great numbers, were continually added to the Lord. The people carried the sick into the streets and laid them on cots and mattresses, so that when Peter passed by at least his shadow might fall on one or another of them. Crowds from the towns around Jerusalem would gather, too, bringing their sick and those who were troubled by unclean spirits, all of whom were cured.

Masaccio's authorship of the entire scene has never been doubted.

Beginning with Vasari, who copied the likeness of the man wearing the cowled red hat for Masolino's portrait at the beginning of this artist's biography in the 1568 edition of the *Vite*, scholars have believed that contemporary individuals can be identified among those represented in the scene. Without specifying his identity, Poggi (1903) noted the resemblance of the bearded man with clasped hands to one of the Magi on the predella of the altarpiece painted by Masaccio in 1426 for the Carmelite Church in Pisa (predella panel now in Berlin, Painting Gallery).[1] Meller (1961) believed that this bearded man was a portrait of Donatello, whereas Berti (1966) identified as Donatello the elderly bearded man seen between the figures of Saint Peter and Saint John the Evangelist. As for Saint John, Parronchi (1966) claimed to recognize in him the features of Masaccio's brother Giovanni, nicknamed *lo Scheggia* ("Chip"), while Meller (1962) thought the young apostle was a self-portrait of Masaccio.

The removal of the marble altar in the recent restoration uncovered a hidden portion of the fresco at the right edge of the picture, which proved to be of primary importance in the "reading" of the scene. According to U. Baldini (1986):

> The discovery behind the figure of Saint John of a church facade, a campanile, some blue sky and a column with a Corinthian capital is more than just an extensive recovery. It, in fact, lends such a new character to the scene that it overturns frequent past descriptions and acclamations of the physiognomy of the pictorial space as "humble." Rather than a poor, existential village, the view opened up beyond the narrow street now clearly bears the mark of a great city—a classical city of beautiful buildings whose architectonic, materialistic and decorative elements speak plainly of an "Albertian" architecture predating Alberti. Perhaps once again Masaccio was able to deduce the most genuine aspects from certain "classical" models in Florence in his time (some rhythmic assonances with the interior of the Baptistry are evident, for example). Or else, gathered here is evidence of a preceding trip of his to Rome to measure and copy columns, entablatures, capitals and windows sought out in the "mine" of the Imperial Forum, [and the whole transformed then into a "Florentine" vision].[2]

Of utmost importance, too, is the solution devised by Masaccio—and revealed by Baldini (1986)—to remedy the deviation from the vertical of the right edge of the picture due to a variation in the width or splay of the adjacent window. By means of "an extremely rigorous optical and perspectival illusion, seen at the lower part of the window, the artist graphically resolved the problem in the wall structure pictorially, adjusting the imperfect arris or juncture angle of the window inset by continuing the painted architecture of the background around the corner onto the window jamb."[3]

The street view is characterized by typical medieval Florentine houses in which can be recognized, according to Berti (1988), the area around the Church of San Felice in Piazza, especially now that the Corinthian street column has been exposed. The ground level of the superb palace of cut stone[4] recalls the high base of the Palazzo Vecchio on the side that descends along the Via della Ninna with the enclosed portico, while the upper level with windows framed in stonework has the Brunelleschian rhythm and measure of the Palazzo Pitti (which would be a significant document for accepting an earlier dating of the design of the palace done originally for Cosimo il Vecchio).[5] The precise geometric dis-

Masaccio, Saint Peter Healing with His Shadow, *detail*

tribution of the concave elements already elaborates a design that will have success in future facades, foremost of which is that of the Palazzo Antinori picturesquely situated at the lower end of the Via Tornabuoni. In Masaccio's scene, the church facade terminating the street has a "classicism" that makes it appear almost an Albertian construction, obtained by blending together classicistic architectural elements drawn from such sources as the Florence Baptistry, where the interior ambulatory is reflected on the exterior in the continuous arcade of the clerestory above the door level. The result is an entirely dignified fifteenth-century facade, which will be found again in Fra Angelico's predella scene of *The Calling of Saint Nicholas* (predella panel now in the Vatican Museums) from the Perugia polyptych (1437), specifically in the oculus, the crowning with a pediment and the portal.

Insofar as Cavalcaselle (1864) referred to the condition of this fresco, he noted that "some of the buildings appear damaged in coloration; but, taken as a whole and apart from ordinary wear on the coloring which has darkened in general tone over time, this painting can nevertheless be regarded as in a satisfactory state of preservation." Evidently, in the restoration after the fire, the *beverone* or varnish preservative covered up the changes in color produced by the flames. Since the recent cleaning, these can be seen quite clearly on the entire left half of the palazzo, the lower section of the corner pilaster, the crippled man's legs and part of the ground, all of which exhibit chromatic changes where the original colors turned reddish from the oxidation of the yellow ocher and *terra verde* pigments. Also, a patch of flaked-off intonaco, that had been reattached in part and "poorly restored" (M. Salmi, 1947) after the fire, was removed and replaced in its proper position, then unified with the rest of the fresco with selective pictorial restoration.

There are ten *giornate*:[6] (1) the "entablature" across the top and the capital of the corner pilaster at the left, (2) the rest of the pilaster and its base, (3) that part of the palazzo above the door level and the projecting side of the overhang of the house to the right of it, (4) the rest of the architecture to the right, including the campanile and church, as well as the scrollwork on the window jamb, going up past the dividing strip along the side of Masolino's scene in the second register above to the height of the rectangle with the female head previously painted by Masolino, an indisputable confirmation of this part of the window decoration as Masaccio's, (5) the rest of the palazzo at the left up to the contours of the figures, (6) the heads of the standing supplicant and the man in the red hat (supposedly Masolino), as well as the wall and support struts under the house projection above them, (7) the heads of Saint Peter, Saint John, and the white-bearded man, (8) the bodies of the two standing figures on the left, the kneeling figure with his arms crossed and the crippled man's head, (9) the bodies of Saint Peter and Saint John, except for their feet, and (10) the crippled man's body, the ground and the feet of the two saints.

[1] G. Poggi, "La tavola di Masaccio per il Carmine di Pisa," *Miscellanea d'Arte* 1, 1903, p. 182.

[2] U. Baldini, "Restauro della Cappella Brancacci, primi risultati," *Critica d'Arte*, 9, 1986, p. 66.

[3] Baldini, "Restauro," p. 71.

[4] O. Casazza, "La grande gabbia architettonica di Masaccio," *Critica d'Arte*, 9, 1986, p. 66.

[5] This would confirm C. L. Ragghianti's suggestion of a date around 1420 for the design, which was rejected and later used for the Palazzo Pitti (*Filippo Brunelleschi, un uomo, un universo*, Florence, 1977, pp. 326–27).

[6] The Tintori survey, published by L. Berti (*Masaccio*, Milan, 1964, p. 149, n. 257), counts nine *giornate*. Not included is the first one, comprising the entablature dividing strip and the pilaster capital, which overlays *Saint Peter Preaching* already painted in the register above it by Masolino.

FILIPPINO LIPPI

Saint Peter Visited in Prison by Saint Paul

Pilaster to the left of the chapel's entrance arch, first register, 2.32 × 0.89 meters

This scene immediately precedes the miraculous event depicted in the adjacent fresco of *The Raising of the Son of Theophilus*, according to the story told in the *Golden Legend* (*Legenda aurea*), a medieval compilation of the lore of the saints by Jacobus de Voragine (1230–1298). In the apocryphal narration, Theophilus, the ruler of Antioch, had Saint Peter thrown into prison, where he certainly would have remained had it not been for the intercession of Saint Paul, who visited him, took care of him and spoke to Theophilus, telling the ruler that Peter was capable of resurrecting the dead. This interested Theophilus, who responded that he would liberate Paul's friend if he could resurrect his son, who had been dead for fourteen years (or, in another interpretation, had died at the age of fourteen years). Paul passed along Theophilus's proposal to Peter who answered: "It is a great miracle which is required of me, but God's grace will do this for me. You have promised a lot, Paul, but everything is easy with the help of God."[1] The scene painted by Filippino catches the exact moment when Saint Peter is responding to Saint Paul.

For a long time, this fresco was attributed to Masaccio. It is indeed the work of Filippino, but it appears so overtly Masacciesque that both M. Salmi (1947) and G. Fiocco (1957) proposed that Filippino may have used the existing *sinopia* already drawn by Masaccio but not yet executed in fresco. Cavalcaselle (1864) was the first to return the painting to Filippino on the basis of Vasari's attribution to him of the scene "when Saint Paul was visiting Saint Peter in prison" in the first edition of *Le vite de' più eccellenti architetti, pittori et scultori italiani* (Florence, 1550). Thus, the painting was added to the others already recognized as Filippino's by Rumohr (1827) and Gaye (1838), and the attribution, promptly reported in Florentine guidebooks of the second half of the nineteenth century, was accepted unanimously by the scholars who ceased to object or propose variations with regard to it. Only Brockhaus (1930) still maintained that Filippino was not the author of this fresco or of the *Raising of the Son of Theophilus*, but rather served only as a "restorer" whose intervention was to be considered nothing more or less than that of repairing those areas of the paintings worn away over time.

Following the fire of 1771 and successive restorations, Cavalcaselle (1864) noted the fact that "the dress of Saint Peter is discolored and shows the ashen preparation. . . . The red cloak is faded. . . . Both the figures of Saint Peter and Saint Paul have golden haloes but these are partially deteriorated." In a drawing in his Notebook, he also indicated a bulging area of the intonaco in the lower part of the picture, which still exists today.[2]

Filippino's intervention in the Brancacci Chapel frescoes was indicated by A. Scharf (1935) as covering a period beginning in 1484 and ending in 1488.[3] Berti and Baldini (1957), however, arrived at a different dating based on Vasari's story that Filippino's model for the resurrected boy in the *Raising of the Son of Theophilus* was the young artist Francesco Granacci, whose birth date is documented as 1469. Considering that Granacci appeared to be between the ages of twelve and fourteen, they pushed back Filippino's intervention to the years of 1481 to 1483, a time that better explains Filippino's new dialectic. In those years, he was in the process of breaking away from his master, Botticelli (in Rome in 1481 working on the Sistine Chapel with other major Florentine painters of the day), and resolutely heading towards a more personal artistic language.[4] The presence of Piero Soderini among the individuals portrayed by Filippino in the *Theophilus* scene

Filippino Lippi, Saint Peter Visited in Prison by Saint Paul, *detail*

indicates a *terminus ante quem* of 1485 for the painting, since that was the year of his death (G. Fiocco, 1957). But it must be remembered that Meller[5] has identified the portraits of other "deceased" individuals from different time periods among those Filippino had gathered for the purpose of witnessing Saint Peter's miracle of resurrecting the dead boy.

There are three *giornate*, in the following sequence: (1) all the architecture with the exception of the prison window, (2) Saint Peter behind the prison bars and that part of Saint Paul's raised arm in the space circumscribed by the window and (3) the figure of Saint Paul. The first *giornata* extends onto the right side of the entrance pilaster, meeting in the corner with and overlaying the painted pilaster that delimits the left edge of the adjacent scene of *The Raising of the Son of Theophilus*. This gives evidence that here in the first register of the cycle the order of execution of the frescoes was from right to left beginning on the back wall, the same sequence used in the register above it. Obviously, this chronological succession is also confirmed by the fact, previously mentioned, that if Masaccio and Masolino had initiated the pictures starting with the entrance arch (moving from left to right), this episode would not have been left unfinished.

[1] J. de Voragine, *The Golden Legend*, trans. G. Ryan and H. Ripperger (1941), New York, 1969, pp. 168–69.

[2] O. Casazza and P. Cassinelli Lazzeri, *La Capella Brancacci, conservazione e restauro nei documenti della grafica antica*, Modena, 1989, p. 31.

See also Appendix, p. 346.

[3] A. Scharf, *Filippino Lippi*, Vienna, 1935.

[4] L. Berti and U. Baldini, *Filippino Lippi*, Florence, 1957.

In support of the earlier dating, it should be added that Filippino's specific choice of young Granacci as a model could be justified as a response to the ambiguous Latin text of the *Golden Legend*. There, the "fourteen years" mentioned could be interpreted as the age of the boy when he died, rather than as the number of years he had been dead at the time of his resurrection.

[5] See the following entry on *The Raising of the Son of Theophilus*.

MASACCIO AND FILIPPINO LIPPI

The Raising of the Son of Theophilus and Saint Peter in the Chair

Left wall, first register, 2.32 × 5.97 meters

Two related events in the city of Antioch are depicted in this scene. The story is told in the *Golden Legend* (*Legenda Aurea*) by Jacobus de Voragine (c. 1230–1298) that Peter, once outside prison, was taken before the open tomb of the young son of Theophilus, the ruler of Antioch. With the aid of Saint Paul, Peter quickly revived the youth who had been dead for fourteen years (or, according to another interpretation, had died at the age of fourteen). This caused Theophilus, all the people of Antioch and many others to profess belief in God and to build a magnificent church. At the center of the church, a chair was raised for Peter so that everyone could see and hear him. He remained in the chair (in Antioch) for seven years. Then he went to Rome, where he sat on the chair of the Roman church for twenty-five years.[1]

In the Masaccio painting, the main scene unfolds outdoors with a crowd of people before the enthroned Theophilus. In showing Saint Peter *in cathedra* (seated on the chair or throne of the church) at the far right, Masaccio alludes to the two "chairs" of Peter—that of Antioch in celebrating the miracle of the narrative, and that of Rome for the truth and universality that came from Peter's subsequent arrival there and the founding of its church, for which he was the first bishop. This is represented by elements of a new contemporaneity, not tied to the historical event but perceived in the Church of the present. Its priests are conspicuous in the attendance at the event of the Carmelite brothers of the Church of the Madonna del Carmine. And among the "believers" are portrayed contemporary counterparts in the group to the right of Peter—the artists Masaccio and Masolino da Panicale, and the Early Renaissance architect-theorists Filippo Brunelleschi and Leon Battista Alberti.

In his biography of Masaccio, Vasari refers to the intervention of Filippino Lippi in the fresco: "[Masaccio] painted there also the raising of the king's son by Saint Peter and Saint Paul; though at Masaccio's death the work was left imperfect and it was finished by Filippino."[2] Vasari's reference to Filippino is more specific in his biography of that artist: "This man in his early youth completed [the frescoes] in the Chapel of the Brancacci in the Church of the Carmine in Florence, begun by Masolino and left unfinished by Masaccio at his death. Filippino then brought it to its final perfection; and he made there the rest of a scene that was missing, where Saint Peter and Paul revive the grandson of the emperor. In the figure of the nude boy is portrayed Francesco Granacci, a young artist; and similarly Mister Tommaso Soderini, a knight, Piero Guicciardini, father of Mister Francesco the historian, Piero del Pugliese, and Luigi Pulci, a poet."[3]

Vasari's recording of Filippino's intervention in the frescoes was soon forgotten, and Bocchi (1591) attributed all the frescoes in the chapel to Masaccio.[4] His attribution was then repeated in guidebooks for Florence by Antinori (1689), Carlieri (1745), Riccardi (1767) and Cambiagi (1778). Among the few which mentioned Filippino were guides by Borghini (1584), Richa (1754–1762) and a *Guida* of 1765 which stated that he "finished the frescoes begun by Masaccio in the church of the Carmelites."[5]

Rumohr (1827), followed by Gaye (1838), brought back to light the intervention of Filippino and defined for the first time with care the problem of distinguishing between the two hands, decisively attributing to him the central part of the scene described above. Not until Cavalcaselle (1864 and 1896), however, was the distinction between the two hands made with exactitude in the pictorial context of the work. He was the first to make the succinct observation, not always properly perceived by subsequent scholars (as Fiammetta Gamba has pointed out),[6] regarding the perfect compositional harmony of this painting in comparison to the one facing it of *The Dispute with Simon Magus and the Crucifixion of Peter*. Divided into two scenes also, the composition lacks unity mainly because of the imbalance between the two groups of figures, one of which is larger than the other. This observation led Cavalcaselle to put forth the hypothesis that Filippino, when confronted with the *Theophilus* scene left unfinished by Masaccio, was limited to

Masaccio and Filippino Lippi, The Raising of the Son of Theophilus and Saint Peter in the Chair, *detail*

following the outlines of the *sinopie* already traced on the wall for the central figures and four others at the left. Cavalcaselle also was the first to assign to Masaccio, in the group at the far left, the fourth head from the left of the Carmelite friar.

The attribution by Cavalcaselle of the individual parts of the scene was not doubted and scholars unanimously accepted it without objections or new proposals. One exception was Hamann (1941), who accepted the attribution of the various figures but gave to Filippino the wall backdrop with the trees and the urns on top, because it was not consistent with the style of Masaccio.[7] Burckhardt (1855), followed by Woermann (1882) and Müntz (1889), maintained that all of the frescoes done by Filippino were executed either from Masaccio's cartoons or over the *sinopie* that had already been traced onto the rough plaster (*arriccio*).[8]

Apart from what has already been mentioned in the sections on the individual scenes, the question arises here as to why Masaccio left the fresco cycle unfinished to go to Rome. Sortais (1905) proposed that the reason was either financial difficulties or the prospect of a more lucrative commission.[9] Later, Brockhaus (1930) speculated that this entire scene had actually been finished by Masaccio, after which some of the figures were obliterated at the time of the condemnation of Felice Brancacci—who was probably portrayed in it with his relatives and friends—in a true act of *damnatio memoriae*. Support for this can be found in the anomalous presence, isolated from the rest of the unified context of work by Masaccio, of the head of a Carmelite friar, definitively by Masaccio and respectfully restored and preserved by Filippino in the group he painted at the far left. (There are only four pairs of feet for the five figures in the group, since Filippino neglected to add those for the body of the Carmelite.) In the face of the total absence of individuals from the Brancacci family and their circle, this would also support a contemporaneous "recovery" on Filippino's part of harmonious substitutes for the already existing figures, rather than the creation of totally new ones.

Brockhaus's opinion that the completed fresco was subsequently defaced was recently revived by Baldini (1984), who connected it with the discovery made behind the eighteenth-century altar that revealed a "historical condemnation" of the scene of the *Crucifixion of Saint Peter*, painted by Masaccio in this location originally, in favor of the altarpiece of the *Madonna del Popolo*. He has also related it to the fact that there are examples of Filippino having intervened to "repair" damages suffered by the frescoes as well as to complete them, as seen in his intervention in *The Distribution of Goods*.[10]

In addition to the portraits already cited from Vasari's description, many others have been pointed out. Meller (1961), in his iconographic study of the portraits, confirmed the presence of the people cited by Vasari and identified others in the context of Masaccio's work who would have lent to the original scene an intentional political symbolism.[11] The head of the Carmelite friar mentioned above could be identified as having the features of Cardinal Branda Castiglione, a contemporary of Masaccio; Theophilus might be a portrait of Gian Galeazzo Visconti (1347–1402), the first duke of Milan; and the person sitting below Theophilus at the left is supposedly Coluccio Salutati (1331–1406), a well-known humanist and chancellor of Florence. To the portraits painted by Filippino, Meller adds the identification of the hatless man directly above the resurrected youth as the Florentine banker Lemmo di Balduccio (14th c.),[12] and the man standing behind the blond child as Niccolò Solderini. These identifications suggest an allusion in the scene to the efforts of Pope Martin V (reign 1417–1431), in the guise of Saint Peter, as mediator in confrontation with the tyrannical Visconti regime still in power in Milan. The dating proposed by Meller for the execution of the scene by Masaccio hinges on the presence in the scene of Gian Galeazzo, whose firstborn son Giovanni Maria (2nd duke of Milan) was assassinated in 1412. Adding to that date fourteen years, the amount of time which transpired before Saint Peter resurrected the son of Theophilus, one arrives at 1426 or 1427 by the Florentine method of dating. But scholars in general lean more toward a date of around 1428 for this painting. Added to the identifications of other contemporary individuals in this painting should be those for members of the group standing at the far right. From the right, they are

Masaccio and Filippino Lippi, The Raising of the Son of Theophilus and Saint Peter in the Chair, *detail*

Masaccio and Filippino Lippi, The Raising of the Son of Theophilus and Saint Peter in the Chair, *detail*

recognized as Brunelleschi, Alberti, Masaccio and Masolino.[13]

The condition of this fresco in the last century is of unusual interest and can be discovered in both the Italian edition of Cavalcaselle's text (1895–1909), written after a renewed direct study of the frescoes, and from the drawings in his Notebook that succeeded the English-language edition (1864–71). The state of conservation is defined in the Italian editon as "still satisfactory, with the exception of the head of the figure seen in profile standing to the left of the king, which in the past had been varnished to bring out the color.[14] On the right side of the picture, the lower area of the clothing of the three figures kneeling before Saint Peter is altered in color. Here and there, some areas of the clothing of other figures and the background appear faded, as well. Due to his method of painting, which differs from that of Masaccio, the parts by Filippino in comparison are lower in tone, less transparent and more full-bodied in color."

Additional notes on this painting, gathered by Cavalcaselle in a new study of the frescoes done especially for the Italian edition of his text, were recorded by him directly on two prints of an engraving of the scene by Thompson made for the 1864 English edition. On one he noted many technical details such as the "discolored" face of the figure to the immediate right of Theophilus, the "missing tree" to the left of the central vase on the background wall and the "damaged" sky near the roof on the right. He also deleted the entire, precisely circumscribed central group of figures from a Masaccian context, except for the standing man in green, noting the "effort" Filippino had made in this area "to imitate Masaccio." He also acknowledged as the work of Masaccio the head of the Carmelite "friar in profile" in the group at the far left.

On the other print, richer in details on the colors, he assigned the *giornate*. Also, he isolated from the Masaccian context the group kneeling in veneration in the scene at the far right, noting that "the lower section of the three figures before Saint Peter has been damaged due to repainting." He again confirmed the head of the Carmelite as being by Masaccio, and he indicated the high quality of some pictorial renderings by writing "perfection of pink color" on the sleeve of Theophilus and "perfection" for the face of Saint Peter on the chair. Moreover, on one of the two engravings, it is of great interest to note the repeated underscoring in pen on the pilasters framing the scene, demonstrating that Cavalcaselle recognized the importance of the painted architecture in the spatial organization of the scenes.

The present restoration, freeing the painted surface from substances that modified it and prevented a correct reading, has allowed scholars to confirm with absolute clarity the division of the work between Masaccio and Filippino by differentiating the techniques of the two artists. The sure identification of the sequences of the *giornate* has erased all doubts regarding Masaccio's authorship of the following areas: the buildings in perspective above the level of the background wall, the background wall itself with the urns and the trees above it,[15] the head of the man to the right of Theophilus with curly black hair and olive complexion (once thought to have been the work of Filippino) and the head of the seated man in the hat who looks up at the ruler, which was erroneously hypothesized as a later addition.[16]

The number of people in the group standing at the right of Peter on his chair was augmented by one, owing to the recovery of a figure in a red cap from under some repainting done probably after the fire to repair a loss of intonaco.[17] A very important fact emerged from the restoration on this part of the fresco, which finally made it possible to understand the reason for the area of "confused" color and outline found between Peter's chair and the figure of Masaccio in the group to the right. Here, Filippino had intervened to cover and mask the arm and hand of Masaccio that had originally been painted in the act of reaching out to touch the Saint. This data appeared in the examination of the fresco made with thermo-reflectographic infrared equipment. Perhaps such a gesture was regarded as irreverent and it was altered for that reason. The fact is not without importance, and the gesture has been considered[18] as a reference to the devotional act made by pilgrims in touching the foot of the bronze statue of *Saint Peter in cathedra* which, at that time, was in Old St. Peter's, the Early Christian basilica church in Rome that was destroyed and replaced in the sixteenth century.[19] Possibly, the gesture was more than just a reminder to those acquainted with the devotional custom; perhaps it was also a remembrance of the actual event in which Masaccio touched this statue while on his hypothesized trip to Rome with Brunelleschi in the Jubilee year of 1423. Certainly the connection with Rome is obvious, as is the pointed emphasis given to Peter's foot clearly outlined under the robe covering it.

Concerning the intervention by Filippino in this fresco with regard to the figure of the resurrected youth, some scholars have questioned whether or not he repeated Masaccio's exact design in the original *sinopia*, which would have been seen either because Masaccio had not yet covered it with intonaco or because it showed up on the *arriccio* when Filippino added new intonaco to the work surface. Salmi (1947) believed that Filippino's work corresponded with Masaccio's original plan, while Mariani (1957), Berti (1964) and Becherucci (in conversation) thought that perhaps Masaccio's figure had been depicted arising from a foreshortened catafalque, thus anticipating a powerful motif subsequently used in the miraculous resurrection depicted in the *Recognition of the True Cross* by Piero della Francesca in his fresco cycle of 1453–54 for the Church of San Francesco, Arezzo. It was used also in a fresco by Andrea del Castagno in the Chapel of Sant'Egidio, Hospital of Santa Maria Nuova, Florence, and by a great many others.[20] Parronchi (1975), on the other hand, thought that the revived youth would have been presented by Masaccio in profile on a bed in the same manner as Tabitha on the opposite wall, or like Drusiana in the relief by Donatello in the Old Sacristy of the Church of San Lorenzo.[21]

Masaccio did thirty-two *giornate* in the following succession, beginning from right to left: (1) the capitals of the pilasters and the horizontal cornice separating the scene from *The Tribute Money* above it, (2) the rest of the pilaster on the right, (3) part of the roof over Saint Peter on his chair and the wall above it, (4) the rest of the building behind him and a portion of the sky, (5) the rest of the sky, the trees and the urns atop the

Masaccio and Filippino Lippi, The Raising of the Son of Theophilus and Saint Peter in the Chair, *detail*

wall, (6) the upper parts of the buildings on the left above the projecting roof and (7) the rest of the building above the heads but excluding Theophilus's niche. Then moving right to left, (8) the wall above the figures, (9) the top of Saint Peter's cloth of honor and his head, followed by (10) his torso and the rest of the backdrop. At this point, the execution of the figures begins from right to left in the following sequence: (11) the heads of Brunelleschi and the man in the red hat, (12) the heads of Masolino, Masaccio and Alberti, (13) their clothes, (14) the kneeling figure farthest to the right, and (15) the section with Masaccio's arm along the lower vertical edge of the chair. (This section is especially difficult to read due to the repainting and modification of Masaccio's gesture already discussed.) To the left of Saint Peter on his chair, (16) the heads of two standing Carmelite friars, and possibly (17) the friar's head in profile, if indeed this served as a "double herm" for Masaccio to separate the two scenes, (18) the two friars' robes, (19) the rest of the figure of Saint Peter, (20) the kneeling figure seen from behind, and (21) the kneeling figure in profile on the left. Then jumping to the center, (22) the head of the standing figure in green, (23) to its left, the heads of six onlookers and the head of the kneeling Saint Paul, (24) Saint Peter's head, (25) four more heads to the left, (26) Theophilus's head in the niche, (27) the head between Theophilus's and the heads in (25), (28) their clothing and the head of the seated man in the hat looking up, (29) Saint Peter's clothes, (30) the body of Theophilus, the head of the man seated at the left, identified as Coluccio Salutati, and the clothing of the man looking up, then (31) Salutati's body. The final Masaccian *giornata* is (32) the fourth head from the far left, identified as possibly Cardinal Branda Castiglione.

Filippino's intervention includes twenty-two *giornate* and begins with (33) the left pilaster and continues from left to right with (34) the first head next to the pilaster, (35) the head in profile identified as Luigi Pulci, (36) the head turned toward the left of Piero del Pugliese and the adjacent piece of the collar on the Carmelite friar,[22] (37) the last head on the right of the group, (38) the body of Pulci, (39) the body of Pugliese, and (40) the body of the next man with the ground and building in front of him. In the central area moving to the right, (41) the body of the kneeling Saint Paul and the arm and hand of Saint Peter, (42) the two onlookers next to the standing man in green, (43) the head of the man identified as Lemmo di Balduccio, (44) the clothing of the man in green, (45) the head of the man next to Lemmo in the red hat, (46) the head of the man considered to be Niccolò Soderini with his clothing and that of the man next to him, (47) two more heads, the first a portrait of Tommaso Soderini, (48) another head and (49) the last head in profile facing left, linked by way of the "double herm" with the friar's head by Masaccio facing right in the group around Saint Peter *in cathedra*. Next came (50) the body of this figure, then, moving left again, (51) the clothing of the next two people, (52) the little boy held back by Niccolò Soderini, (53) the son of Theophilus and, (54) the ground with Saint Peter's feet, the winding sheet and the human skulls and bones.

[1] J. de Voragine, *The Golden Legend*, trans. G. Ryan and H. Ripperger (1941), New York, 1969, pp. 169–70.
[2] G. Vasari, *Le vite de' più eccellenti pittori, scultori ed archittetori* (1568), ed. G. Milanesi, Florence, 1878–81, 2, p. 298.
[3] Vasari, *Le vite*, 3, pp. 462–63. Pulci was tutor to the sons of Lorenzo de' Medici, and Soderini, an elected city official, was related by marriage to Lorenzo. Guicciardini, a prominent Florentine, was also a Medici supporter.
[4] F. Bocci, *Le bellezze della città di Firenze*, 1591, p. 14.
[5] *Guida per osservare con metodo le cose notabili della città di Firenze*, Florence, 1765.
[6] F. Gamba, *Filippino Lippi nella storia della critica*, Florence, 1958, p. 33.
[7] R. Hamann, "Masaccio und Filippino Lippi," in *Festschrift für Wilhelm Waetzoldt*, 1941, pp. 81ff.
[8] J. Burckhardt, *Der Cicerone*, (Basel, 1855), Italian reprint, Florence, 1952, p. 880; A. Woltmann and K. Woermann, *Geschichte der Malerei; die Malerei der Renaissance*, Leipsig, 1882, 2, p. 171ff.; and E. Müntz, *Histoire de l'Art pendant la Renaissance*, Paris, 1889, 1, pp. 612ff.
[9] G. Sortais, "Masaccio et la Chapelle Brancacci," *Etudes*, 42, no. 104, August 1906, pp. 343ff. [1905 in bibliography.]
[10] U. Baldini, "Prime risultanze per il restauro," in "La Cappella Brancacci nella chiesa del Carmine a Firenze," *Quaderni del restauro*, 1, 1984, p. 24; Baldini, "Nuovi affreschi nella Cappella Brancacci: Masaccio e Masolino," *Critica d'Arte*, 49, no. 1, 1984, p. 70; Baldini, "Restauro della Cappella Brancacci, primi risultati," *Critica d'Arte*, 9, 1986, p. 66; and Baldini, "Sui restauri della Cappella Brancacci," in L. Berti, *Masaccio*, Florence, 1988, p. 108.

For Filippino's intervention in the *Distribution of Goods*, see entry related to it.
[11] P. Meller, "La Cappella Brancacci: Problemi ritrattistici e iconografici," *Acropoli*, 1961, 3, pp. 186ff. and 4, pp. 273ff.
[12] The face of this individual was damaged by scratching on the surface for the purpose of erasing the identifying features, a sign that the use of the *damnatio memoriae* was a common act even after the time of Filippino.
[13] We owe the identification of Brunelleschi to Meller ("Cappella Brancacci," 3, pp. 186ff. and 4, pp. 273ff.), of Alberti to Berti (*Masaccio*, Milan, 1964), of Masaccio to Salmi ("L'autoritratto di Masaccio nella Cappella Brancacci," *Rivista Storica Carmelitana*, 1929, p. 99ff.), and of Masolino to Berti (1989).
[14] Perhaps this refers to varnishing operation in 1770 by Thomas Patch, English artist working in Italy c. 1768–1782.
[15] Baldini, "Restauro," p. 65; O. Casazza, "Il ciclo delle Storie di San Pietro e la "Historia Salutis": Nuova lettura della Cappella Brancacci, *Critica d'Arte*, 51, no. 9, 1986, p. 95; and Baldini, "Sui restauri," p. 104.
[16] M. Marcucci and A. Parronchi, *Marcucci, imitazioni di Masaccio*, Florence, 1975, p. 7.
[17] This figure does not appear in Piroli's engraving done around 1798 in light of early restoration work already accomplished. The Lasinios in their engraving, faced with the area that had been covered with a layer of plaster, invented the existence of two figures to correspond with the number of feet shown for the group at the right.
[18] O. Casazza, "La grande gabbia architettonica di Masaccio", *Critica d'Arte*, 53, no. 16, 1988, p.95; Baldini, "Sui restauri," p. 108; and Casazza and Cassinelli Lazzeri, *La Cappella Brancacci, conservazione e restauro nei documenti della grafica antica*, Modena, 1989, p. 15, p. 66ff. and fig. 62.
[19] The foot is heavily worn due to constant touching by the devout. Regarding the circumstances of the placement of the bronze statue in Old St. Peter's, see M. Guarducci ("Riflessioni sulla statua bronzea di S. Pietro nella Basilica Vaticana," *Xenia*, 18, 1988, p. 57ff.), who publishes documents and ancient testimonies to prove its execution in the Late Antique-Early Christian period, around the first half of the fifth century, and to confirm its presence in Old St. Peter's where it was brought from the nearby Monastery of San Martino, in existence before the end of the 13th century. This contradicts Wickhoff's attribution of the statue to Arnolfo di Cambio, a sculptor from the Pisano workshop active in Rome c. 1270 ("Die Fresken der Katharinen Kapelle in S. Clemente zu Rom," *Zeitschrift für bildende Kunst*, 1889, pp. 301–10). Salmi concurred with the attribution to Arnolfo (*Civilità fiorentina del primo Rinascimento*, Florence, 1967), which was most resently proposed again by A.M. Romanini ("Arnolfo e gli 'Arnolfo' apocrifi," *Roma Anno 1300*, Acts of the 24th International Congress of Medieval Art History, Rome, May 19–24, 1980). See also G. Cuccini, *Arnolfo di Cambio*, Perugia, 1989, p.78.

C. Cecchelli (*Iconografia dei Papi*, Rome, 1937, pp. 54–62, 68–71 and 75ff; and Plate XII) discusses the iconography of the figure and its similarity to a marble statue of Saint Peter in the Vatican Crypts once attributed to Arnolfo. This attribution too was overturned by convincing documents brought to light by Guarducci ("Riflessioni," p. 111–118) showing that the marble image was salvaged from an eminent Imperial mausoleum of the Anicia family.
[20] M. Salmi (*Masaccio*, Milan, 1947, p. 70) sees a reflection of Masaccio's work in a fresco by Niccolò Alunno in the Church of Santa Maria in Campi, Foligno, dated 1458. V. Mariani ("L'arte di Filippino Lippi," in *Saggi su Filippino Lippi*, Florence, 1957, p. 76) maintains that the nude is a derivation from the Classical, as is the Isaac in Brunelleschi's competition panel, *The Sacrifice of Isaac* (1401-02, Florence, Bargello) for the North Doors of the Florence Baptistry. See also L. Berti, *Masaccio*, 1988, p. 106.
[21] Marcucci and Parronchi, *Marcucci*, p. 5.
[22] See Casazza and Lazzeri, *Cappella Brancacci*, p. 28.

FILIPPINO LIPPI

Saint Peter Liberated from Prison

Pilaster to the right of the entrance arch of the chapel, first register, 2.32 × 0.89 meters

This scene is taken from Acts 12:

During that period, King Herod started to harass some of the members of the church. He beheaded James the brother of John, and when he saw that this pleased certain of the Jews, he took Peter into custody too. During the feast of the Unleavened Bread he had him arrested and thrown into prison, with four squads of soldiers to guard him. Herod intended to bring him before the people after the Passover (12:1–4). . . . During the night before Herod was to bring him to trial, Peter was sleeping between two soldiers, fastened with double chains, while guards kept watch at the door. Suddenly an angel of the Lord stood nearby and light shone in the cell. He tapped Peter on the side and woke him. "Hurry, get up!" he said (12:6–7). . . . Peter followed him out, but with no clear realization that this was taking place through the angel's help. The whole thing seemed to him a mirage. They passed the first guard, then the second, and finally came to the iron gate leading out to the city, which opened for them by itself. They emerged and made their way down a narrow alley, when suddenly the angel left him (12:9–11).

The scene shows Saint Peter walking out of the prison past the sleeping guard accompanied by the angel. As were all the others, this fresco was once attributed to Masaccio. Gaye (1838) first ascribed it to Filippino,[1] and the attribution was quickly accepted by the commentators for the Vasari edition published in Florence in 1848, but not by Rosini (1850).[2] After Cavalcaselle's reaffirmation of Filippino's authorship (1864), the attribution of the work was unanimously accepted.

The condition of the fresco is generally good, except for some losses, compensated for in the nineteenth-century restoration but now reworked by chromatic selection along the left edge of the pilaster face in the areas of the angel's hair and the clasped hands of the angel and Peter. There was also a loss of color pigments on the upper part of the soldier's lance and on the long feather in his hat. These had been added *a secco* and subsequently flaked off, either due to the deterioration of the holding power of the medium or because of the cleaning to which the painting was subjected after the 1771 fire. Cavalcaselle, who saw the frescoes after the nineteenth-century renovation, pointed out losses still evident, such as "part of the color of the Angel's wings" and "here and there, both the Angel's and Saint Peter's haloes." On a sketch in his Notebook, he also wrote a note of reference to the "Baptizing" next to Peter's feet. This may have been a *lapsus* for the *Distribution of Goods*, since Saint John's feet there resemble those of Peter in this scene, a fact that is now clearer and more indisputable.[3]

Due to the darkening of the varnish on this fresco, Sacher's analysis (1929) in terms of the symbolic value of the colors was flawed, when he contrasted the "dark and faded" colors used to represent the prison walls and the sleeping guard with Peter's luminous yellow mantle and the angel's pristine white costume with touches of light blue—the colors of "liberty" as the two figures head for freedom.[4] Now, of course, all the colors are shown to be equally light and clear.

There are four *giornate*, beginning at the top: (1) all the architecture down to the contour of the figures, (2) the heads of the angel and Peter, (3) their bodies and the ground in front of them, and (4) the soldier and the ground in front of him. Indications for the superimpositions of the *giornate* are very clear in this fresco. The half of the painted pilaster on the left side of the real pilaster projection meets up with and overlays the other half that marks the right edge of the adjacent *Dispute with Simon Magus*. This proves once more that the succession of work in the first register of this side wall was from left to right, starting at the back wall, with the *Liberation from Prison* the last scene to be executed.

[1] G. Gaye, *Carteggio inedito di artisti dei secoli XIV, XV e XVI*, Florence, 1838, 1, p. 581 and 2, p. 469.

[2] C. Milanesi, G. Milanesi, C. Pini and V. Marchese, "Sulle pitture della Cappella Brancacci," in G. Vasari, *Le vite de' più eccellenti pittori, scultori ed architettori* (1568), Florence 1848, 3, pp. 165ff. and 5, pp. 255ff.

[3] O. Casazza and P. Cassinelli Lazzeri, *La Cappella Brancacci, conservazione e restauro nei documenti della grafica antica*, Modena, 1989, p. 31; and U. Baldini, "Restauro della cappella Brancacci, primi risultati," *Critica d'Arte*, 9, 1986, p. 66ff.

[4] H. Sacher, *Die Ausdruckskraft der Farbe bei Filippino*, Strassburg, 1929. See also F. Gamba, *Filippino Lippi nella storia della critica*, Florence, 1958, pp. 72ff.

FILIPPINO LIPPI

The Dispute with Simon Magus and the Crucifixion of Saint Peter

Right wall, first register, 2.32 × 5.88 meters

The last two episodes in the life of Saint Peter are represented in this fresco. On the right, along with Saint Paul, Peter appears before Emperor Nero in a confrontation with Simon Magus (the Magician), and on the left, Peter suffers death by crucifixion. Both stories are drawn from Jacobus de Voragine's *Golden Legend* containing the lore of the saints. Simon the Magician, a well-known sorcerer and a convert to Christianity with a large following in Jersualem, offered Peter money in exchange for the secrets of his power (whence the term "simony" for the buying and selling of positions in the Church). Simon then went to Rome where, with his magic arts, he persuaded Emperor Nero to have faith in his powers. Subsequently, he challenged Peter and Paul in various demonstrations of ability, but, unlike the two saints, he could not manage to revive the dead. To prove his powers, however, Simon, in Nero's presence, threw himself off a tower and began to fly about supported by demons. But Peter prayed for the demons to drop him, and the sorcerer fell to the ground and died. The legend continues that, during the height of Nero's persecutions, Peter had left Rome but Christ appeared to him along the Appian Way. Peter asked him, "Where are you going, sir?" Christ answered, "I am going to Rome to be crucified a second time." Hearing these words, Peter understood that he had to return to the city and prepare for his own martyrdom. Ultimately, he was crucified with his head down, according to his own wishes, on the Janiculum, a hill outside Rome.[1]

At the time of the recovery of parts of a fresco scene on the back wall of the chapel, above the altar and below the window in the recent restoration, U. Baldini (1984) formulated the hypothesis that Masaccio had originally painted in that location the concluding scene of the Life of Saint Peter cycle, the martyrdom by crucifixion. This fresco was destroyed around 1460–61, so that a thirteenth-century panel painting of the *Madonna del Popolo* could be installed there instead as the altarpiece. When young Filippino Lippi was called in two decades later to repair the damaged frescoes and complete those that had never been finished, he revived the scene of the crucifixion of Peter by including it here in the two-part scene with the *Dispute with Simon Magus*.[2]

With regard to the painting that might have been intended for this space on the right wall in the original overall plan of the fresco project by Masolino and Masaccio, it very probably would have been conceived in the same way as the two-part scene of *The Raising of the Son of Theophilus and Saint Peter in the Chair* on the wall facing it. That is, the two scenes joined in one space would be closely related in terms of the narrative sequence, as Peter's miracle of raising the dead boy was immediately followed by the veneration of Peter in the church built by the people of Antioch. In view of the subject of the first scenic action in Lippi's painting of the dispute between Peter and Simon before Nero, it may then be proposed that, rather than Peter's crucifixion, the subject of the second scene would logically have been that of the fall of Simon Magus to the ground in his attempt to fly, since it followed sequentially the scene of the dispute in the *Legend* narrative.

Filippino's whole composition for the *Dispute* could have been developed in the manner theorized by Parronchi (1975), as a derivation from a predella scene containing the same subjects belonging to an altarpiece by Benozzo Gozzoli, at that time in the Alessandri Chapel in the Church of San Pietro Maggiore (predella panel, The Metropolitan Museum of Art, New York), or from a later predella of 1461 by Benozzo, now in the Royal Collection of Buckingham Palace, London.[3] The two episodes depicted in the Lippi fresco painting are indeed merged in these predella scenes, but, with regard to their scenic plan, while the crucifixion has assonances with that in the Lippi work, the depictions on the panels of the fallen figure of Simon Magus have such analogies with that of the dead Ananias in Masaccio's *Distribution of Goods and the Death of Ananias* that Benozzo's predellas may themselves have been derived from the original Brancacci frescoes.

It should be mentioned here that, in our opinion, Masaccio had carried to its completion the *Theophilus* scene on the lower register of the left wall and had even drawn the *sinopia* for the scene of *Saint Peter Visited in Prison by Saint Paul* on the left entrance pilaster, which is far too Masaccio-like to be called only an intentional imitation by

Filippino. Similarly, he could also have drawn the *sinopie* for the two scenes of the Simon Magus composition. The lack of "Masaccian quality" in the fresco, and its lack of adherence to the probable underdrawing already executed by Masaccio, can best be explained by Filippino's painting of the entire composition *ex novo*, without having to compensate by restoring and completing the work using parts of the fresco already done on the intonaco. Nevertheless, the balancing of the groups in the same way on either side of Peter's cross is not, upon close inspection, so new as to exclude both Benozzo's and Filippino's dependence upon Masaccio's original design perhaps visible to both in the *sinopie*.

Filippino shows that he wished to create, beyond the usual iconography for the scene, an exact rendering of the historical setting of the event. The architecture of the wall and portal arch, with the wall embedded in the pyramid, seems to have been taken from real life. Despite changes over time, a similar view can still be observed outside the ancient Porta Ostia, where the Pyramid of Caius Cestius on the left backs up against the Wall of Aurelian. Pertinent to this is a medieval building just inside the gate that bears the inscription: *S. Petre ora pro nobis* (Saint Peter pray for us). Whether or not this exact site was the scene of Peter's martyrdom, the presence of the pyramid justifies it as the model for the background in Filippino's crucifixion scene.

In the first edition of his *Vite* (Florence, 1550), Vasari declared Filippino's authorship for "the entire Dispute of Simon the Magician and Saint Peter before Nero and his crucifixion." In the second edition of 1568, however, this phrase did not appear, which fueled the nineteenth-century debates about whether to attribute the work to Masaccio or Filippino. But actually—as well noted by Rumohr (1827) who defended the fresco as Filippino's[4]—even if the scene was not mentioned with its title, it was comparably identified with the citation of some of the people portrayed in it by Filippino, among whom were "Antonio Pollaiuolo, and himself who, as young as he was, never made another for the rest of his life, therefore one could not have a portrait of him at a better age; and in the scene that follows he portrayed Sandro Botticelli, his master, and many other friends and great men, and among the others Raggio the broker."[5] In spite of this, the painting was still attributed to Masaccio by Patch (1770), Lastri (1766 and 1775), D'Agincourt (1811), Lasinio (1812) and so many others that even Filippino's self-portrait in the scene was identified as a self-portrait of Masaccio. Rumohr (1827), followed by Gaye (1838), proposed Filippino's name for the whole work, and Cavalcaselle (1864) definitively confirmed this. Subsequently, it was accepted unanimously by scholars.

Among the portraits Filippino included here, already partly identified in the literature, are: his self-portrait at the far right with his face turned out toward the viewer; in the group of three standing to the left of Nero, Antonio Pollaiuolo on the right wearing a red hat; on the left of the same trio, erroneously identified at one time as Botticelli, may be "Raggio the broker" referred to by Vasari (Berti, 1957); and the portrait now identified as Botticelli in the figure looking out at the spectator from between the two men in the group of three at the right of the crucifixion scene.

The condition of the fresco in many areas does not appear good because of pigment losses and abrasions, especially in the corner of the chapel adjacent to the back wall. Cavalcaselle recorded that the painting had suffered a fair amount of damage, specifying several areas of missing color and indicating for the section with the crucifixion the fact that "the tones are discolored." Preserved among Cavalcaselle's papers is a print of Thompson's engraving of the scene on which he noted the salient points of his visual analysis, inscribing negative aspects such as "flat color without marked shadows," "hasty perspective lines" and a general judgment that, in the Italian text, ended in a losing battle for Filippino in comparison with Masaccio: "All this painting by Filippino is flat, it does not breathe and the figures do not dominate, as in the badly done foreshortened nude or the man in front of him."

Cavalcaselle's own drawings of the scene are more precise, and they also delineate the *giornate*. He not only indicates the colors but he also identifies the portraits as follows: "Filippino" on the far right, "Polajuolo" standing in profile to the left of Nero, and "Granacci" (the young artist who posed for the nude boy in *Theophilus*) to the right of Saint Peter in that same group. Noting the "damaged" condition of the painting, he jotted down comments about figures in the group at the far left, such as "mannered," "flat head," etc. For the onlooker at the crucifixion with his back turned, he recorded, "reminds us of Andrea del Sarto at the Annunziata." He elaborated on this in his text, writing, "The posture of this figure is, with very slight variations, repeated in one of the frescoes by Andrea del Sarto in the cloister of the Santissima Annunziata Church."[6]

Here in this fresco, compared with the rhythm and vitality of Masaccio's and Masolino's large formats, Filippino is less in tune with these artists than he is in the *Raising of the Son of Theophilus* and the two scenes of Peter in prison on the entrance pilasters. This is evident in certain details of strong, realistic rendering, done with less differentiation, and a perspective scaling of the figures that is not very effective. Also, Filippino did not preserve the spatial relationships of the preceding scenes. Instead, he increased the height and size of his figures, bringing them forward almost to the edge of the "stage front" of the space opened up by Masaccio's architectural framework. The difference in Filippino's painting technique, now more evident than ever, renders obsolete the hypothesis offered by more than one scholar regarding restorations made on the scenes in the second register of the frescoes, for which Filippino's participation must now be absolutely excluded.[7]

There are forty-two *giornate* for the painting, a large number but justified by the many figures and portraits present in this scene. The work proceeded as follows: (1) the dividing strip across the top that serves as an "entablature," (2) one-half of the painted pilaster in the corner at the left, which overlays the other half already painted on the wall perpendicular to it, adjacent to *The Distribution of Goods*, and then, perhaps (3) the painted pilaster section at the far right of the scene. Moving from the top left to the right, (4) the architectural background with the pyramid, the crenellated walls and part of the arch, (5) the rest of the portal arch with the landscape view and the foreshortened wall to the right of it, (6) the wall with the window, and (7) the rest of the

Filippino Lippi, The Dispute with Simon Magus and the Crucifixion of Saint Peter, *detail*

Filippino Lippi, The Dispute with Simon Magus and the Crucifixion of Saint Peter, *detail*

wall above the figures with the canopy. Returning to the far left and moving right, (8) the head of the first figure and (9) his body, (10) the next two heads, (11) the soldier's head and (12) his body, (13) the next head and (14) his entire body extending behind and not including the arm of the cross and (15) the head of the next figure with a lance (for which only traces of its incised outline remain, since it was painted *a secco* extending upward on top of the architectural background done in *giornata* (4). Continuing to the left, (16) the executioner, the left arm of the cross with Peter's arm nailed to it, and the ground below, (17) Saint Peter's body, (18) the executioner on the right supporting Peter and (19) the man raising the cross on a pulley, except for (20) his foot under the arm of the cross. This scene concludes with the trio on the right of (21) the man with his back turned, (22) the head of the man now identified as Botticelli, (23) the head and body of the man in profile with the ground immediately behind him and (24) the carved stone base of the foreshortened wall, which has been aligned with the base of the right-hand framing pilaster in terms of perspective.

The scene of the *Dispute* then proceeds on toward the right with (25) the figure of Simon Magus, (26) the figure of Saint Paul, (27) the head of Saint Peter, (28) his body and (29) his feet, (30) the head of the man proposed to be "Raggio the broker," (31) the head of the next figure and (32) his body, (33) the head in profile (Pollaiuolo), (34) Nero's head, (35) the head and body of the bearded man seated at the left, (36) the surrounding floor,[8] (37) Nero's body, (38) the head of the man seated on the right and (39) his body. This scene was concluded with (40–41) the heads of the last two figures with Filippino's being the farthest to the right, (42) the rest of their bodies and feet, and the strip of foreground back to and including the step on Nero's throne.

[1] J. de Voragine, *Golden Legend*, trans. G. Ryan and H. Ripperger (1941), New York, 1969, pp. 332, 335–37.

[2] U. Baldini, "Nuovi affreschi nella Cappella Brancacci: Masaccio e Masolino," *Critica d'Arte*, 49, no. 1, 1984, pp. 69ff.; O. Casazza, "Il ciclo delle Storie di San Pietro e la 'Historia Salutis': Nuova lettura della Cappella Brancacci," *Critica d'Arte*, 51, no. 9, 1986, pp. 69 and 88, and note 10; and O. Casazza and P. Cassinelli Lazzeri, *La Cappella Brancacci, conservazione e restauro nei documenti della grafica antica*, Modena, 1989, p. 33 and note 2.

[3] M. Marcucci and A. Parronchi, *Marcucci, imitazione di Masaccio*, Florence, 1975, p. 13.

[4] C. Rumohr, *Italienische Forschungen* (Berlin-Stettino, 1827), ed. J. von Schlosser, Frankfort, 1920, pp. 378–80, 394–97 and 416.

[5] G. Vasari, *Le vite de' più eccellenti pittori, scultori ed architettori* (1568), ed. G. Milanesi, Florence, 1878–81, 3, p. 463.

[6] Casazza and Cassinelli Lazzeri, *La Cappella Brancacci*, p. 31. Editor's note: In the Annunziata frescoes, painted in 1510, Del Sarto made frequent use of the device of a robed figure in the foreground with his back to the viewer, similar to Filippino's model. Perhaps the closest replica is that of the man on the right in *The Death of Saint Philip*.

[7] U. Baldini, "Dalla scoperta di San Giovenale a quella della Brancacci," *Gli Uffizi, studi e ricerche*, no. 5, 1989, p. 18.

[8] Editor's note: The terra-cotta statue on the ground may be explained by a passage in *The Golden Legend* (p. 332), which says that Simon the Magician "caused stone statues to laugh."

SIGNUM
SALUTIS

VINCENZO MEUCCI

The Madonna del Carmine

Ceiling

Vincenzo Meucci (1699–1766) was already a very successful and prolific painter of frescoes in Tuscany when he received the commission to restore the Brancacci Chapel in the context of a larger program of decoration promoted between 1746 and 1748 by Lorenzo Gaspare Masini, the prior of the Church of Santa Maria del Carmine.[1] The first project, however, was the execution of a decoration in masonry and stucco at the front of the chapel, completed in 1747. This did not meet with approval, and it was removed and replaced with another in stone designed by the French architect Chaman.[2] Inside, the groin-vaulted ceiling, which, according to the reports by Richa, had suffered greatly from moisture,[3] was completely demolished along with the frescoes of the Evangelists painted there, according to the sources, by Masolino. The frescoes in the lunettes suffered a similar fate, because, as it was said at the time, "they had no value." Vincenzo Meucci then decorated the new domed ceiling with *The Virgin Giving the Scapular to Saint Simon Stock* (*The Madonna del Carmine*), and Carlo Sacconi painted decorative architectural designs in the lunettes on the side walls.

From our examination and research done before the restoration work, it appeared to be impossible to recover even partially the old structure of the groin vault, because the new ceiling was installed at a higher level than the previous vaulting. There was some probability, nevertheless, of finding at least traces of the original painted scenes in the lunettes, since the archival documents indicated a "covering up" of the "figures on the third register," not the destruction of them.[4] Nothing was found under the decorations in the side lunettes, however, and it was discovered that both the original intonaco surfaces and the underlying *arricci* in those areas had been destroyed. But under the frescoes on the back wall on either side of the window, below the *arriccio* with the *sinopie* done by Meucci, were discovered two fragments of underdrawing related to the cycle of the Life of Saint Peter by Masaccio and Masolino. The two *sinopie* by Meucci, for figures of angels at the sides of the window, were really "notes" made directly on the *arriccio*, rather than actual canonical "*sinopie*" in the sense of a rigid and synthetic indication of forms.[5]

The frescoes by Meucci and Sacconi underwent extensive restoration after the fire of 1771. These restorations have been preserved not only because they are still chromatically harmonious with the whole, but also because they were made as sutures for the losses and lacerations that occurred after the fire. They are presumed, therefore, to be interventions in the context of the existing work that maintain the original image from recollections, as opposed to arbitrary reconstructions.

The fire of 1771 had a very serious effect on the architectural motifs decorating the side-wall lunettes that had been executed by Carlo Sacconi using calcimine paint (*bianco di calce*). The heat of the fire, generated with great intensity toward the top of the chapel, attacked this thin, painted layer to the point of producing a "bubbling" of the plaster. This necessitated the creation of a new pictorial "veil" over the surface, which totally modified the design and overall aspect of the architectural decorations by Sacconi. The design can still be determined because of the existence on the old layer of intonaco of the incised lines defining it, which no longer relate to the overpainted decoration. That this was not the result of a modification made during the course of the work, or of a change of plan at the time, is proved by the existence of the burnt picture surface underneath the "veil" of the present pictorial surface. In addition, a *sinopia* was found on the *arriccio* of the lunette on the right wall that shows the exact architectural motif of the balustrade corresponding with that of the incised lines still visible below the actual pictorial surface.

Interesting from the point of view of technique is the fact that the drawing of the balustrade on the right wall was developed in black chalk for only the left half of the space. This was then transferred onto paper, which was flipped over and used to register the image in reverse on the intonaco of the rest of the wall. From the evidence of the incised lines of Sacconi's version, as seen in a drawing made from the lines still visible in the lunette of the left wall, the overall geometric plan could be reconstructed. What emerged was a complex architectural design consisting of a balustrade, embellished at the center by a motif of a vase of flowers with masks, and three wide arches expanding the space, which was closed at the top by a coffered ceiling decoration.

During the work of putting the chapel back into order following the fire, completed in 1782, the paintings by Meucci and Sacconi also underwent restoration at the direction of the marquis Gabriello Riccardi, who had acquired the patronage of the chapel after it had been renounced by the French descendants of the Brancacci family.[6] Two artists were involved—Giuseppe Romei, who also painted the ceiling of the transept of the church in 1780, and Domenico Stagi, who worked on the architecture. Actually, we think the painting of the lunettes was done by the latter, while Romei was given the responsibility for the restorative intervention on the painting in the dome.[7]

At this time, the inscription, *Signum Salutis in Periculis*, was placed on the ceiling over the entrance arch in two large painted escutcheons in the spandrels at the base of the illusionistic "oculus." Thus, in the rededication of the renovated chapel to the Madonna del Carmine, a precise "historical" reference was made to the miraculous power of the Virgin in saving the chapel from complete destruction in the fire of the 1771, a miracle that extended, of course, to the saving of the frescoes by Masaccio, Masolino and Filippino.[8]

[1] C. Caneva, "L'ultimo della Brancacci," *Gli Uffizi, studi e ricerche*, no. 5, 1988, pp. 85ff, (with bibliography).

[2] J. Mesnil, "Per la storia della cappella Brancacci," *Rivista d'Arte*, 7, 1912, pp. 34ff.

[3] G. Richa, *Notizie storiche delle chiese fiorentine divise ne' suoi quartieri*, Florence, 1754–62, 10 (1762) of 10 vols., p. 40.

[4] Citing contemporary documents, Mesnil ("Per la storia," pp. 34ff.) reports that Meucci, "strongly warning that the chapel suffered from dimness, tried therefore to lighten it up as much as possible, adopting the brightest colors that would act to reflect the largest amount of light rays, and because the figures on the third level did not have any value, covered them over with his own work." Also, the Carmelite prior Lorenzo Masini had opened up "that beautiful window . . . worked and embellished with such perfection." The cost of this whole operation, that brought irremedial destruction to the original fresco cycle in the top register and on the ceiling of the chapel, was "one thousand five hundred *belli ducatoni*," including the expense of demolishing the first facade, and it was finished in July, 1748.

[5] U. Baldini, "Nuovi affreschi nella cappella Brancacci: Masaccio e Masolino," *Critica d'Arte*, 49, no. 1, 1984, p. 70; and O. Casazza, "Il ciclo delle Storie di San Pietro e la 'Historia Salutis': nuova lettura della Cappella Brancacci," *Critica d'Arte*, 51, no. 9, 1986, p. 69.

[6] U. Procacci, "La Cappella Brancacci: vicende storiche," in "La Cappella Brancacci," *Quaderni del restauro*, 1, 1984, pp. 9ff.

[7] For the documents and further bibliography, see W. and E. Paatz, *Die Kirchen von Florenz*, Frankfort, 1940–54, 3 (1952) of 6 vols., pp. 209 and 271, n. 107.

[8] O. Casazza, "Settecento nella Cappella Brancacci," *Critica d'Arte*, 51, no. 11, 1986, pp. 68ff.

THE HISTORY OF THE BRANCACCI CHAPEL AND ITS RESTORATION

THE RESTORATION: HISTORY, RESEARCH AND METHODOLOGY

Umberto Baldini

While the restoration of the Brancacci Chapel was a necessary intervention due to its precarious conditions, we believe that it can also be considered an important lesson in method for all those who worked on it. The ways and means with which it proceeded, from documentations and analyses to the actual work and its conclusions, have been discussed on many occasions. Yet in a volume such as this, designed to report all the facts of the completed project to the public at large, along with its advancements and discoveries, these must be reiterated in order to present the whole of our work and observations.

By the 1970s, due to the rapid process of "obscuration" of the frescoes caused by the degeneration of substances applied to their surfaces and accentuated by atmospheric pollution, the chapel had been placed under inspection on the part of the Opificio delle Pietre Dure, through my instigation and direction, starting with a study of the humidity and temperature extensive enough to allow for a "real time" reading of the variations in and behavior of the frescoes through the changes of the seasons. The beginning of the actual operational project and thus the initiation of the restoration work on the chapel did not take place, however, until July 1981.

At that time the state of preservation of the chapel was verified by means of the most modern instrumentation available to furnish us with objective, concrete data to study and analyze. From the in-depth analyses a "clinical portfolio" was developed, on the basis of which we could rigorously and responsibly formulate the requirements, and therefore the methodologies, of the interventions to be carried out. In advance of these, it was also necessary to proceed with exhaustive research and examinations to collect the information still to be found on the walls of the chapel, outside the context of the restorations and modifications done before and after the fire of 1771. Every possible examination of the structures and the surfaces was accomplished sufficiently for us to acquire all the data still extant, in spite of the regrettable Baroque transformation of the chapel, and to arrive at the most complete and conclusive speculation ever made on the status of the chapel. These operations post-dated by fifty years Ugo Procacci's recovery, from behind two small marble sections removed from the top of the altar pediment, the first two fragments of the painted surface of the chapel still in the chromatic state that prevailed after 1734, subsequent to the cleaning of the frescoes by Antonio Pillori, and before the fire of 1771.

The schedule of preliminary operations included testing performed as follows:

(1) Above the eighteenth-century ceiling to verify the existence or not of parts of the ceiling, ribs and lunettes of the original Gothic structure of the chapel.

(2) Underneath the intonaco of the two large lunettes on the side walls to verify the existence or not of paint residue from the original frescoes and whether or not an original *arriccio* still existed on which might be preserved traces of a probable *sinopia*.

(3) Underneath the intonaco on the back wall at the same height as the side wall lunettes, on either side of the Baroque window above the frescoes of *Saint Peter Preaching* and *The Baptizing of the Neophytes*, in order to verify whether or not an original *arriccio* still existed on which traces of a probable *sinopia* might be preserved.

(4) Behind the eighteenth-century marble altar, which was removed in order to (a) verify the existence and therefore the extent of possible earlier paintings on sections of the wall surface covered over since their execution, (b) verify from inside the chapel the original Gothic window opening still visible from the outside and (c) verify the existence or not of the original window jambs in the hope that pictorial decorations had been executed on them.[1]

(5) Behind the marble revetments forming the eighteenth-century dado, which were removed completely on the back wall and partially from the side walls to test for the existence or not of a previous dado and to check the appearance and condition of the underlying walls toward a possible rehabilitation.

Masaccio, The Raising of the Son of Theophilus and Saint Peter in the Chair *(copy after), detail*

(6) On the inside surface (intrados) of the triumphal entrance arch above its supporting corbels in order to verify the existence or not of the original Gothic arch that might preserve traces of pictorial decoration.

At the conclusion of the above examinations carried out between July and November of 1981, the following results were obtained:

(1) The entire original Gothic ceiling, including the ribs of the groin with their corbels, had been completely destroyed during the renovation of 1746–48, because the new semicircular dome for Meucci's frescoes was built at a higher level than the original ceiling. For the same reason, no trace of Masolino's ceiling frescoes were found.

(2) Acting on the consensus expressed by the Regional Committee of the National Council for Cultural and Environmental Properties,[2] the two side-wall lunettes were removed entirely, but no traces of painted intonaco nor consistent signs of the fifteenth-century *arriccio* were found. The fact that they once existed was manifested in some very small fragments of *arriccio* showing traces of red chalk, preserved by chance and thereby confirming the total destruction of both the frescoes and the *arriccio* with the *sinopie*.

(3) After tests on the back wall of the intonaco underneath the eighteenth-century cornice, painted to simulate architecture and surmounting the second register of frescoes, it was possible to recover the original *arriccio* on the fifteenth-century masonry at the top level where numerous obvious traces of the underdrawing were found. The subsequent removal of Meucci's frescoes in this area, authorized by the same Regional Committee, allowed for the recuperation of two *sinopie* related to two original scenes which had disappeared.

(4) The jambs of the original window were found and almost completely recovered. They turned out to be painted with a geometric design comprised of leafy rinceaux and two medallions, each containing a head. There were signs of two other medallions located in the upper parts of the jambs, but without any remains or pictorial fragments from the time of the application of the intonaco connected with them. Since the intonacos were completely absent, perhaps they were removed in a rushed attempt to save the images painted there, before the jambs were subjected to damage by the insertion of the new altar and the enlarged window frame in the Baroque renovation.

The original Gothic window was longer, as shown by the continuation of the jambs below the measurements of the present window. This opening had been reduced in height by raising the level of the sill, at the time of the painting of the original fresco series, to provide Masaccio with wall space for a scene that, due to its location, was meant to function as the altarpiece. Fragments of this scene, painted just below the ornamental band that runs across under the present windowsill, show parts of a landscape, a fragmentary figure on the right and other figural elements on the left. Even in their fragmentary state, they lead us to believe that they might be part of the Saint Peter cycle, specifically of the scene depicting that final glorification of his life—*The Crucifixion*.

This was the most important recovery of the operations, both new and unexpected, since there was no previous knowledge of such a scene painted in this location over the altar. The discovery of these pictorial excerpts, enlarging and confirming what Procacci had found in 1932, provided us with

Masaccio and Filippino Lippi, The Raising of the Son of Theophilus and Saint Peter in the Chair *(copy after), detail*

knowledge of the state of the frescoes as they were before the fire and successive interventions. From the brilliance and clear luminosity of this painting we were given an entirely new Masaccio, at last revealed as the founder of a new "school" characterized by a pictorial voice not only formalist but also colorist and luminist, that bore so much fruit in future generations.

(5) Although there was no trace of a previous dado, the investigation allowed us to observe the conditions of the entire masonry base of the wall system, which turned out to be in good condition and perfectly preserved.

(6) No positive data resulted from the tests of the round arch, which was constructed at a higher level and therefore destroyed the Gothic entrance arch at the same time that the ceiling was removed.

Contemporary with and following upon the recoveries made, we initiated a series of analyses capable of furnishing us with objective data useful in preparing the remedies and the means for the most appropriate interventions to rehabilitate and restore the whole complex. All of this preliminary work, from the actual initiation of the restoration project to its completion, was the official responsibility of the Central Institute for Restoration in Rome, which I had the honor of directing. With the financial support of the Olivetti Corporation, which was not new to this type of "enterprise," we were able to accomplish rapidly the scientific collaboration and coordination needed for the project. In addition to the regular and almost daily relations with the specialized satellites of the National Restoration Center of Florence, the Institute also availed itself of qualified specialists and additional equipment at the University of Florence, as well as technicians and researchers from the Donegani Institute, Novara, coordinated and directed by the Syremont of Milan. This attests once again to the scientific, moral and civic responsibility brought to bear in the safeguarding of a work of such great value.

With regard to the compilations of data that emerged from our studies and tests, it should be emphasized that this project was not done just for the purpose of putting together an abstract "hyperamnesis." As Antonio Paolucci has written, "Diagnostics which are ends unto themselves can become a manneristic mode of self-gratification and almost a form of sublime tautology that in some cases can complicate and inhibit operations and even be used as 'another' alibi to justify a mediocre operation."[3] Instead, this project was articulated, shaped and frequently oriented and directed towards clarifying, documenting, stating, managing and conceding a requisite objectivity to our work.

The objective documentation and analyses, the essential areas and points of which have been assembled for a forthcoming second publication on the chapel restoration,[4] comprised the following:

(1) Photographic documentation in direct light, blanketing the surfaces using black-and-white and color film at various measurements and in different dimensions, done prior to intervention on the frescoes.

(2) Photographic documentation in raking light, blanketing the surfaces using black-and-white and color film at various measurements and in different dimensions, done prior to intervention on the frescoes.

(3) Ultraviolet fluorescent examination to identify cognitive elements of the condition of the painted surfaces and to detect the presence of fixatives

and efflorescences present at the pigment layer level, or otherwise superficial in nature. This was done both before and after the cleaning, thus a clear analysis of the nature, extent and methodology of the intervention was able to be made through an exact and objective comparison with the previous state of the frescoes.

(4) Preliminary diagnostic investigation by infrared color photography oriented toward the acquisition of data correlating the characteristics of reflection, absorption and transmission of the different pigments present and their stratification. These were used to draw up a map of probable nonhomogenous elements and to acquire further information on the technique of execution, the type of pigments used and the condition of preservation or possible existence of retouchings, insertions, restorations, etc.

(5) Study of the micro-environment of the chapel space with particular reference to the measurement of concentration of anhydrous sulphur in the air and the quantity and nature of suspended dust particles. (The latter proved to be high in carbon, which also accounts for the considerable deterioration of the frescoes.)

(6) Study of the intonaco, its binders and the mineral salts present, coming from the masonry and old restorations, by means of chemical analysis and examination with an electron scansion microscope.

(7) Chemical and physiochemical analyses to determine the state of preservation of the frescoes. For the first time, an original, nondestructive method was utilized for measuring sulphurization, the principal cause of degradation of such works. A study of the values obtained allowed us to prepare for the appropriate, correct method of cleaning.

(8) Photospectroscopic studies of the colors using a device with fiber optics capable of analyzing the light diffused from the fresco surface in varying wave lengths. The goal of this research was to document the colors of various parts of the fresco before and after restoration and to identify statistically the "noise" that was attributable to the dirt deposit itself on the fresco surface.

(9) Infrared reflectographic analysis penetrating the paint layers in a noninvasive examination. Among the latest of such methods to be applied to the scientific study of works of art, it was used experimentally on frescoed surfaces for the first time on the walls of the Brancacci Chapel. Reading through the layer of obscuration from dirt and varnish, it was possible to study the status of the original pigment at various levels, using a scale of grays, and therefore to know in advance how it would appear after the removal of the dirty layer.

(10) Microbiological analyses conducted by taking samples directly from the walls with wet and dry buffers and a scalpel and, at the same time, aerobiological analyses to furnish a baseline orientation regarding the microbic content of the chapel environment. A comparison was then made of the biological pollutants in the atmosphere with those on the walls.

(11) Holographic analyses using double exposure of the two-dimensional surfaces were performed. This extremely sensitive investigative technique, capable of finding deformations of the surface up to a fraction of a micron, was carried out by setting up a small holographic laboratory inside the chapel itself, complete with optical components and materials for photographic development. This study constituted the first attempt to apply double exposure holography to an on-site diagnostic study of frescoed walls. It was found to be quite feasible and permitted the study of local behavior, as well as the visualization of the dynamics of the internal structures. All of this was possible without even minimally disturbing the phenomena themselves, due to the completely noninvasive character of the procedure. The information extracted had to do with the recurrence of movements in the surface related to structural settling, the determination of slow drifts and periodic shifts, and the identification of surface areas with anomalous behavior.

(12) Photogrammetric projection in order to construct a graphic-numeric model of the frescoed walls intended to objectify the geometric and dimensional aspects and to determine latent characteristics and phenomena, or whatever else was uncertain from direct analyses. In photogrammetry, a noninvasive method of investigation, the field of observation and documentation of data is the visible surface of the object. The relationship that exists between the surface geometry and the physical mass of the frescoed walls, however, imposed the need for integrated investigation procedures, particularly of combined photogrammetric and thermographic analyses. Every verification of such an interdisciplinary nature requires, of course, the predisposition of common points of reference, both in the data acquisition phase and successively in the interpretation phase. In the course of a restorative intervention, after localizing and quantifying all the deformation phenomena of interest in the fresco and the underlying masonry, it is especially important to determine height differentials at various points on the surface. An early, significant outcome of the study was the creation of a planometric model with these height differences expressed both graphically by means of a linear curve and also as numerical functions for the corresponding points of measurement.

(13) Thermographic readings to determine data related to the mechanisms of exchange of thermal energy between the structure and the environment, as well as data concerning the structural makeup of the chapel, including material discontinuities present in it and phenomena acting upon it. It was thus possible to determine the areas of detachment of the intonaco which, studied and interpreted in relation to other readings of the same areas—photogrammetric, ecographic, etc.—allowed and will continue to allow for a correct preservation intervention.

(14) Determination, finally, of an appropriate method of cleaning that would not alter the colored pigments and the surface of the frescoes in any way, while, at the same time, it would succeed in chemically removing all traces of organic substances which were the residuals of earlier restorations. This method exploits the property of some types of resins for ionic exchange and the reactivity of ammonium carbonate.

(15) Study and plan to put into operation a system for cleansing the atmosphere of pollutants continuously in real time, so as to lower as much as possible the flow or the persistence of negative agents inside the chapel, especially during the presence of visitors.

We believe that it is of the utmost importance to emphasize that we did not stop with the restoration work on the chapel proper. Once the problems of historical, philological and analytical documentation and management were resolved, our work extended into the entire structural complex of which the chapel is a part, in order to isolate the chapel and protect it from the negative effects of external agents. Taking advantage of the permission to operate freely in the monastery rooms adjacent to the chapel, we accomplished a complete rehabilitation there also, to ensure the most appropriate and secure defensive buffer zone for the structures and environment of the chapel itself. This type of approach is of great importance, considering the short time that restored works resist new degradation without these provisions, as it can be and has been recorded in entirely correct interventions carried out in our own day.[5] This is the reason why our work must be followed up with a program of constant maintenance and inspection, which is the minimum that can be asked in the case of an art monument like the Brancacci Chapel that has risked "death" so often in the past. The most secure means for a precise and exact future diagnostic evaluation is rigid inspection and testing that makes use of the valuable baseline "checkup" data left in the form of the digitalized images and graphics. Such are the methodological ramifications of this kind of "global" intervention that leaves nothing out, since the very concept of maintenance has been linked to the restoration process itself.

On the operational level of the restoration, understood as the recuperation of the painting of Masaccio, Masolino and Filippino, a key factor was the development of a feasible, safe method for removing the substances obscuring the original fresco surface by way of critical comparison with the recovered fragments from behind the altar and on the window jambs. These were quickly taken as a model and a measure of comparison, to refer to at least initially, since our target context was completely concealed under the dark pall of dirt. The first attempts to discover and liberate the original "fabric" or context from the *beverone*, done in direct rapport and reconciled with these fragments, were the adjacent frescoes of *The Baptizing of the Neophytes* by Masaccio and *Saint Peter Preaching* by Masolino, to see if the "veiled" areas would even respond in the same way—that is, with the same tones as those found to be so bright and clear in the fragments. To quote O. Casazza in the chapter that follows: "As in an archaeological excavation where the research advances slowly through thinly stratified layers of the earth, so evolved our first cognitive moment of the original fresco fabric. Testing here and there on all the scenes, we sought to arrive gradually, identifying the various pigments and the different techniques of the three artists in order to accomplish those equilibrations necessary to a correct and well-balanced 'restitution' of the work."[6]

Out of this came another lesson in method that reconfirmed for us the value of approaching the cleaning as an act of constant critical evaluation, thus removing it from servility to the mechanical act that, all too often, ends without conceding any qualitative benefit to the work. The condition remains the same except for a better "clarity" of the images—clean but not bright, no longer obscured but uniformly flat and unresolved in the definition of forms by light. That is the risk of a too-often praised and exalted "scientific approach" to the removal process. Frequently, once a specific solvent is discovered that behaves well, that is, "functions" for the removal, uncritical workers do not preoccupy themselves further. They proceed mechanically on all the surfaces, simply applying more solvent where more resistance is encountered without making adjustments for what is actually found in the process. The often misunderstood and debated theory of "proportional cleaning," which we have favored as the basis of the removal process since the early years of our career in the restoration laboratory, and that we put at the base of our *Theory of Restoration*,[7] proved again, not unexpectedly, to be a valuable method of choice for the Brancacci frescoes. For the recuperation of proper chromatic values, attention must be given in the act of removal to the relationship between color values and the formal values with which the work of art is configured in terms of its volumes and overall design. The thinning of the veil of dirt and varnishes should therefore be effected gradually in juxtaposed squares or "plugs" and executed little by little on corresponding parts of the surface defined by the *giornate*. The process of "excavation" to reveal the original surface occurs in a harmonious way on those parts of the intonaco that, by virtue of their creation, retain a genetic unity and a physical similarity derived from and established by the carbonation process in the setting of the plaster. The objective of this approach is to better recognize, discover and reconstitute the same equilibriums that the artist knew how to achieve in the linking up of the successions of the *giornate*.

If the restitution of the original contexts of the known scenes was carried out with great zeal, no less effort was expended with regard to the aforementioned historical and technical discoveries and recoveries: the two *sinopie* on the top register of the back wall, the jamb decorations of the Gothic window and the fragments of a fresco scene, not known about until now, painted above the altar by Masaccio. The *sinopie* were done by two obviously different hands. We have attributed to Masolino the drawing at the right of the window, above Masaccio's *Baptizing* scene, because of its recognizable and irrefutable Masolinian "handwriting" closely related to the *sinopie* in the Church of Saint Augustine at Empoli. We have assigned to Masaccio the scene on the left, above Masolino's *Saint Peter Preaching*, on the basis of the carefully modeled, powerful figure marked with strong features.[8] G. Briganti (1987) and R. Foggi (1989)[9] share in this distinction of hands, but L. Berti (1988) is of a differing opinion. While recognizing a greater incisiveness in the work on the left, he is still inclined toward Masolino as its author, citing its similarities with Masolino's *Madonna of Humility* (1423) in the Kunsthalle, Bremen, another *Madonna* in Berlin, the Virgin in the Empoli *Pietà* and even the old, dozing listener in the foreground of the *Preaching* on the second register of the Brancacci frescoes just below the *sinopia*. Berti maintains that these two underdrawings were done during a period when Masolino worked alone on the top register without the assistance of Masaccio.[10]

The cleaning of the *sinopie* has allowed us to distinguish with certainty the subjects of the two scenes as *The Repentance of Saint Peter* on the left and *Feed My Lambs, Feed My Sheep* on the right.[11] With regard to the latter scene, because of the fragmented and deteriorated state of the *sinopia*, one cannot make a precise identification of the individuals as they appear delineated here. Undoubtedly, the protagonists of the scene (Jesus and Peter) are placed at the center of the drawing with the spectators ranked subordinate to them on the edge of the action. The presence and symbolic value of the sheep are sufficient, of course, to make an identification of the scene as that in which Christ, after his resurrection, conveys to Peter this very important eccle-

Masaccio, The Repentance of Peter, *sinopia drawing*

Masolino, Feed My Lambs, Feed My Sheep, *sinopia drawing*

siastical charge, "Feed my lambs . . . feed my sheep," as related in the Gospels (John 21: 15–23). This fresco is not mentioned in any of the early sources for the chapel, but the historical event has notable weight in the Life of Saint Peter and, in the context of the other stories that are illustrated here, becomes absolutely indispensable to the painted cycle.[12]

The heads in the two medallions that decorate the window jambs also appear to us to be by different hands, with the feminine head at the left surely by Masolino and the masculine one on the right, to our mind, by Masaccio.[13] Those not sharing this opinion and leaning toward the attribution of both heads to Masolino are M. Boskovits (1987), E. Wakayama (1987), L. Berti (1988) and F. Bologna (1989).[14] In opposing the doubts expressed, even by some who climbed the scaffolding with us during the work of restoration, we wish to reiterate the differences in technique—absolutely determinant in our view—between the two heads with regard to line, light and modeling. The head by Masolino has been realized and painted within a graphic contour carefully delineated and indicated with the point of the brush, while the other head is constructed in a painterly way without contour lines and resolved graphically and volumetrically with color that varies with the light.[15] These same stylistic differences are distinguishable in the Sant'Ambrogio altarpiece, *The Virgin with Saint Anne* (1424; now in the Uffizi Gallery), through a comparison of the angel at the top right painted by Masaccio with the other three done by Masolino. In either case, we can speak of a Masaccian "execution" but not actually "invention," because, in both instances, Masaccio seems to have executed the painting in a context that had already been formally invented and drawn by Masolino.[16] The use of pouncing on the masculine head in the Brancacci decoration for direct transfer from the drawing could have allowed for the utilization of an actual design by Masolino, interpreted and executed by Masaccio for the sake of expediency because he was already there on the spot, on the level of the scaffolding from which he worked on the adjacent *Baptizing of the Neophytes*. The two different hands therefore could be explained in an objective sense by the simultaneous presence of the painters on the scaffolding, working independently of each other in a precise alternation and division of the tasks and surfaces.

In terms of the enormous difference of pictorial rendering between Masolino and Masaccio in the definition of volumes and the use of light, a conclusive comparison can also be made between Masaccio's medallion head and a nearly similar one, graphically, on one of the two gentlemen at the center of the piazza in the scene of the *Raising of Tabitha* done by Masolino. Here the light caresses and weakens the sculptural form, delightfully softening it to read as a very smooth surface. In Masaccio's head, however, the light builds and sharpens the form, achieving that unambiguous effect through a variation in style and approach to painting. As seen in the angel of the Uffizi *Virgin with Saint Anne*, from Masolino's initial "graphic" concept, the work is transformed into "painting" by Masaccio by way of a new, natural intensity in the play of light and a different way of refining volumes. A difference of worksmanship is even observed in the geometric decoration and leafy scrollwork on the jambs, justifying the supposition that the sections above the two heads and the horizontal band under the window are by Masolino, while the sections below the medallions are assignable to Masaccio. The difference between them is that between painting and "sculpting."[17]

Absolutely attributed to Masaccio—and here all are in agreement—is the scene that now, unfortunately, is reduced to two fragments of fresco depicting, as previously discussed, *The Crucifixion of Saint Peter*. This relies not only on the rigor of the form and light and the amazing landscape, but also on evident analogies with the *Crucifixion of Saint Peter* from the predella of Masaccio's altarpiece for the Church of the Madonna del Carmine in Pisa (1426, panel now in Berlin Painting Gallery). It has been possible to determine with certainty that the upper three-quarters of the scene in height was painted on a surface obtained by filling in the lower part of the original Gothic double-cusped lancet and the lower quarter on the inclined plane of the window inset that slopes downward from the old sill to meet the vertical plane of the back wall. The rediscovered fresco fragments were uncovered in the upper part of the flat surface and consist of bits of sky, the landscape horizon and a fragmentary figure on the right, with elements of another figure (an arm?) on the left. Also preserved directly above the fresco fragments is a horizontal ornamental band with geometric decoration and scrollwork running under the new sill that was created for the truncated lancet.

This recovery was the most important one made, both new and unexpected, since there was no prior knowledge of such a scene having been painted above the altar. It is neither recorded by the early sources nor mentioned by Vasari. Nor is it presumed that its destruction occurred at the time or by the hand of Filippino, who painted the martydom of Peter, along with Peter's dispute with Simon the Magician, in the lower register of the right wall precisely because it was not accounted for elsewhere. From this, it may be concluded that the destruction of this fresco altarpiece was tied in with the changes to which the whole chapel was subjected, especially the back wall, as a direct result of the reversal of the fortunes of the Brancacci family already in the fifteenth century. It is known that from the time of the exile in 1435 of the chapel's patron Felice Brancacci, who was declared a "rebel" in 1458, no other member of the family assumed responsibility for the chapel. Very soon, and evidently by will of the Carmelite friars whether directed to do so or not, it was transferred to the cult of the Madonna del Popolo. This took place probably around 1460, the year in which the Company of the Madonna del Popolo was founded.

Considering the fall into disgrace of the Brancacci family between 1435 and 1458, it may be proposed that the destruction of the scene glorifying Peter, already painted over the altar, became necessary in order to permit the placement in that location of the thirteenth-century panel painting of *The Madonna del Popolo* with its canopy. This could not have been done without obliterating the whole lower area of the frescoed scene painted on the slope of the window inset that ended in direct contact with the top of the altar. This forced destruction thereby negated the dedication of the chapel to Saint Peter and transferred it to the cult of the Madonna del Popolo, with all that had been or could be derived from this on the political level. This was done as well as for the convenience of the Carmelites, who surely wished to eliminate all possible suspicion of connivance or nostalgic links with the Brancacci family.

This fact is not without importance and ulterior consequences. This new

discovery of "destruction" points up and makes more credible a similar destruction occurring at the same time and for the same reason in the "hot zones" of the scene of the *Raising of the Son of Theophilus*, where presumably were portrayed Felice Brancacci, members of his family and others in his sociopolitical circle. These areas of the fresco were mended and restored, although much later, by Filippino Lippi, who replaced the obliterated features with those of individuals of his own time in harmony with the group and the individuals previously executed there by Masaccio.

That these rediscovered fragments above the altar on the back wall were connected to the scene of *The Crucifixion of Saint Peter* seems evident to us not only from the similarities already mentioned with the same scene on the predella panel in Berlin, but also because no other episode in the cycle of Saint Peter would work so well as the altarpiece than this final event of his life, his unification with Christ through martyrdom. Citing the absence of the pyramids depicted in the Berlin panel scene and the fact that the fresco scene appears to take place against nothing more than a landscape view, some scholars have presented a hypothesis that the altarpiece depicts *The Giving of the Keys to Saint Peter*. But if that is so, what do we make of the figure with all the air of an executioner by its obvious resemblance to one in the Berlin predella scene? Moreover, isn't the episode of the "giving of the keys" already expressed in the now rediscovered *sinopia* from the top register above, *Feed My Lambs, Feed My Sheep*? And as for the proposal that the altarpiece depicts *The Fall of Simon the Magician*, that subject is certainly interesting figuratively but not to the point of meriting glorification over the altar, as if it were the principal and conclusive scene in the Life of Saint Peter cycle.[18]

In truth, it is the comparison of the fresco with the Berlin panel which suggests to us that Masaccio may well have carried out here a graphic expedient pictorially similar to the one he used to handle the "defect" of the variation from the vertical of the left outside edge of the window inset, corresponding to the right edge of the scene *Saint Peter Healing with His Shadow*. It seems probable that Masaccio overcame the aberrant, trapezoidal flaring of the inclined plane below the original Gothic windowsill by placing the two pyramids in the triangular areas on either side, locating them in the foreground nearly at the planar surface and on the extreme edges of the composition, as seen on the predella panel.[19]

The analytical study of the *giornate* for the window area is of extreme importance and interest, since it defines and ratifies a sequence of the working sessions with regard to both the figural fragments and the decoration of the jambs that demonstrate specific technical links with the adjacent fresco scenes on the back wall. The schema derived from the study, illustrated in the *giornata* diagram in the Appendix, shows a logical procession of the work moving from the top to the bottom on the scaffold in direct correlation and simultaneously with work on the scenes on either side of the window. The ornamental scrolls at the top of the left window jamb followed after the painting of *Saint Peter Preaching*, adjacent to the left of them on the wall, because their intonacos overlay it. These intonacos were created in four distinct sessions: the now fragmentary scroll at the top (1), the lost medallion (2), the scroll above the preserved medallion (3) and the medallion with the feminine head (4).

The scrolls opposite on the right jamb (1A, 2A and 3A on the diagram) were painted before the *Baptizing of the Neophytes* adjacent on the right. The horizontal scroll decoration under the windowsill (5) came next in succession, since it is superimposed over the vertical scroll (3A) contiguous to it on the right jamb. At this point the decoration of the jambs by Masolino was taken over by Masaccio working alone on the lower level of the scaffold in the first register, where he had begun by painting the scene to the left of the window of *Saint Peter Healing with His Shadow*. While working on it, he integrated into its fourth *giornata* the adjacent part of the jamb (6), thereby creating on the same section of intonaco both the architecture of the right half of the scene and the scrollwork on.the left jamb. This intonaco overlays the medallion with the female head (4) and the lower part of the standing figure on the right in the *Preaching* scene in the second register, both of which had already been painted by Masolino. There is no doubt from this incontrovertible evidence that this area of the decorative jamb motifs is by Masaccio, who then, we found, repeated them in the same technique in the same area on the right jamb.

The work by Masaccio therefore proceeded from left to right with the execution of the scene we have hypothesized as *The Crucifixion of Saint Peter* in the space directly above the fifteenth-century altar. Of its two discovered fragments (7), the one on the left overlays the scroll (6) on the left jamb, and the one on the right overlays both the scroll beneath the windowsill (5) and that part of the scroll (3A) above the medallion on the right jamb. He subsequently executed this medallion with the masculine head (8), whose intonaco overlays the scroll decoration above it (3A), as well as the landscape fragment to the left from the supposed *Crucifixion* and the adjacent scene to the right of the *Baptizing of the Neophytes*. This was followed by the scroll in the lower part of the jamb (9) whose intonaco overlays the *Crucifixion* fragment adjacent on the left, the medallion with the male head (8), the *Baptizing* on the right above in the second register, and the "trabeated" border separating the two registers. The intonaco of *giornata* (9) was then, in turn, overlaid by that of the third *giornata* (containing the landscape and architecture) of *The Distribution of Goods* adjacent on the right in the first register.

These important findings clarify the phases of the work on the back wall on the two levels of the respective registers, bringing back into new consideration the phases of the work on the chapel as a whole. Leaving aside the first phase of decoration executed on the ceiling and in the top register lunettes, for which the fresco surfaces no longer exist, various proposals have been put forth for the work sequences of the scenes in the middle (second) and lower (first) registers. Salmi, for example, believes that Masolino was involved in these frescoes in a sequence that would have seen the completion between 1424 and 1425 of the following scenes: *The Fall* at the entrance, *Saint Peter Preaching* on the back wall and *The Healing of the Crippled Man and the Raising of Tabitha* on the right wall. In the last can be verified the first intervention by collaboration of Masaccio on the architectural background. Masaccio then continued the cycle between 1426 and 1428, according to Salmi, beginning with *The Baptizing of the Neophytes* and following with *The Expulsion*, *The Tribute Money* and, on the register below, *Peter Healing with His Shadow*, *The Distribution of Goods* and *The Raising of the Son of Theophilus and Saint Peter in the Chair*, with the last left unfinished.

Masolino, Decoration of the window jamb, detail

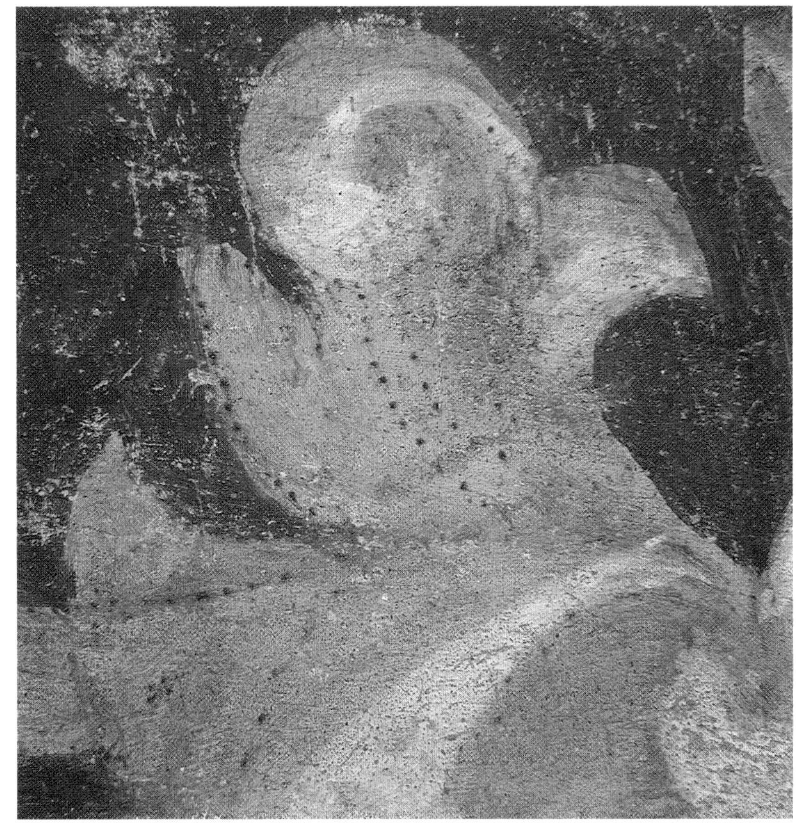

Others following Berti's lead propose another sequence of work, beginning on the second register with *The Fall* and *The Expulsion* painted on the opposing pilasters of the entrance arch, followed by *The Raising of Tabitha* and *The Tribute Money* on the right and left walls, respectively, and ending with the *Baptizing* and the *Preaching* on the back wall. From there, work was taken up below on the first register moving from right to left with *The Distribution of Goods* and *Peter Healing with His Shadow* on the back wall followed by *The Raising of the Son of Theophilus* on the left wall, with this last scene never completed.

Proof however that the fresco painting in the bottom register was done first on the back wall exists in the fact, supported by the study of the *giornate*, that the scenes on either side of the window and the scene above the altar done in sequence with them were brought to completion, while the scenes on the adjacent long walls and the entrance pilasters at that level were not painted, except for *The Raising of the Son of Theophilus* which was only partially done, according to general opinion.

If this was the system and the manner of working at the lower level, then one cannot understand why it would be otherwise above. Proceeding from what was derived regarding the bottom register, it becomes even more logical to think of a similar sequence on the second register, with the two artists working in alternation beginning with the *Preaching* and the *Baptizing* on the back wall. From there they continued on the long walls, resuming their work by attaching it to the two scenes on the back wall, as the sequences of the *giornate* for *The Tribute Money* and *The Raising of Tabitha* would also suggest. Therefore a movement on the scaffold from the back wall toward the entrance arch of the chapel seems evident, with the whole register concluded there in the painting of *The Fall* and *The Expulsion*. To theorize the start of the works at the entrance arch is not logical, since the pilaster scene on the left in the lower register, *Saint Peter Visited in Prison by Saint Paul*, was not painted by Masaccio, as it would have been in that case, but by Filippino Lippi, called in to bring to a conclusion the work that had been left unfinished.

These, in our opinion, are the critical findings based on what was recovered after the removal of the eighteenth-century altar installation. This restoration has further importance, however, with regard to the exceptional "spatial projection" created illusionistically by the painted architecture of the chapel, once it was no longer interrupted or debased by the large canopy of the altar. This gives obvious evidence for the original conception—as Paolo A. Rossi has emphasized[20]—that ties together intimately the three walls and predisposes them to receive the paintings, thereby obtaining an extremely unified visual effect independently of the subjects depicted and even before the scenes were executed. The painted scenes are not set off with decorative framing bands in the manner seen in earlier fresco cycles, nor do they appear as paintings placed on the wall to fill it up. Instead, the material structure and solidity of the wall surface has been "dissolved" by an articulation of the two-dimensional space with painted pilasters in the corners of the room supporting painted architraves that extend the full length of the walls. These elements create the visual effect of a rectangular architectural loggia open on all sides. For the observer who enters the chapel, the scenes appear not as paintings on the walls but rather as direct views into real external space. The continuity of these views along the horizon line is not interrupted, and indeed is accented, by the vertical elements at the corners.

The spatial and structural conception of these painted pilasters and architraves is so identical with that rendered in stone by Brunelleschi in his "ideal" structures, the Pazzi Chapel in the Church of Santa Croce (begun c. 1440) and the Old Sacristy in the Church of San Lorenzo (designed by him and begun 1421–25), that it is difficult not to feel here in the Brancacci Chapel the determined presence of this architect, to whom is also owed the perspective definition of the space in Masaccio's *The Tribute Money*.

Even the Gothic window in the center of the back wall does not constitute a break in the continuity of the walls. Instead, its concavity acts to the contrary, putting us in a delicate relationship with real space, not as a view to the outside but only as an effective source of light that both illuminates the frescoes and functions in a pictorial sense to lend three-dimensional solidity to the figures governed by light and shadow. Thus the light source unifies the spectator with the illusionistic architectural space defined by the painted pilasters, with the real external space and, finally, with the scenes depicted, putting him/her into a relationship of maximum intensity with them all.

New Conservation Ideology and Its Effects: A Professional Opinion

We maintain that the Baroque canopy of the altar, destined by official decision to be reinstalled in the Brancacci Chapel at the time of this writing, is a completely foreign body, intrusive in its convex form and brutally interruptive of the continuity of the "Brunelleschian" space created by the original artists. Needless to say, it is also a disturbance with regard to the fragmentary recoveries in the window area, which will be hidden again in part by the altarpiece of *The Madonna del Popolo*, also to be returned to its former position in the chapel. The long work of recuperation and restoration that has "resurrected," in the real sense of the word, the most admirable pictorial cycle that Italy possesses will be ruined if, the day after the inauguration, the canopy is reinstalled, bringing about a most unhappy conclusion to the consciously planned destruction of the Brancacci Chapel initiated in the eighteenth century. This altar installation has been defended, preserved and lent a historic value so high that it permits nothing less than the renewed exclusion or covering up of so many precious bits of authentic Masaccian painting. Moreover, it will once again subvert the rehabilitation of the original illumination of the chapel and the frescoes that has been effected through the near-complete recovery of the dimensions of the old window. This window was the actual source of light for Masaccio and Masolino, who regarded it also as the pictorial source for the illumination of their scenes.

In the decision-making process, a long and tormented bureaucratic *iter*, the incredible plan emerged to reinstall the canopy not in its original location but in a "detached" position—that is, set out from the wall about twenty-five centimeters and thereby providing "stratagems to allow a glimpse of the important recovered fragments." Such an unbelievable action would upset and arbitrarily modify the very historic value that has been attributed to this Baroque "monument" deigned to be worthy of preservation at all cost. Historicity, once ascertained and validated, is not subject to modification; it cannot be manipulated at will—otherwise "farewell" to historicity.[21]

The replacement of the Baroque canopy in the Brancacci Chapel in a different manner from its "historical" one will be a serious architectural and structural absurdity. Created to be incorporated into the wall as a bas-relief and defined with pilasters and half-columns, it cannot be transformed into a freestanding structure detached from the wall. It literally won't stand up on its own, and its lateral surfaces are of rough, unfinished stone meant not to be seen but imbedded in the wall. From being a low-relief element on a wall adapted to receive it, and thereby diminishing the amount of its projection from the plane of the frescoed surface, it will become an obstructive monstrosity even more intrusive and foreign to the chapel space. Above all, it will block and detract from a frontal, unified visual experience of the fresco scenes and decorations of the back wall.

If this is a case of "as it was, where it was," absurd as that may be to us, then this dictum ought absolutely to be applied and guaranteed with regard to the historicity claimed for this object. To approach its reinstallation differently will elude the meaning and the significance of the avowed historical worth of the object, which, unfortunately, we recall as sustained only by its avowed mediocrity. It has been said that this moving of the canopy out from the wall and these modifications to its integrity are acceptable and justified, because in this way it will be possible to see what is left of the work of Masaccio and Masolino once covered by the canopy. Unfortunately, this "seeing" will be

Fragments of the decoration of the left window jamb

Fragments of the decoration of the right window jamb

OPPOSITE, LEFT:
Masolino, Female head, left window jamb

OPPOSITE, RIGHT:
Masaccio, Male head, right window jamb

Masolino, Female head, detail

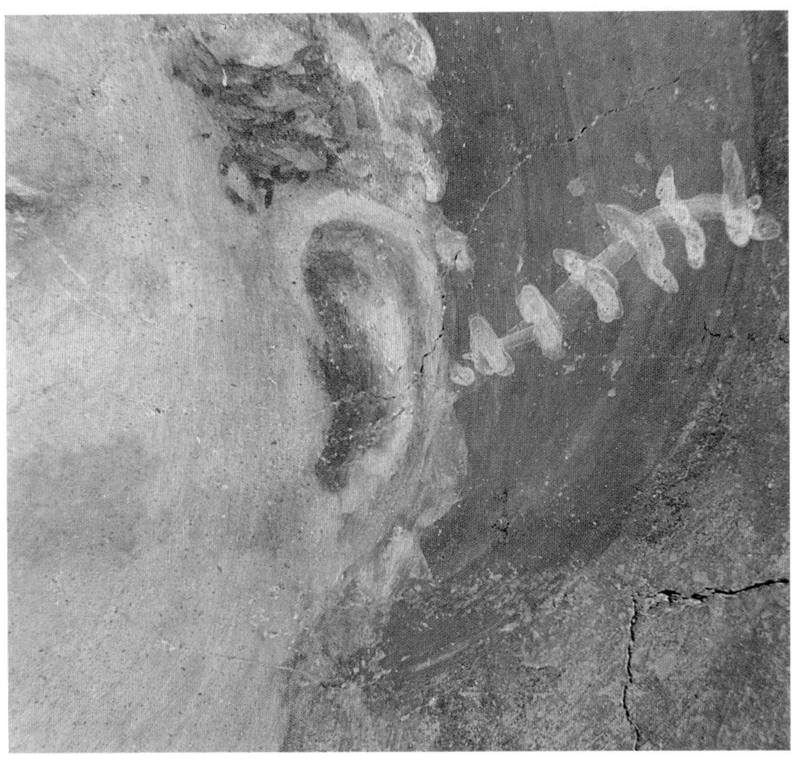

Masaccio, Male head, detail

ABOVE:
Masaccio, Saint Peter Healing with His Shadow, *detail*

BELOW:
Masaccio, The Distribution of Goods and the Death of Ananias, *detail*

neither "seeing" nor "understanding," because the scenes and decorations lose their worth if seen only partially and divided. The value of this window area, in point of fact, is its contribution to the articulation of the space of the chapel. Rather than seeing it in isolated parts and out of context, it would be better to see it in a photograph or illustration. There it could be presented full-size or even enlarged so that it would be possible to analyze thoroughly its definition by color and line. But to understand it as it truly was meant to exist, it must be seen in conjunction with the rest of the wall and connected with the other frescoes, now revealed to us with their true chromatic values.

The recovery of these fragments has provided not only the key to evaluating the reliability of the recently cleaned fresco colors, but also the key for an adequate reading of the spatial design, both architectural and illusionistic, for the whole chapel. And whereas the loss of the unified "reading" of the two fragments that remain from the destroyed scene of *The Crucifixion of Saint Peter* might be accepted as unimportant, the loss of the pictorial adjustment made by Masaccio to the imperfect vertical alignment of the outer edge of the window inset, by bringing part of the jamb into the plane of the wall surface in *Peter Healing with His Shadow*, would be a serious loss of an optical-pictorial invention of great importance and relevance. An equal exchange simply cannot be made here in allowing the survival of a liturgical relic that compromises the clarity of the reading of the spatial values (chapel space—fresco space) created in this place originally by Masaccio.

We wish to emphasize the fact that during the course of the construction of this canopy, decreed by the cult of the Madonna for the ornamentation and spiritual enhancement of the chapel following upon and connected with the destruction and consequent modification of the ceiling and the lunettes, the thirteenth-century icon of the Madonna del Popolo (before which the mother of Andrea Corsini had prayed in 1299) was altered at the top "by the unfortunate necessity of adapting it to the semicircular arch of the canopy and redoing it with a devoted repainting." This changed its appearance completely, conforming it with the style and language of the new decorum according to "a criterion of normalization of the original context, of which we are aware of other examples in Tuscany in the late eighteenth century."[22] Therefore, if equal historical value is given to the canopy in the context of the eighteenth-century church, then why was the "devoted repainting" of the altarpiece considered "stylistically incongruous and disfiguring" and subsequently removed in a recent restoration? Doesn't such a change qualify for as much consideration as "history" and "unmodifiable history" as the canopy itself, not to mention the stucco decoration on the entrance facade of the chapel, the marble dado with its wreathed litany, the figured marble flooring, the enlarged back window and the fresco by Meucci on the ceiling?

Viewed with rigorous logic, if "to restore" signifies only "to preserve," we would like to have explained to us why the dismantling and removal of the altar was not stopped before the opening up of the back wall resulted in discoveries that, no matter how valuable they were, would have to be covered up again? Why were we given permission at all to clean the painted surfaces of the frescoed walls, and why were we allowed to take the leaves off the Adam and Eve nudes? Why was the dark patina removed from the painted surfaces if it had been "historically acquired" by the images? Thus obscured and monochromatic, dim and smoke-blackened, were not the frescoes taken as a model and a pattern of salvation in our own twentieth century by a society of strong, hard-working and impoverished people, who found in them a very positive and sublime exaltation of humanity? Why then, once restored to a good physical and material state, were the frescoes not immediately covered over again with dirt, if that patina (whether false or not) should be considered "historical" from some points of view? It would not have surprised us if this had happened. The times may even be ripe for such occurrences, since, for a long time now in our profession, we no longer speak of "*restauro*" (restoration) but of "*restaurazione*" (reparation), defined as the return to and re-establishment of the preceding situation in a remedial action undertaken almost as "repairmen" to restore that which preceded, ignoring and erasing with one swipe of the sponge all progress and advancements. I am not speaking of technological discoveries, which upon close scrutiny are more often than not used as "screens" to defend and approve sometimes ill-advised operations, but rather of those advances at the ideological level.

So, instead of moving forward on the basis of indisputable advances recorded in these last decades, restoration does an about-face. It gets more and more caught up with personal taste and fashion, turning with the wind and caring nothing for the integrity and inviolability of the work of art, making a series of compromises and playing more and more frequently that convenient, facile card called "historicity." Thus, from reparation one moves to the most unconstrained conservativism, where those ideological advancements and actions that superseded the facts and errors of the past through research and knowledge are ignored in favor of a "political" return to the status quo.[23]

No longer is the fact even taken into consideration that the preservation of a historical change in a work of art—as Cesare Brandi[24] wrote in this regard—is required only when the subsequent additions are of such quality as to surpass in importance the work to which they were applied. To elevate this mediocre altar in the Brancacci Chapel "to the supreme level of the fresco cycle by Masaccio and Masolino" in order to adhere to a general rule of restoration offends the very theory that sanctions respect for different historical phases and disregards the higher imperative of respect for the integrity of the original work itself.

While "reparation" in place of restoration has nevertheless asserted itself as being nearly a providential and irrefutable "call to order," it cannot play havoc with the inviolability of the work of art and its significance.[25] Restoration must not run after fashion, as it has in the past, aligning itself time and again with the fragile prevailing esthetic. A work of art is an absolute unity and should not be dressed up in different clothes according to the requirements of our fluctuating tastes. This does not mean that a work of art is "immutable"; as we ourselves have declared many times, it is linked, quite apart from any modification of the material of which it is composed, to that "lifetime" of existence which has relevance to and for us as its viewers. "Unmodifiability" is something different; it has nothing to do with the comprehension of the work and the circumstances surrounding it, by which we resolve our participation in it in our own time. Instead, it means the inviolability of the elements with which the work of art was originally formed, elements that should be safe from any change of fashion and that we cannot or, in any case, ought not to alter in the slightest through arbitrary action or personal desire.

We are convinced that one cannot reverse certain actions, and we proclaim emphatically that whatever our operations achieved in a responsible way over the last decades—outside of mechanical interventions, which are always perfectable—it was never attained through change as a result of changing taste toward propositions of individual solution. Instead, it has been achievement and acquisition within the rigorous bounds of an ideology by which it will be substantiated in the future. For example, we cannot accept the practice of "reconstructing" missing areas of a work of art after the fact, that were arbitrarily and carelessly reconstructed in the past. Also, we would never employ interventions which might alter inappropriately the originality of the pictorial context.[26] We do not want to have considered as "integrations" by reparation, however, those formal figural recuperations that had been made in the areas of the Brancacci frescoes deprived of original painting in the fire of 1771. As O. Casazza explains in the section on the restoration of the paintings in the following chapter, these replacements, conscientiously carried out, were presumably not "inventions" but true and faithful "recoveries" from memory of the original frescoes that were completely legible and visible prior to their traumatic modification. Possibly the restored areas were even derived, in a close examination of the damaged surfaces, by tracing. This is quite a different situation from invention and arbitrary reconstruction.

Returning to the subject of the altar, if, after all, the historical instances are held to be valid that it should be brought back and reintegrated into the church, then it will be time to proceed as well with a similar "reparation" regarding Masaccio's fresco, *The Trinity* (c. 1428), in the Church of Santa Maria Novella, Florence. It too should be subjected to the same methods and means that, by ministerial decision, are to be used in the Brancacci Chapel "so as not to alter the spatiality of the environment and its historical connotations."[27] Yet to be uncovered, if they still exist, are the original colors and vivid "lights" that remain obscured by nineteenth-century restoration materials. These were not wholly eliminated when the *Trinity* fresco was restored following its detachment from inside the entrance wall of the church and returned, in 1951, to its original location in a bay of the left side aisle. But plans must be made now, if they are to be consequent and in line with the "save history" method as we understand it, for the reparation of the highly irresponsible damage done at that same time to the harmony of the architecture and space of the "Neo-Gothic" renovation of Santa Maria Novella.

And perhaps "Adam's skeleton" ought to be moved and reconnected at the bottom of the *Trinity* fresco, from which it was separated in 1861 when the top part of the fresco was moved to the entrance wall. Unless, of course, it is not desirable "to historically restore" it to its place underneath the altar table, because for us—as for the nineteenth century—it is unimportant. In any case, once the unity of the fresco has been reconstituted, its removal from the side-aisle bay and reattachment to the vestibule wall ought to be planned and carried out in the name of the "history" that was arbitrarily violated forty years ago. Only then, according to the new "call to order," will the fresco have been reestablished in its proper place. To continue, that Neo-Gothic altar which was dismantled so recklessly and taken out of the bay by Ugo Procacci will now find its place again in the rebalancing of the rhythms of the bays along this side aisle. Unless, of course, the bureaucratic decision-making process takes another eleven years, at which time the 1951 intervention will catch up with the Neo-Gothic one and the present installation will also meet the fifty-year requirement under law to be considered an "antique" work. Procacci's intervention can then be ceded *ope legis* (*dura lex, sed lex*) the historical value that it now lacks. Only then, thank God, will we finally be able to consider it protected from modifications, once its historical worth has been obtained in this manner.

[1] Plans for the removal of the altar and other research were introduced and adopted unanimously in a session of the Superior Council on April 4, 1970, by its members Giulio C. Argan, Cesare Brandi, Cesare Gnudi and Ugo Procacci, with Mario Salmi presiding.

[2] The decision of the Regional Committee was reached in December, 1982 by members Giorgio Bassani, Maurizio Calvesi, Michele D'Elia, Marco Rosci and Bruno Toscano, with Decio Gioseffi presiding.

[3] A. Paolucci, "Considerazioni sulle indagini svolte per il progetto Piero," in *Un progetto per Piero della Francesca*, Florence, 1989, p. 76.

[4] U. Baldini, "Procedimenti del restauro," *Critica d'Arte*, 52, no. 13, p. 66.

[5] In the case of the frescoes by Piero della Francesco in the Church of Saint Francis of Assisi in Arezzo, this would not have happened if, at the time of the rehabilitation, a contingency system of access for visitors had been provided. Perhaps it could also have been prevented regarding Andrea Mantegna's frescoes in the Camera degli Sposi in Mantua, or in the case now emerging with respect to Giotto's fresco cycle in the Scrovegni Chapel in Padua, if such provisions, for so long desired, had actually been implemented for these projects. In the Scrovegni, for example, the unreliable external walls of "decorticated" brick were left too long without a protective plaster seal, which favored a negative flux of external atmospheric agents toward the interior.

The responsible decision must be made, once and for all, to put an end to this unfortunate state of affairs where, every twenty years or less, another intervention is called for due to constant unpredicted occurrences and an almost unavoidable negative cycle of effects.

[6] See next chapter by O. Casazza, section on "Cleaning."

[7] U. Baldini, *Teoria del restauro e unità di metodologia*, Florence, 1 (1978), pp. 24ff. and 2 (1981), pp. 5ff.

[8] U. Baldini, "Nuovi affreschi nella Cappella Brancacci: Masaccio e Masolino," *Critica d'Arte*, 49, no. 1, 1984, p. 68.

[9] G. Briganti, "E Masaccio torna a brillare," *La Repubblica*, January 2, 1987; and R. Foggi, "Catalogo delle opere," in L. Berti and R. Foggi, *Masaccio*, Florence, 1989, p. 88.

[10] L. Berti, *Masaccio*, Florence, 1988, p. 37.

[11] O. Casazza, "Il ciclo delle Storie di San Pietro e la 'Historia Salutis': nuovo lettura della Cappella Brancacci," *Critica d'Arte*, 9, 1986, pp. 68ff.

[12] G. Vasari (*Le vite de' più eccellenti pittori, scultori ed architettori*, Florence, 1568, 3, p. 88) could possibly have seen and interpreted this scene as the start of Peter's preaching, when he wrote: "And after his weeping over his error of denying [Christ] and next the preaching to convert the people" (*E dopo il suo piangere il pecatto fatto, quando lo negò e appresso la sua predicazione per convertire i popoli*). Since Masolino's *Saint Peter Preaching* is in the register below (directly under "his weeping over the sin of denying Christ"), the word *appresso* (next) might logically signify *vicino* (nearby), and in this case *sotto* (below). Then, the "preaching to convert the people" described by him is in effect the *Preaching* still *in situ*.

[13] Baldini, "Nuovi affreschi," p. 70.

[14] M. Boskovits, "Il percorso di Masolino: precisazioni sulla cronologia e sul catalogo," *Arte Cristiana*, 718, 1987, pp. 47–66; E. Wakayama, "Masolino o non Masolino," *Arte Cristiana*, 719, 1987, pp. 125–36; Berti, *Masaccio*, 1988, pp. 37ff. and F. Bologna, Note in *La Nazione*, December 7, 1989, p. 9.

[15] U. Baldini, "Dalla scoperta di San Giovenale e quella della Brancacci," *Gli Uffizi, studi e ricerche*, no. 5, 1988, p. 16.

[16] Exactly how much is attributed to the collaboration of the two in the *Virgin with Saint Anne* can be seen from the radiographic and reflectographic analyses and judged by the hypotheses about the work already done by Masolino before the intervention of Masaccio (O. Casazza, "Al di là dell'immagine," *Gli Uffizi, studi e ricerche*, no. 5, 1988, pp. 93ff.).

[17] Baldini, "Nuovi affreschi," pp. 70ff.

[18] Berti, *Masaccio*, 1988, p. 38. Further doubts have been expressed by R. Foggi, who proposed that, due to the state of extreme fragmentation and the fact that the scene with the same subject had been painted about fifty years later by Filippino, a hypothesis for the *Crucifixion* seemed not to have value (Foggi, "Catalogo," in Berti and Foggi, *Masaccio*, p. 88).

The altarpiece of *The Madonna del Popolo*, when placed in direct contact with this wall, settles perfectly into the space and entirely covers the destroyed area of the fresco. This appears to us to confirm that Masaccio's painting was indeed destroyed to make a place for the *Madonna*, and, therefore the fragments are not proof of a "cancellation" made by Masaccio himself out of dissatisfaction with the work, as some have suggested.

For the effects of this matter related to Filippino's fresco, see the entry for *The Dispute with Simon Magus and the Crucifixion of Saint Peter*. Also see O. Casazza, "La documentazione grafica della Cappella Brancacci. . . ," in O. Casazza and P. Casinelli Lazzeri, *La Cappella Brancacci, conservazione e restauro nei documenti della grafica antica*, Modena, 1989, p. 33.

[19] Casazza, "Il ciclo," pp. 9, 69 and 88, n. 8.

[20] P. Rossi, "Cappella Brancacci, una proposta: facciamola vedere 'vuota,'" *La Nazione*, November 23, 1989. See also A. Parronchi, "Cappella Brancacci: no all'altare," *La Nazione*, November 12, 1989; C. Cresti, "Cappella Brancacci, una proposta: di quell'altare farne un paravento," *La Nazione*, November 15, 1989; A. Paolucci, "Cappella Brancacci, è gia deciso," *La Nazione*, November 15, 1989; and G. Nardi, "Cappella Brancacci: la storicizzazione, restauri e valori," *La Nazione*, November 23, 1989.

[21] When the campanile of San Marco in Venice fell at the beginning of this century, it posed only a problem of whether or not to reconstruct it. It didn't enter anyone's mind, once its reconstruction was established, to want to have it moved from its original site because then, maybe, it would give more space to the piazza or to allow for a better view of the facade of the Ducal Palace next to San Marco.

[22] A. Paolucci, in *Capolavori e restauri*, exhib. cat., Florence, 1986, p. 425.

[23] All over Italy, actions are being taken every day that indicate a continuous shift away from the ideology and methodology at the base of the great dictates of Cesare Brandi (*Teoria del restauro*, Rome, 1963), which, I will point out, did not constitute changing taste or fashion but rather a secure achievement on a solid foundation from which one goes forward and never backward. (Too often Brandi's maxims are exalted, while, at the same time, the work is carried out in a completely contrary way.)

His involvement *in extremis* in *Arte e Dossier* (no. 2, 1986, pp. 12ff.) was welcomed because it convinced us to "rethink" the historical value of Giovan Battista Regazzini's image of Saint Catherine of Alexandria inserted in 1568 into Gentile da Fabriano's fresco of *The Madonna and Child* (1425) in Orvieto Cathedral. He justified and insisted upon the removal of the figure, retained because of historically unfounded scruples. We do not know what he would have said about the fact that the modern framing, "completely false and arbitrary in proportions and shape," has been reattached to the panels of Fra Angelico's polyptych, *Virgin and Child Enthroned with Angels and Saints* (c. 1437), in the National Gallery of Umbria, Perugia. Also, reintegrated into the altarpiece were copies of the two missing predella panels, the originals of which have been in the Vatican Museums since the beginning of the last century. A museum, inasmuch as it is the prime institution of preservation and exhibition, ought, however, to show the original contexts of the works of art and not spurious ones. Of course, the next director of the Gallery will surely take off the frames, and his successor will probably put them back on, proceeding in the "reparation" mode and according to the now-established practice in all our museums whereby a change of directors calls for immediate exhibition changes, even if works are only moved from one room to another, in order to make a show of presence.

And if false and unauthentic renovations or copies of originals are to be remounted, then why not remove the areas restored with "neutral" in-painting on Giotto's fresco cycle, *The Life of Saint Francis* (c. 1310), in the Bardi Chapel of Santa Croce in Florence, and, with the aid of photographs, redo the previous "reconstructions" made by Gaetano Bianchi? Shouldn't the same be done for Piero della Francesca's *Legend of the True Cross* (c. 1450) in the Church of San Francesco in Arezzo? Quite probably—since an act of "reparation" has already been happily completed there (no matter that it is antihistorical) by the relocation of the *Crucifix* (13th c.) by the Master of Saint Francis, associated from 1961 with the Dezzi Bardeschi altar. With its removal, the *Crucifix* was then installed on the left wall of the church where, suspended perpendicular to the main altar, it does not correspond with any historical precedent (as does the *Crucifix* by the Master of the Fogg *Pietà* in Santa Croce in Florence). No crucifix was ever in this location. It would have hung on the *iconostasis* or icon screen between the choir and the sacristy, as seen in Giotto's fresco, *Saint Francis at Greccio*, in the Upper Church of San Francesco at Assisi, which certainly would not have been depicted it that way if it weren't in line with Franciscan tradition.

Thus absurdly relocated at Arezzo (although we have to be thankful that it was not hung from the keystone of the choir vault, as some believed it should be), the crucifix seriously damages the "proportions" of Piero's design by intruding on a space whose perfect "order" is achieved through the painted architecture and the placement of the figures in the scenes. This crucifix is no substitute for that Renaissance symbol of centralized space, the egg hanging suspended, immobilized by the light and emerging from the shadows below, in the niche depicted in Piero's *Madonna and Child with Saints* painted for the Church of Saint Bernardino, Urbino (after 1472, Brera Museum, Milan).

[24] See Note 23 above.

[25] If this were the case, why not return the *Captives* by Michelangelo (Academy of Fine Arts, Florence) to the Grotto in the Boboli Gardens? It was Buontalenti who, with "great genius," constructed this fantastic vision, placing them on pilasters with a new and splendid creativity, where they remained in complete harmony from 1576 to 1908. Wasn't Michelangelo's *Victory* in the Great Hall (Salone dei Cinquecento) of the Palazzo Vecchio taken away in 1980 from its high position of privilege in the central niche of the nineteenth-century partition across the entrance wall? Wasn't the valuable balance of that partition, modeled by De Fabris on that in the Audience Hall of the Palazzo, tampered with when Michelangelo's sculpture was removed and returned to its original position against the long wall of the Great Hall? (P. Barocchi, *Palazzo Vecchio: committenza e collezionismo medicei*, exhib. cat., Florence, 1980, p. 15).

[26] Unfortunately, this still happens, as it did in the case of a famous work in the Uffizi Gallery that recently emerged from an exemplary cleaning operation performed on such a level as to signal a major accomplishment of recent times. In spite of the splendid formal recuperation, the painting was debased by and lost its essential quality as a result of the curiously "historicized" retention of an incorrect alteration made in the nineteenth century. At that time, gaps in the paint surface, caused by the separation of the boards that make up the panel, were filled in with plaster and integrated with the whole as if these were "missing" parts of the original painting. Not taken into consideration was the fact that these arbitrary additions deformed the original line and dimension of the image through the elongation of the painting.

"Reparation" and not "restoration" was thus the case even here, in the replacement of something that had been eliminated in the course of the operation because it was considered false and not in keeping with the reality of the work of art. Therefore, the feet and the arm of the Christ Child, and the other areas affected by the separation of the boards, now have "measurements" that retain nothing of the appearance created by the artist. Actually, he has been penalized, where there should have been more effort by us to recognize and preserve the verity of his line and color.

[27] Opinion given on June 16, 1989 by the Joint Committee of the National Council for Cultural and Environmental Properties comprised of: the Regional Committee for Environmental and Architectural Properties: Roberto Di Stefano (president), Alberto Spigaroli, Giuseppe Infranca, Ruggero Martines, Amerigo Restucci, Mario Manieri Elia, Margherita Asso and Vincenzo Regino; and the Regional Committee for Artistic and Historical Properties: Francesco Negri Arnoldi (president), Michele Cordaro, Vettore Spalletti, Luigi Spezzaferro, Bruno Passamani, Andrea Cavalli and Pietro Amato.

THE BRANCACCI CHAPEL FROM ITS ORIGINS TO THE PRESENT

Ornella Casazza

The chapel is located in the Church of Santa Maria del Carmine in Florence, at the end of the right transept arm. Rectangular in plan, it measures 5.68 meters wide by 6.84 meters deep, including the entrance pilaster.

Dedicated to the Madonna del Carmine (Our Lady of Mount Carmel) or the Madonna del Popolo (Our Lady of the People), the chapel was under the patronage of the Brancacci family from the second half of the fourteenth century until 1780, when it passed into the hands of the Riccardi family.

Its history begins with Piero di Piuvichese Brancacci, who, in his will of February 20, 1367, provided for "the founding of an ancestral chapel as proof and recognition of the social prestige of the family and an indication of its satisfactory financial condition."[1] This is spoken of in his son Antonio's will, recorded in 1370–71, as the chapel "that Piero di Piuvichese, his deceased father, had *left behind* [author's italics] in said church,"[2] thus providing definite evidence for the start of the work. For the progress of construction on the chapel, there is only one other reliable early document, an entry in the accounts of the Carmelite Convent for March 28, 1387: "Pittances to the brothers who are excavating the vault under the Brancacci Chapel" and "to those who assist and who build the wall during that time."[3]

By 1422, Felice di Michele Brancacci, not Antonio Brancacci as Vasari claimed,[4] was the patron of the chapel, as clearly affirmed by Felice's will dictated on June 26, 1422, before his departure for the Embassy in Cairo.[5] He was patron until at least 1436, the year of his exile.

Among all the Brancacci, Felice was the highest in the ranks of the Florentine ruling class and held important public positions. In 1412, he was an elected member of the Council of the Sixteen Standard-Bearers (Sedici Gonfalonieri) representing the sixteen districts (*gonfaloni*) of Florence, and in 1418 he was elected to the Council of Twelve Goodfellows (Dodici Buonuomini), which also acted to advise the Signoria, the central government of the Commune of Florence, on legislation and foreign policy. Following this, he served as ambassador to Lunigiana on the Genoa coast and, in 1422, as ambassador to Egypt in Cairo, along with Carlo Federighi, a man of culture, a "philosopher" and a "doctor of law."

In 1426, Felice was an agent for Florentine troops holding Brescia under siege during the war against Milan. In 1427, he was head of a silk trading company, and in 1433 he married Lena Strozzi, daughter of the Florentine aristocrat Palla Strozzi. A rich and powerful man,[6] it was Felice who commissioned Masolino and Masaccio to decorate the Brancacci family chapel after his return from Cairo in February, 1423.[7] And certainly it was he who chose the theme of the Life of Saint Peter for its many aspects associated with his own mercantile interests.

The actual appearance of the chapel and its decoration is the result of a series of alterations and modifications: (1) those done initially to facilitate the execution of the frescoes by Masaccio and Masolino, (2) those that occurred in the time immediately associated with Felice Brancacci's fall into disgrace (exiled in 1436 and declared a rebel in 1458), and (3) those made subsequently in the eighteenth and nineteenth centuries.

The original Gothic chapel was groin-vaulted with pointed arches and illuminated by a tall, narrow, double-cusped lancet in the outside wall. This window was uncovered at the beginning of our restoration work in 1982, during the dismantling of the eighteenth-century altar. The lower part had been filled in from the original sill up to a height of 1.60 meters, reducing the size of the opening and providing a new wall surface over the altar to accommodate the final scene in the Life of Saint Peter, his martyrdom by crucifixion, which was painted there by Masaccio to serve as the altarpiece.

Other changes took place between 1435 and 1458. In a veritable act of *damnatio memoriae* to erase the "memory" of a patron who had become politically embarrassing to them, if not dangerous, the Carmelite brothers changed the name of the Chapel of Saint Peter to the Chapel of the Madonna del Popolo, and placed over its altar a thirteenth-century panel painting of the Virgin Mary referred to as "Our Lady of the People."[8] Also at this time and in

Masolino, Adam and Eve: The Fall, *during restoration*

connection with the *damnatio*, the portraits of all the people related to the Brancacci painted by Masaccio in *The Raising of the Son of Theophilus* were obliterated. The Carmelites thereby eliminated all possible trace or presumption of anti-Medici connivance with the Brancacci. Left unfinished by Masaccio, the *Theophilus* fresco was then completed in 1481–82 by Filippino Lippi, who also restored with fidelity the areas where the troublesome portraits were removed.[9] At the same time, he painted three scenes in the bottom (first) register that were never executed by Masaccio or Masolino—two on the entrance pilasters and one on the right wall of the chapel.

Not only was the cult of the Madonna responsible for the diminished importance of the Life of Saint Peter cycle, but also, due to its ritual practices, the frescoes suffered excessive blackening and obscuration from the smoke produced by the very large number of votive lamps kept burning in this small chapel. Church records for 1516, for example, show that half a barrel of oil was required to fill the lamps every morning.[10] A complete cleaning of the frescoes has been documented as early as the second half of the sixteenth century.[11]

Other modifications carried out in the chapel are traced to the early 1670s. "In the division of the first level, a beautiful carved and gilded wood cornice with four large matching figures supporting the ends" was installed in 1670; executed soon after, in 1674, was "the dado that runs around the Chapel, all of white marble, together with the floor and steps up to the altar similarly of marble, and the railing."[12] The altar was then furnished in silver with candlesticks of different sizes, urns and two little angels in the act of crowning the Virgin on the altarpiece. Also, eleven silver lamps were suspended from an iron chandelier. On this occasion of general refurbishing and embellishment of the chapel, it is probable that the nudity of Adam and Eve was covered up with leaves in the two frescoes, *The Fall* by Masolino and *The Expulsion* by Masaccio. These leaves were definitely not original to the frescoes, as proved by the fact that their materials existed only on the surface

Masaccio, Adam and Eve: The Expulsion, *detail, during restoration*

of the intonaco. Macro- and microphotographs of the surface show that these materials covered and clogged up those areas where the original pigment had cracked from age and flaked off. Moreover, in an examination effected by infrared reflectography penetrating through the various layers, it was possible to "see" with exactitude the original underlying picture surface showing the bodies as completely nude.

There is no precise information as to the year and the name of the person involved in the addition of the leaves. It can only be stated that in 1652 the leaves did not exist, as clearly indicated in a description from that year, which serves as the *terminus post quem*: "Masaccio was a talented man and following Giotto worked very freely, as seen in his figures of Adam and Eve formed completely nude in a chapel in a major church in Florence."[13] It is important to note in this same treatise the reply given to the question of whether or not "the nude images were obscene or hazardous to the soul": "[These pictures were declared] not lascivious or obscene, although there is nudity, nor does the Church hold them as such, as can clearly be seen in these [figures] of Adam and Eve and Others."[14] This opinion was written on the eve of the reign of Cosimo de' Medici III, Grand Duke of Tuscany from 1670 to 1723, about whose bigotry ample evidence has been brought to light, and the leafy cover on the Adam and Eve figures was no doubt added during this time period. Even if no specific documentation for it exists, it is a supposition supported by comparison with other incredible acts of censorship effected in that time.[15]

In 1680, Marquis Francesco Ferroni, wishing to acquire the chapel, offered to renovate it in a manner similar to that of the Corsini Chapel on the other side of the transept. He proposed to destroy the frescoes, considered old-fashioned according to current taste which abhorred "those ugly characters dressed in long robes and cloaks in the manner of the antique."[16] But his patronage was opposed by the mother-grandduchess Vittoria della Rovere who "either made a commotion about it on her own or was instigated to do so by the Academy of Painters, or more likely by a noble family who did not wish to make its name known."[17] Therefore nothing was done, even though Ferroni said that he was willing "to have the frescoes cut from the wall on the first register where the most famous paintings are" and to preserve them elsewhere, thus accomplishing the renovation of the chapel without great damage to them. Fortunately, even that proposal was not accepted.[18]

The poor state of preservation of the frescoes was mentioned in a record of the period, from which it is clear that the Saint Peter cycle was no longer an object of religious devotion, and the pictures were valued only as being "very old."[19] Thus, the words of G. Bottari, written in 1730, appear significant and even courageous: "Another harm came to the good paintings from those who, wishing to adorn particular figures there with royal or imperial crowns and diadems or similar trifles, began by ruining them in general. . . . By such expedients, some of the beautiful pictures by Masaccio suffered grave detriment. . . . After the image of the Our Lady was placed there, to which the devoted faithful celebrated many feasts, and for that reason, there was affixed over said paintings ornaments of carved wood and such frivolous bric-a-brac, therefore by this, and by the frequent coming and going in this chapel to light the lamps and similar needs, they were greatly scratched and it is feared that they will be scratched more."[20] Four years after this sharp warning, when a new architectural decoration of the church was carried out in 1734, the painter Antonio Pillori cleaned many of its wall murals, including "recleaning likewise those in the Chapel of Our Lady."[21]

The final, inconsiderate transformation of the chapel happened between 1747 and 1748 under the direction, interestingly, of Angiola Tempesti, mother of Lorenzo Gasparo Masini, the prior and head supervisor for the Carmelite church. First, on the entrance facade of the chapel a stucco and masonry decoration was completed in 1747, which was not liked. Subsequently, it was removed and replaced by one of stone designed by the French architect Chaman.[22] Another change was the complete destruction of the ceiling vault that, according to Richa,[23] had suffered greatly from dampness and, along with it, the frescoes of the four Evangelists painted there supposedly by Masolino.[24] The lunette frescoes on the top register of the walls also disappeared because, as it was said, "they had no worth." The new round dome of the ceiling was then completed by Vincenzo Meuci, who painted on it *The Virgin Giving the Scapular to Saint Simon Stock*. The bare lunette areas of the side walls were repainted with an architectural design by Carlo Santoni.

An archival reference found by Mesnil held out the possibility of something remaining of the original lunette paintings below these eighteenth-century decorations. It states that Meucci, "strongly advising that the chapel suffered from a lack of light, brightened it up as much as possible, adopting the brightest colors to draw and reflect a better amount of the light rays; and because the figures on the third level had no worth, he covered them up with his work."[25] Mesnil also cites from these archival documents that Meucci "retouched all the lost and broken plaster of the good pictures, but with so much delicacy that nothing he did was known to be touched," and that Prior Lorenzo Masini had "that beautiful window opened up and embellished with so much perfection." The cost of this whole operation that brought irremedial destruction to the frescoes in the top register and on the ceiling was "one thousand five hundred *belli ducatoni*," including the expense of demolishing the first facade decoration. The renovation was completed in July 1748.[26]

While nothing was found of the original fresco work in the lunettes of the side walls, two fragmentary *sinopie* (red chalk underdrawings) on the *arriccio* (base coat of plaster) belonging to the Life of Saint Peter cycle by Masolino and Masaccio were discovered under the frescoes in the top register of the back wall on either side of the window.[27] Obviously, Meucci did not limit himself to covering the work up; first he destroyed it and then covered over the space at his disposal. Also, the enlargement of the window "to let more light into the chapel," in spite of being "beautiful, worked and embellished with all perfection," destroyed forever the top of the original lancet, although the lower part remained *in situ* but hidden in the construction of the new marble altar.[28] It also modified in a serious way the original "light" so highly significant to the comprehension of the innovative use of incident light in the paintings by the two artists, especially in those of Masaccio.

Added to the records was a terrible fire that, in the night between January 28 and 29, 1771, devastated the church but did not produce very serious or irreparable damage to the Brancacci Chapel itself. The documentation for this event with respect to the chapel and frescoes is as follows:[29]

1. "The firemen made a hole in the roof of the crossing of our church on the side of the altar of Our Lady [the Brancacci Chapel], which had commenced to catch on fire, and thus the course of the fire was interrupted, because it did not reach the roof of the altar of Our Lady, the sacristy and the convent. . . . In the crossing, no trace was found of the lumber [wood for the scaffolds and the work that had been going on, which had filled the whole nave], by which the fire had been able to penetrate into the chapels themselves; that is, the heat was of such intensity it caused whatever there was of a combustible nature in each and every chapel to burst into flame. . . . The facade of the chapel of the Most Serene Lady of Mount Carmel at the head of the crossing suffered greatly, with the falling of a good many pieces of the cornices and of the capitals of the *pietra serena* columns, the burning of the two beautiful doors framed and veneered with walnut [probably at the sides of the entrance to the chapel] and the demolishing of the marble railings. Inside the chapel, the Carrara marble floor was damaged, as was the marble dado that surrounded it and even the marble altar. . . . Burnt also were the gilded cornices dividing the pictures between the first and second registers, along with the harpy figures that supported them in the corners [presumably seriously damaging the intonaco in these areas and altering the color there as well] and the large glazed window above the altar. The very famous pictures on the walls were left in existence, with the exception of two pieces of intonaco which fell in the sacristy area [from *The Tribute Money* at the far right in the area of the steps, where the perspective was incorrectly repaired in the eighteenth-century restoration, and from the first house at the left in *Saint Peter Healing with His Shadow*; there was also a third lacuna, not spoken of here, in the loggia above the crippled man in the *Raising of Tabitha*]."[30]

2. "The pictures that are in the Chapel of Our Lady of Mount Carmel, painted by Masolino da Panicale, Masaccio and Filippino Lippi . . . are partly damaged but not totally lost."[31]

3. "The chapel called the Brancacci, dedicated to the cult of the Our Lady of Carmel, which was decorated with perfection by the renowned Masaccio . . . is also in a condition such that, blackened and terribly spoiled from the smoke, only a few of the pictures, done by Masolino da Panicale, Masaccio and Filippino Lippi, are recognizable."[32]

4. "The pictures on the sides of the chapel of Our Lady by Masolino, Masaccio and Filippino Lippi were left damaged."[33]

5. "The pictures by Masolino, Masaccio and Filippo Lippi . . . were left very damaged."[34]

6. The flames "did not however act to cause irreparable damage to that [painting] in the chapel previously of the Brancacci and now called of Our Lady."[35]

By "irreparable damage" is understood here to mean a loss in which the painting has completely disappeared. It is difficult to know from the descriptions if circumscribed losses of this type also occurred, since it is not possible to trace the precise causes for those lacunae still visible on the walls, and variously restored in the past, that have now reappeared in their full extent during the recent restoration work. Considered as irreparable is the damage now brought to light that can be attributed to the flames and the heat of the fire, affecting more than one section of the fresco cycle and resulting in notable and irreversible changes in some colors. The heat altered the colors according to the different percentages of iron present in the intonacos of the various *giornate*, changing the ochers on the ground to a pinkish color (especially in *The Tribute Money*) and reddening the flesh tones (as on the baptized neophyte), the walls of the buildings (the stone palace in *Saint Peter Healing with His Shadow*) and the yellow in Saint Peter's cloak (in *The Tribute Money*). Changes of this kind, pointed out in detail in the commentaries on the individual frescoed scenes, were first published in *Critica d'Arte* by the present author.[36]

The wooden cornices separating the registers on the walls of the chapel and the wooden stands at the corners for votive lamps were especially deleterious to the surrounding areas during the fire. As seen from the outlines, the cornices were responsible for irreparable damage to the color pigments, since, wherever they caught fire, they burned slowly like coals and generated a very high level of heat. In other areas, however, the frames did not catch fire but cracked and fell to the floor before burning. The severe damage encountered in the corners of the chapel was clearly due to the burning of the stands and, in the corner on the left, perhaps also of wooden poles leaning there, which were used for candle snuffers, crosses, banners and other things. The fire did not touch the altarpiece, *The Madonna del Popolo*, which had been removed to the convent about a year earlier.

A few days after the fire, on February 3, the architects Giuseppe Salvetti and Romualdo Morozzi were called in by the highest authority to perform a survey of the premises. It was then decided that the Brancacci Chapel would immediately have its window reglazed and the gap in the entrance facade boarded up. On February 10, the Grand Duke Pietro Leopoldo, who was in Pisa at the time of the fire, personally came to see the condition of the church.

Of great interest is an exchange of letters which demonstrates the very high importance that the German-born painter Raphael Mengs (1728–1779) attached to the frescoes of the Brancacci Chapel.[37] For Mengs, a proponent of the neoclassicism emerging at that time in Rome, Masaccio was a primary figure in the history of artistic innovation. The exact date of the first letter is unknown, but it was written around February 20 by Canon Giuseppe Querci, director of the Royal Gallery, to the counselor Angiolo Tavanti, in Pisa with the Grand Duke who was staying in that city again: "I must then beseech Your Excellency, for the love that You have for our country's heritage, to do Your utmost for the preservation of the celebrated paintings by Masaccio in the Church of the Carmelites, so that, after having been saved in part from the furor of the fire, these precious souvenirs of the art of design do not perish entirely in another grim mishap, as will surely happen if they are not promptly provided with protection. The painter Cavalier Mengs, upon leaving Florence, exhorted me most warmly to concentrate on reiterating to His Royal Highness those concerns he expressed regarding this matter immediately after the fire [it seems therefore that Mengs spoke directly to the Grand Duke], and he told me that he had left the painters Ferri and Pacini [Gesualdo Ferri and Santi Pacini, the latter known as one of the most esteemed restoration painters of the period] with the appropriate instructions concerning the actions to be taken for such work, and which will be executed as soon as His Royal Highness deems it well to order it done."

Tavanti responded on February 25: "With respect then to Masaccio's paintings, which escaped the furor of the fire's flames in the burned Carmelite Church, I would like Your Most Illustrious Lordship to suggest to me what might be done to assure their preservation, so that His Royal Highness may give His orders."

Canon Querci quickly replied on February 27: "As for the request made by Your Excellency in His much esteemed letter of the 27th of this month [meaning the 25th], concerning the protection and relief that could be brought to Masaccio's paintings, I have the honor of replying that before all else, it would be best to make a wooden partition for the entire entrance of the chapel where said pictures are located, so that they remain defended from inclement conditions, and to the same end, it is necessary to repair the glass window above the altar [two things that had already been decided in the survey of the premises done on February 3 by the architects Salvetti and Morozzi]. This extrinsic remedy is necessary because, as the fire has caused the intonaco to separate on many parts of the walls, the winds, sometimes humid and sometimes dry, which freely pass through the afflicted Carmelite Church can easily accelerate their deterioration. With regard, then, to the actual repair of the paintings, I would gladly support what Cavalier Mengs has told me he suggested to the painters Ferri and Pacini. All the same, since this is a very delicate thing and constitutes a problem of whether it is better to do or not do, or at least to be certain that one needs to do little, I believe that the commission to execute any work should be preceded with an appraisal by two of the most highly accredited professors."

And here finally is a letter from Mengs himself, written from Rome on March 23 to Canon Querci: "Concerning the chapel by Masaccio, I remember it with sorrow, but to help as much as possible with this esteemed souvenir of the renaissance of painting, the glory of the Florentine nation, not only should said pictures be cleaned but, before putting a hand to them, precautions should be taken, since one finds in many places that the intonaco is detached and calcinated, wherefore it is necessary to carry out two different operations before proceeding with the cleaning. As for the actual ways and means to be employed, I have already discussed this with Mr. Pacini and Mr. Ferri, and, if it pleases the Sovereign, I could explain everything to them that seems to me the most necessary to be done."

These valuable documents not only show us how important the involvement of Mengs was in the restoration of the Brancacci Chapel paintings, given the great authority that he possessed, but they also inform us, better than any other source, about the damages incurred by the frescoes due to the fire other than the blackening due to the smoke. Unfortunately, we know nothing of Mengs's instructions to the two Florentine restoration painters.

Procacci, who published these documents, believes in any case that a speedy intervention by Ferri and Pacini to consolidate the separated plaster surfaces can safely be maintained. The two most certainly would not have gone against the opinion and advice of a man with so much authority, as the letters cited seem to well demonstrate. The cleaning and retouching of the frescoes, according to information provided by the abbot Vincenzo Follini,[38] an eyewitness to these events, were entrusted to Giuseppe Romei, the artist responsible for painting the vaulted ceiling of the church's transept.

This all occurred when the marquis Gabriello Riccardi, a subdeacon of the Carmelite church, acquired the patronage of the chapel on August 18, 1780, for two thousand *scudi* after negotiations with the Grand Duke's agent, Giovanni Battista Cangini. After the fire and at the time of the Brancacci family's renunciation of its patronage, Cangini had been named intermediary between old and new owners of the various chapels of the church.[39] Among Riccardi's immediate restoration projects was the complete revamping of the burial vault underneath the chapel. According to the Riccardi household records, it was the only one to have suffered serious damage from the fire nine years earlier.[40]

During the reconstruction, the floor and the revetments on the lower part of the chapel walls were also redone with variegated marbles. Riccardi decided to leave unaltered all of the painted decorations, including those by Meucci and Sacconi from the eighteenth century, except for a cleaning and touch-up by the painter Giuseppe Romei (as noted in a church record book) and by Domenico Stagi.[41] Canon Gabriello did not limit his interventions just to reviving and putting in good order all of the paintings located in the chapel. He also redecorated the space in a way that would honor the prestige of his family and, for this reason, decided to construct a new altar to substitute for the existing one badly damaged by the fire. At the same time, he also had made sixteen bronze candlesticks with the family coat of arms on their bases, which still exist today.[42]

At the conclusion of the restoration work in 1782, two years after he acquired ownership of the chapel, Gabriello had a memorial tablet placed on the floor before the altar. This still exists. Although it has worn away over the years,[43] it bears witness to one of the greatest acts of patronage performed by the Riccardi family, that of preserving Masaccio's precious frescoes in the full awareness that they were saving a very important part of Florentine history, which had been imperiled by time and man so often in the past.

The Madonna del Popolo was also returned to its place on the altar, but in his Memoirs, Father Ranieri Chiti[44] recalls how the pointed arch of the Gothic frame had been rounded off. He was pleased, however, that the "face of the Divine Savior crowned with thorns" painted in the gable remained quite visible[45] and that Christ's name abbreviated with Greek letters had been retained in the recent reduction of the arch, attributable to the 1780–82 restoration carried out by the Riccardi family. It is reasonable to date also to this period "the devoted repainting that had been done over almost all of the altarpiece, according to a criterion of academic normalization of early works, of which we know other examples in Tuscany in the late 18th century."[46]

Concerning developments during the nineteenth century, in 1830 the chapel caught the attention of a noted scholar, Attilio Zuccagni Orlandini, who was working at the time on Plate X of the *Atlas of Tuscany* which contained the map of Florence. Orlandini wrote that he was "strongly in favor of providing special means of restoration and preservation for one of the most precious monuments among the many this city is privileged to have."[47] But nothing was done.

In 1832, the restorer, Luigi Scotti, of the Royal Gallery wrote that "the immortal works of Masaccio," as a result of the fire, had been "smoked over as noted by Casentino, and then were diligently and patiently restored to their former condition, as can now be seen." On April 19, 1834, Antonio Ramirez di Montalvo, the director of the Royal Gallery, mentioned that the chapel's frescoes had been damaged by the decorations and by copyists, and, about the same time, the Provincial of the Carmelite Order expressed hope that the chapel would be placed under the guardianship of the Academy of Fine Arts.[48]

At the end of August, 1864, Orlandini proposed the idea of forming a committee, with himself as its secretary, "to record its deliberations and keep alive the enthusiasm of its members." In his opinion, the following three aspects were to be deplored in the chapel: "(1) a cornice of gilded wood running horizontally across the pilasters, as well as the walls of the chapel, perhaps covering a part of the paintings. Those Reverend Fathers are ignorant of the cause that produced such a barbarism, but it is very probable that this wide wooden band was used for attaching lights and draperies during Feast Days, thereby substituting wretched cloths in bright colors for those divine frescoes!; (2) lights fed by wax and oil that burn continuously, and their combustion produces that blackish patina which disfigures its lineaments and coloring; and, added to this, the dust rising from the floor has formed a dirty deposit that hides many traits of those divine frescoes; and (3) appearing above the arch of the chapel, the face of a clock to which is attached its metal casing, and said clock is very near to the church bells; all conduct electrical current, and this could one day be the cause of very severe and irreparable damage."

It was not until December 13, however, that the project got underway, when the Carmelite prior, Giuseppe Fiaschi, wrote to the director of the Royal Galleries and president of the Commission for the Preservation of Art Objects. "To keep always the memory of the very celebrated professors Masaccio and Masolino everlasting," Fiaschi asked that a member of the Commission perform a survey of the premises, given that the frescoes "have suffered some slight damage . . . wherefore, following its wise judgment those remedies can be made that are necessary to prevent greater damage." Immediately afterwards, Orlandini met personally with the director of the Galleries to whom he had written a letter on December 16, recalling among other things the vow he had made in 1830 to restore the frescoes. He also described the events of past months during which his efforts to form a committee had been unsuccessful. At any rate, the inspector Ferdinando Rondoni was given the responsibility of making a survey of the premises at the Carmelite Church on December 17, and two days later, he submitted his extremely interesting report. He wrote: "[I entered the Chapel] to evaluate the present condition of the noted and celebrated frescoes by Masaccio, which make up the main part of the walls of the Brancacci Chapel in the aforesaid church. After a very intensive examination of them, I am able to testify that, overall, they appear as they did many, many years ago, that is, they are covered over with a generalized film produced by abuse of the votive lamps, together with many small blistered areas of color. At the bottom of the scene where Saint Peter is reviving a boy, there is a bulging of the plaster surface approximately 0.17 meters high and 0.44 meters wide, demonstrated by various means, which must quickly be repaired so that it does not detach from the rest of the surface. Another slight damage exists in the scene of the calling [*sic*] of Saint Peter, where a really very long, nearly vertical crack in the plaster between Saint Peter and a disciple must also be repaired. Finally, let me say that the Carmelite monks expressed the idea to me of removing entirely a very awkward gilded bar affixed horizontally on both side walls of this Chapel in the last century, put there perhaps to divide the individual scenes or even to hang tapestries, and whatever the original reason may have been, they only serve to disrupt the harmony of those paintings; the Royal Commission will decide on what I have presented above."

January 16, 1865, following up on this report, the restorer Pietro Pezzati was designated head of the restoration project. But this was not followed up because, on May 6 of that year, the Commission resigned due to its lack of authority and power to operate, and especially because it was unable to finance the restoration work. On February 22 of the following year, Prior Fiaschi requested that the director of the Galleries send over Pezzati; thus Orlandini's scepticism in the previously cited letter appears to have been justified, when he wrote that, due to the usual bureaucratic delays, "the provisions will be very late and then forgotten."[49]

Nevertheless, something was certainly done around this date, because, in a letter dated about fifty years later, the head architect of the Regional Office for the Preservation of the Monuments of Tuscany mentions explicitly that "the celebrated frescoes have not been cleaned since they were consolidated about forty years ago."[50]

"Consolidation" of the fresco surfaces was in fact spoken of in September, 1860, when new discoveries were made in the cloister, including a fragment of Filippino Lippi's *Confirmation of the Rule* (thought at the time to be a part of Masaccio's *Sagra* or *Consecration of the Church of Santa Maria del Carmine*). Even the "recipe" was recorded then, and it is not improbable that an intervention of this type was also done in the Brancacci Chapel, owing to the materials found connected with the pigments during the analyses conducted before our recent restoration work. This consolidation was not done by Gaetano Bianchi, who rejected the "recipe," but perhaps by Pietro Pezzati, who may have used a similar method to overcome the previously mentioned intonaco blisters.[51]

There is no precise information on this in the contemporaneous *History of Painting in Italy* (London, 1864–71) by J. Crowe and G. B. Cavalcaselle. Nevertheless, this publication, and especially the subsequent Italian edition of 1897, is an outstanding source for surveying the state of preservation of the frescoes. Also from Cavalcaselle's Notebook of drawings, preserved in the Marciana Library, Venice, can be extracted the most valuable notations of great documentary relevance, many of which do not appear in his printed text on the Life of Saint Peter cycle.[52] With these, Cavalcaselle provides important data on the technique, colors, mixtures and formal aspects that could not always be rendered clearly in line drawings themselves, which lacked color. As a fine connoisseur and "reader" of the individual technical qualities of each of the artists who worked in the Carmelite church, Cavalcaselle was able to give us an exact report on the condition of the entire chapel. Therefore, this became an extremely important document for us.

In addition to his comments on the state of preservation of the individual scenes, Cavalcaselle made a valuable appraisal of the condition and the

Masaccio, The Baptizing of the Neophytes, *detail, before restoration*

Masaccio, The Baptizing of the Neophytes, *detail, during restoration*

technique of execution for the whole cycle: "In these frescoes, the coloring, especially of the flesh, is so transparent that it sometimes allows the intonaco to be perceived underneath. This effect is more so in the upper level frescoes, while in the lower register closer to the spectator's eye, the colors are more saturated in the highlighted areas and stronger in the shadows, and the technique is easier and bolder. This approach of painting in broad masses on a very smooth background, using fluid colors applied with great artistic resolve and mastery, was to produce, together with the warmer tints in the shadows and the contrast of the half-tints, that strong tonality of coloring that gives volume to the bodies. As for the imperfection of some parts of the linear perspective, he remedied this with excellent coloring and exactness in the aerial perspective, which lends to the severity of the compositional lines and the figures a greater sense of realism. Also, the easy drapery and wide movement of its folds, together with the masterful way in which the nude forms are created, correspond perfectly with both the grandeur of the figures and the excellence in the coloring. Masaccio's ability is remembered especially for his great quality as a colorist, which bettered considerably the art of both Antonio Veneziano and Masolino, and therefore demonstrated not only his great superiority over the painters of his time, but also, by more or less showing them the way, he was a precursor to those great artists who flourished in the 16th century."

Cavalcaselle concludes: "It is truly deplorable and a great harm to art and its history, that this Chapel was abused in 1774 with the destruction of Masolino's frescoes which disappeared under the work of the whitewasher or were substituted by Vincenzo Meucci's painting. Besides causing the loss of renowned works, damage was caused by the new colors which, by comparison, dulled the tones of the whole chapel."[53]

In 1890, it was reported that "the marble decorations of the walls, which disrupted the harmony of the surroundings with their white mass and impeded the view of these superb frescoes, have been covered over with wooden ones and the floor, also white, will be covered with a rug in subdued colors." Also, a request was made for "the reduction of the roof that protrudes too far and the demolishing of a recently made walkway outside the window that robs the Chapel of most of its light."[54]

On May 18, 1895, an earthquake shook the city of Florence. Damage to the church and convent, documented in a report sent on June 27 by the Regional Office for the Preservation of Monuments to the Ministry, was of little consequence and immediately repaired.[55]

In a letter of January 31, 1902, from the Regional Office for the Preservation of the Monuments of Tuscany to the Commission for the Preservation of Monuments, it was reported that "signs of obvious infiltration of dampness" had been observed by the architect Ezio Cerpi on the back wall of the chapel due to seepage of water from the outside. Steps were then taken to install a glass roof over a loggia and to eliminate a masonry structure in order to give more illumination to the chapel.

When the Head Office of the Ministry expressed its concerns over the "display of lights" and the damage caused by the smoking of the candles and wax splattered on the frescoes, the prior of the convent, Alberto Bertieri, in a letter to the supervisor dated January 2, 1903, assured him that, from this moment on, no such celebrations would be officiated, with the exception of the anniversary of Saint Andrea Corsini. He also requested that the reliquary with the remains of the Blessed Angiolo Mazzinghi be removed from the altar, and he mentioned that the splatterings of wax were not from the "display" but rather were due to the actions of a "servant," now deceased, who used a cane fitted with a taper or a candle to show the frescoes to visitors during the hours of less light or on rainy days.[56] In view of the desires of the scholars, notice was then given that the church would extend its Matins hours to one o'clock in the afternoon.

At a "long delayed" meeting in Florence in January, 1903, of the "very large" committee organized by San Giovanni Valdarno, Masaccio's birthplace, with the aim of celebrating the artist's centenary, the condition of the frescoes was discussed.[57] Guido Carocci pointed out the various provisions already made in recent years to ameliorate its conditions and to guarantee the safety of the paintings by Masaccio, Masolino da Panicale and Filippino Lippi: the covering with wood of the marble dado which clashed with the subdued tonalities of the paintings, the provisions made to arrest the infiltration of dampness and the orders given to prevent decorations and lighting displays in the chapel. He spoke also of the difficulty presented in carrying out the proposal to reopen the original window, since it was backed up on the outside wall of the chapel by construction done in the sixteenth century. He concluded by saying that new studies would be made on the matter, and that, with the agreement of the Commune and the Regional Office, a search would be made for another altar to substitute for the existing one, which would be more in character. He also mentioned that the dusting of the frescoes would be done shortly. This was all repeated in a communication dated January 29, 1903, to the Ministry from the Regional Office for the Preservation of Monuments, where the intention was expressed "to modify the shape of the eighteenth-century altar and to mask the modern decorations that constitute so many notes of brilliant color clashing with the low, subdued tonalities of the frescoes."

Brought up again that year, in letters dated June 23 and July 6, from the prefect of the Commune to the director of the Regional Office, was the suggestion that, in the renovation of the atrium outside the chapel wall, work should also be done for the "recovery of the visible remains of the original ogival window that exists behind the present window." After further studies, the Regional Office communicated a status report on the situation to the Ministry, reviewing all the proposals made or discussed and giving a contrary opinion regarding the recovery and repair of the outside of the old window, because of the risk of damaging the stability of the intonacos on the inside wall. For the same reason, it was judged inappropriate to approve the removal of the white marble canopy over the altar situated underneath the present window.[58] It was emphasized that "the frescoes require only precaution and require it daily depending on how many people visit the precious Chapel. Recommended is a scrupulously careful dusting to liberate the frescoes from the layer of dirt that in some areas actually hides essential parts of the compositions. With equal precautions, the old wax drippings wherever encountered ought to be removed, as also should the gilded cornice or wooden fillet fastened along the top edge of the frescoes and that in some places appears loose and falling down."[59]

In February 1904, a new iron frame was made for the window, "with six openings compared to the previous twenty-nine." The light thus acquired, it was noted, was greatly increased. As for the dusting, the elder Fiscali (Domenico) offered to do the job,[60] but it was Filippo Fiscali who drew up the report sent April 15 to the director of the Regional Office, which reads: "[The frescoes] are covered by a layer of dirt that has overshadowed them for more than forty years, when they were last repaired; they are also spattered with numerous wax droplets, which were recognized as being very old due to their adhesion to the paintings. The condition of the plaster is secure, and the closures done at the time of the above-mentioned repair work continue to hold up on the *arriccio*. The color adheres very well in the intonaco and would permit the safe execution of a scrupulous cleaning of the pictures, provided that the skillful action of the restorer is employed . . . to render them free from all that has disfigured them disgracefully for a long time; and to remove only the dirt that dims their beauty, thus also to remove the numerous wax drippings and to cover up the most visible losses with harmonious tints, as prescribed by the ministerial orders." The minister, in approving the project, expressed his strong hesitation with regard to the preselected restorer, "given that a Committee of the Superior Council of Fine Arts had recently had to complain about the ill-considered restorations executed by the very same Fiscali on the paintings by Mantegna in the Chapel of the Basilica of Sant'Andrea in Mantua, to remedy which studies are being done for the most appropriate means to adopt so that the disfigurements suffered by those illustrious pictures could at least be attenuated." In this instance, he continued, it was necessary that the work be done "by a person whose scrupulous diligence and capabilities do not evoke the slightest doubt of this kind."[61]

In a meeting on June 17, the Curatorial Commission for Monuments and Archaeological Excavations of the Prefecture "expressed the opinion that the frescoes of the Brancacci Chapel . . . must be cleaned according to the norms that will be dictated, after examination of these frescoes, by a Sub-Committee including Tito Conti, Edoardo Gelli and Riccardo Mazzanti together with Agenore Socini from the Regional Office for the Preservation of Monuments." The sub-committee was also asked to select the artist to whom "the cleaning of the frescoes under the surveillance of the Regional Office should be entrusted."[62] On June 30, the survey was done at the Carmelite Church, and after their "careful inspection," the members of the committee "were pleased to affirm unanimously the good state of preservation there. Even the upper scenes on either side of the altar, which had suffered the most in the past from the dampness in the walls, were in better shape after the isolation work had been done recently on the outside to protect them. This precautionary measure not only procured more light for the Chapel but also left the frescoes in a condition such that further deterioration was no longer feared. Even the damage decried due to some old, limited wax droplets and some very small, light scratches was such that it was barely noticed when contemplating the grandiose beauty of the whole Chapel." In summation, the committee expressed unanimously the following opinion in its report to the prefect on July 5: "(1) That, for the best result, the work on the frescoes must be limited to a simple general dusting and a partial cleaning with bread crumbs in the areas that need it; (2) that any other operation must absolutely be excluded, maximal or even minimal touch-ups, in neutral colors, on the scratches; (3) that for the greatest safety the agent for the prescribed and explicit project must adhere to it in an absolute manner, [and] the work of executing must be assigned to him in sections, according to the prior evaluation of the present state of the frescoes to be made jointly by the members of the commission and the regional office; and (4) that, given the minimal work to be done and its specifications, the commission for their execution can be entrusted to the restorer Filippo Fiscali."

The minister, on behalf of the Regional Office, declared his approval "that the simple general dusting of the frescoes be executed" but could not "in any way consent even to a partial cleaning using bread crumbs." This method had yielded a terrible result in the frescoes by Correggio on the ceiling of the Church of San Giovanni in Parma, and, in his estimation, "it certainly should not be tried again on the marvelous paintings by Masaccio." He consented, however, to giving the commission for the work to Fiscali,[63] who began the project on October 17, 1904. The first report, regarding what had been done on *The Tribute Money* and *The Raising of the Son of Theophilus*, emphasized "unanimously" the carefulness of the intervention, and Fiscali was again given "the strongest recommendations, since, in following the preordained method up to the present, he exercised the greatest caution and accuracy so as not to cause even the slightest detriment or alteration to the marvelous paintings."[64] The project was brought to completion on November 29,[65] and in the final inspection report drafted on December 6,[66] the Sub-Committee "expressed, in unanimity, its satisfaction and pleasure with the very accurate and conscientious way in which these [frescoes] were cleaned by Mr. Filippo Fiscali."[67]

In 1908, the Commune Committee for AA and BBA renewed the proposal "to give the chapel back its original light by removing the present altar and reopening the Gothic lancet."[68] In the same year, the installation of a ventilating duct was ordered for the steps on the other side of the back wall.[69]

During World War I, from 1914 to 1918, as part of the program for "the defense of Italian artistic patrimony against the perils of the war," the frescoes were protected with a wall of sandbags covered with strips of cloth or paper.[70] The church was used as a military depot, and a partition was constructed to close off the chapel from the rest of the building. In order to provide for better protection of the existing works of art, however, orders were given "to isolate totally the transept from the rest of the church," and to this end "the partition was torn down and rebuilt at the head of the nave of this same church."[71]

In 1928, a new restoration of the paintings was contemplated,[72] but this was not followed up.

In a letter of January 23, 1929, Alfredo Lenzi of the Office of Fine Arts of the Commune wrote to Giovanni Poggi, the Superintendent of Medieval and Modern Art in Tuscany, that the Committee for the Centenary Celebration of Masaccio was asking for work to be done to enhance the church's appearance, as follows: (1) removal of the stained eighteenth-century altar in white and colored marble, and the reconstruction of the original double-cusped lancet, of which only the lower part remained intact, (2) removal of the modern

Masaccio, Decoration of the right window jamb

wood wainscoting running below the frescoed area, as well as the eighteenth-century wainscoting in colored marble underneath the aforementioned wood one, and the refacing of the dado area with plain plaster painted to simulate marble, modeled upon many fifteenth-century examples, (3) replacement of the present floor of inlaid white marble and *bardiglio* (gray-blue veined marble) with one made of large terra-cotta tiles, (4) recoloring of the external view of the chapel with colors that do not disturb the view of the inside, (5) construction of a plain stone altar corresponding to the style of the Gothic window whose light should not be hindered at all, and the beautiful Byzantine-style altarpiece on which Our Lady of Mount Carmel (or Our Lady of the People) is represented can remain on this altar, and (6) the closure of the chapel with a gate, in a sober design in harmony with the place and time of the construction of the Chapel itself.

The Office of Fine Arts expressed reservations with regard to some of these requests, especially for the removal of the eighteenth-century altar and the wood wainscoting installed in the chapel in 1890. The removal of the altar, or at least of the marble reredos in which the thirteenth-century altarpiece was enclosed, was judged to be dangerous for the safety of the frescoes abutting it. For the same reason, the reconstruction of the lancet would not be easy, since it would require raising the stones of the arch behind the frescoed intonaco. It was noted that the detachment of the smallest piece of painted plaster would be a source for the harshest criticisms. As for the wood wainscoting, installed to cover the colored marble which clashed with the character of the chapel, it was considered preferable to maintain this masking of the marble, rather than to remove it and risk damaging the painted plaster surface above it.

In conclusion and bearing in mind that something should be done to enhance the look of the famous chapel, the Office of Fine Arts proposed the execution of the following work only: (1) removal of the marble altar leaving the reredos in place independent of the altarpiece and the steps. Simplification of the architecture of the reredos itself by the elimination of the pediment and the two angels that overpower it, (2) substitution of large terra-cotta floor tiles for the present geometric design in white marble and *bardiglio*, and the installation of the commemorative epigraph [from the floor] on the outside wall of the chapel, (3) removal of the marble railing closing off the chapel entrance and replacement with an iron gate of plain design in character with the chapel, (4) substitution of larger glass panes in the skylight of the atrium behind the chapel in order to obtain more light, (5) replacement of the glass panes in the chapel window with a single Saint-Gobin pane, which should be slightly milky to impede the view through it of the atrium skylight outside. The question remained of a new altar to put in the chapel, but, before preparing the design for it, the Office solicited the opinion of the Superintendency which responded on February 6 by giving to the Provincial Commission for the Preservation of Monuments the task of returning a decision to the Superior Council of Fine Arts.[73] In any event, between 1929 and 1930, "the light through the existing chapel window was increased, and the Baroque marble altar built in the eighteenth century was reduced in size and the flooring was redone."[74]

In 1932, during the search being conducted, following indications in documentary sources,[75] for evidence of old frescoes in the church, two small projections were removed from the marble altar in the chapel. Revealed behind them were two areas of the frescoed surface in *Saint Peter Baptizing the Neophytes* and *Saint Peter Preaching* which, although considerably darkened due to the soot, showed the tonality of the colors in the time before the altar was built about 1748—that is, in the period when Bottari wrote that the pictures looked "fresh."

In the following years, during World War II, some cautious attempts at cleaning in small areas were made, and, in 1945, when the anti-airstrike protections were removed, a dusting of the frescoes was executed. In November 1946, "the small roof above the Brancacci Chapel caved in due to a broken rafter, which let a great abundance of water penetrate inside the Brancacci Chapel causing it severe damage."[76] This was repaired immediately, however, before any serious damage could occur. No other fact of importance is registered for the several decades following.

By the 1970s, due to the rapid process of the "obscuration" of the frescoes caused by the degeneration of substances applied to their surfaces and accentuated by pollution, the chapel was placed under inspection on the part of the Opificio delle Pietre Dure, through the instigation and direction of Umberto Baldini, starting with a study of humidity and temperature extensive enough to allow for "real time" readings of the variations in and behavior of the frescoes through the changes of the seasons.[77] Thereafter, the state of preservation of the chapel was verified by means of the most modern instrumentation available to furnish us with objective, concrete data to study and analyze. From the in-depth analyses a "clinical portfolio" was developed, on the basis of which we could rigorously and responsibly formulate the requirements, and therefore the methodologies, of the interventions to be carried out. In advance of these, it was also necessary to proceed with exhaustive research and examinations to collect all the information still to be found on the walls of the chapel, outside the context of restorations and modifications done before and after the fire of 1771. In July 1981, work began following a series of operational procedures that are reported and discussed by Umberto Baldini in the preceding chapter.

The discovery of the new pictorial excerpts illustrated herein, enlarging and confirming what Procacci had found in 1932, provided us with knowledge of the state of the frescoes as they were before the fire and successive interventions.[78] From the brilliance and clear luminosity of these painting fragments, we were given an entirely new Masaccio, at last revealed as the founder of a new "school" characterized by a pictorial "voice" not only formalist but also colorist and luminist, that bore so much fruit in future generations. Yet, while he himself moved in a new, modern direction, it was never in violent contrast with, and always within the boundaries of, the sweet imagery and language of the great Masolino. In a sense, Masaccio could change syntax and meanings, but he could not employ a different linguistic vocabulary and still have his painting coexist on the same wall with that of his collaborator. The Masolino-Masaccio relationship cannot be narrowed to a simplistic contrast between *The Fall* and *The Expulsion*; it does not have the impact and the impossibility for coexistence as does the relationship between Brunelleschi and Ghiberti. Yet the differences were such that they opened the way—with Masaccio in the lead—to modern painting.[79]

We are today in a position to specify precisely all of the fresco scenes in the chapel and to forge on this basis a new reading and interpretation of the Life of Saint Peter cycle as a whole.[80] Excluded are the lost decorations of the intrados of the original Gothic entrance arch, which would not have contained scenes but probably consisted of an alternating decoration of heads of saints and stylized foliage, as seen on the original window jambs that were uncovered on the back wall. Despite any trace of the frescoes or their *sinopie* in the lunettes at the tops of the side walls, we do know their subjects from Vasari's descriptions in Masaccio's biography to have been *The Calling of Peter and Andrew* ("where Christ took Andrew and Peter from the nets") and *The Shipwreck* ("the stormy shipwreck of the Apostles"). Vasari also wrote that in the sections of the groin-vaulted ceiling were depicted *The Four Evangelists*. Added to this are the discoveries made during the recent restoration work of a fragmentary scene painted by Masaccio above the altar, the subject of which is recognized as *The Crucifixion of Saint Peter*, and of the *sinopie* for two scenes in the half-lunettes at the top of the back wall identified as *The Repentance of Saint Peter* and *Feed My Lambs, Feed My Sheep*.

In the reconstruction plan of the fresco decorations, the missing scenes are located above and related to those still extant. Beginning at the top of the chapel, in the four sections of the ceiling vault, we have *The Evangelists*; in the lunette of the left wall, *The Calling*; in the half-lunette at the left on the back wall, *The Repentance*; in the half-lunette at the right, *Feed My Lambs, Feed My Sheep*; and in the lunette of the right wall, *The Shipwreck*. For the scenes on the left and right walls, not only were their subjects clearly identified but their locations were also easily determined from Vasari's descriptions.[81] Recent confirmation exists in an article published in 1940 by Longhi, who identified a previously unpublished painting, then in the Giovanelli collection in Venice, as a faithful remembrance of the lost *Calling* by Masolino in the Carmelite church. Noting that the illumination in this painting came from the right, Longhi declared that the original fresco must have been located in the lunette of the left wall of the chapel, where it would correspond with the pictorial "light" from the window on the back wall.[82] The missing scenes, thus recuperated, identified and united with the extant ones, constituted a "cycle" that could now be better analyzed.

The Life of Saint Peter Cycle and the "Historia Salutis"

Masaccio, The Baptizing of the Neophytes, *detail, during restoration*

Looking at the cycle in a context that manifests the message and value of didacticism and reflection, all of the scenes and characters lead us to a profound contemplation of its theological content. This is not to overlook the personal references made that are related to the wishes of the patron, a man of the sea and therefore a sailor-fisherman like Peter (*Calling*), and like Peter begging for Divine help during the tempest (*Shipwreck*) that certainly could have befallen him in his travels as a man of commerce and as a politician. Nor does it dismiss propagandistic motivations with regard to the duty of Florentines to make the Catasto or declaration of income (*Death of Ananias*) and thereby pay taxes (*Tribute Money*), or the condemnation of acts of simony (*Dispute with Simon the Magician*). Ultimately, however, the cycle must be considered for its essential goal of exalting the man and the role of Apostle Peter, the Church and its sacrament of salvation and the universal supremacy of the pope.[83]

From the way in which they were chosen and arranged, all of the scenes appear to illustrate the "mystery of salvation" (*mysterium salutis*), by which is meant the redemption of Man through Christ, which the Church fulfills *in persona Christi* and to which—Church/salvation—"all are called." Beginning with the fresco scenes just inside the chapel entrance, in the second register of the right and left pilasters respectively, the images of our progenitors serve as vignettes presenting the background information needed to understand the fundamental images of the "salvation history" (*historia salutis*). This history can be extracted from a collation of episodes found in the Gospels and the Acts of the Apostles in the New Testament, and from the *Golden Legend* (*Legenda aurea*), a compilation of ancient Church lore emphasizing the lives of the saints. We have been able to reconstruct and analyze our presentation, aided by the precise and theologically irreproachable contribution of Father Ferdinando Batazzi, as follows:

The Fall (Genesis 3:1–15): Sin cannot be defined if a personal relationship between Man and God is not presupposed. Adam and Eve perverted this relationship in their desire "to be like God, who knows good and evil," refusing love and creaturely dependence, breaking the bond of friendship and disfiguring their "image and likeness to God."

Expulsion from Paradise (Genesis 3:23–24): Everything has changed between Man and God. The rewards of Divine friendship ended because sin is evil, the worst of evils, the source of all evils. Sin thus entered into history in the first couple, in the first brothers and in human society. If the initiative for the rupture came from man, it is logical that the initiative for reconciliation can come only from God.

The Evangelists: The Word of God descended from heaven and "for us men and for our salvation It became a man" in order to "reconcile Man with God through the atonement of sin by death on the cross" and to save all of mankind. Jesus is the only savior of mankind (Luke 2:11). In fact, "after God had, many times and in many ways, spoken through the Prophets, he spoke to us through his Son" (Hebrews 1:1–2); and the word of Jesus, which is gospel, "is the power of God for the salvation of all believers" (Romans 1:16). Christ ordered that his gospel be preached to all as "the source of all saving truth and moral teaching" (Constitution on Divine Revelation, "Dei Verbum," 7). Consequently, the redemptive acts and words of Christ extend in a continuum through the Church, which acts *in persona Christi* to reread, interpret and transmit salvation.

Peter Drowning (Matthew 14:28–31): Each possible human liberation assumes the calling out to God, "Lord, save me," but it is Christ who "stretches out his hand and saves." There is only one imprescriptible requirement for salvation—belief in Christ, "truly the Son of God."

The Calling (Luke 5:1–11): Peter is the first to experience the richness of the calling and the first to recognize his own worthlessness and insufficiency before Christ. Peter becomes "the first fisher of living men so that they may live." And each man "from his birth is called into a personal relationship with God," called to "be reborn in the water and in the Holy Spirit—as fish in the waters of Christ—because one cannot be saved (live) if one does not dwell in the water" (Tertullian, *De baptismo*).

Peter's Repentance (Luke 22:54–62): The Gospel says that the Lord "looked at Peter, and Peter remembered . . . , and he went out and cried bitterly." Salvation cannot take place if it is not the Lord "who calls and looks at us." The repentance of sins is the beginning of salvation; it is a seeking of the "face of God" and a recognition of him as the Savior. The invitation to salvation is radical—"reform your lives and believe in the Gospel" (Mark 1:15).

Peter, the Universal Shepherd (John 21:15–23): The Church lives "under the staff of One Shepherd" by whose wounds we have been healed. He "brought our sins in his body to the cross so that all of us, dead to sin, could live in accord with God's will" (I Peter 2:24). Christ transmitted his power of preeminence to Peter and to the Church with the following words, "Feed my lambs, feed my sheep."

The Tribute Money (Matthew 17:24–27): First of all, Peter recognized that Jesus was not obliged to pay the tax because, as he himself had already sworn (Matthew 16:16–20), Christ was the Son of God. The words of Jesus convey an affectionate bonding with the one he chose as his vicar and express Peter's earthly mission: "Give it to them for me and for you." The "tribute" speaks of how the salvific plan relates to historical reality. The mission of the Church is not of a political, economic and social order; the Church transcends temporal realities and respects their autonomy, but the grace of salvation elevates human reality because reconciliation with Christ embraces all the temporal order. Whether the "tribute" is paid to the Temple or to the Romans, one is obliged to "give unto Caesar what is Caesar's, but give to God what is God's" (Luke 20:25), and to "pay each one his due: taxes to whom taxes are due; toll to whom toll is due; respect and honor to everyone who deserves them" (Romans 13:7).

Healing of the Cripple and the Raising of Tabitha (Acts 3:1–10, and Acts 9:36–43): The salvation that the Church proclaims has a concrete name and face: Jesus of Nazareth, crucified, risen again and appointed by God as "author and prince of life." The first miracle, that of the paralytic, fulfulls all expectations—as Jesus had always done—because there is never complete restitution of physical life without repentance of sins and a return to grace which is the "salvation" of all mankind. The redemptive force emanates from Christ, who "is Lord and gives back life."

Peter Preaching and *Peter Baptizing the Neophytes* (Acts 2:14–41): These scenes proclaim salvation and the completion of its promise. The story didn't end with God's action. Instead, with the descent of the Holy Spirit at Pentecost a new era opened up, which was the time of the mission of the Church. Peter was the head of the Church; and in the Church of God there can never be changes. Peter's message was clear and unequivocal: "Reform and be baptized, each one of you, in the name of Jesus Christ, that your sins may be forgiven; then you will receive the gift of the Holy Spirit."

Saint Peter Healing with his Shadow (Acts 5:12–14): Here the metaphor of salvation emanates from the person of Peter. In its "shadow," which covers men with its redemptive power and liberation from physical suffering, is the presence of God which protects the way of the Church today just as it protected those who journeyed in the desert.

Alms for the Poor (Acts 4:32–37) and *The Deceit of Ananias and Saffira* (Acts 5:1–11): The community of salvation is a community of love. Only living by grace creates a union in the deep conviction that "with one heart there is one soul." With a new life there ought to be new relationships of love and sharing. The "poor man"—and this is a sharp moral turn in the life of salvation—is he who puts all his material possessions at the disposal of the needy. It is a way of redistributing wealth. By their greed and deceit over money, Ananias and Saffira sin against the sanctity of Christian life. Peter's reprimand is contained in this phrase: "You have lied not to men but to God."

The Raising of the Son of Theophilus and Saint Peter in the Chair: Apart from Peter's presence in Antioch, described in the letter from Paul to the Galatians (Gal. 2:11–14)—it is not certain that he was the first bishop of that city—the rest is legend. In any case, where Peter dwells, there is the "chair" of unity, truth and love which leads to the Father. Peter guarantees it; the word of truth saves (and can in fact perform miracles as in the *Raising of the Son of Theophilus*), and obedience to truth is necessary. "To grow in salvation, one must be eager for the milk of the word of God, which redeems" (I Peter 2:2).

The Dispute of Peter and Paul with Simon the Magician Before Nero: Except for the meeting between Peter and Simon the Magician (Acts 8:9–24), the rest is based on legend. Peter demonstrated his severity with regard to the magician who had just become a Christian. Salvation cannot be bought with money. No economic investment exists for the gifts of the Holy Spirit. There is no connection between magical acts and the "signs" of salvation that are based completely on faith (*signa fidei*) and whose effects emanate from the efficacious power of Christ.

Paul Visiting Peter in Prison (Acts 12:1–6): Even if this scene is not historical fact, visiting those who are suffering in prison is a required act of love towards one's fellow man. By means of the prison, the mystery of persecution is recalled here as a probationary experience in the plan of salvation. "The Son of God, who came to save the world . . . not condemn it," (John 3:16–17) was not spared persecution, nor were his apostles. "Have no fear of the sufferings to come. The devil will indeed cast some of you into prison to put you to the test. . . . Remain faithful until death and I will give you the crown of life" (Rev. 2:10).

Peter Liberated from Prison (Acts 12:1–19): Freedom is one of the essential aspects of the gospel of salvation. Personal and social freedoms are articulated in the theological freedom from sin, death, and law as an end unto itself. In the profound metaphysics of Christian freedom, there is always a "being freed from" by "being for." The liberated Christian becomes a messenger of freedom "out of love . . . at one another's service" (Gal. 5:13), in the imitation of Christ who, being free, "came not to be served but to serve." Not by chance did Peter's liberation from prison coincide with the Passover, the culmination and source of freedom. As soon as the Apostle realized that he had actually been freed, he said: "Now I know for certain that the Lord has truly sent his angel to rescue me from Herod's clutches." The driving force of freedom is prayer.

The Crucifixion of Peter: During Nero's persecutions, Peter was martyred and "out of humility asked to be crucified with his head down." (Eusebius, *Ecclesiastical History*, 3, pt. 1, p. 2). Thus God's plan of salvation was demonstrated in the mystery of the cross, the instrument of redemption and the evocative and essential conclusion to salvation. The cross, mystery of salvation, is also candidacy for glory and the foundation of moral Christian life.

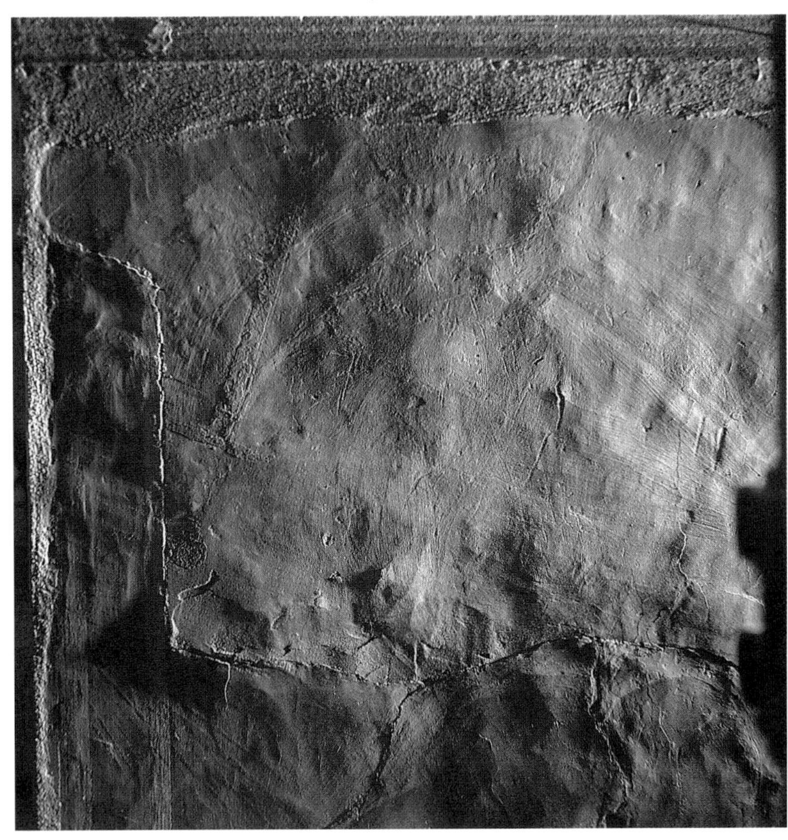

Masaccio, The Expulsion, *detail, in raking light*

Artists at Work: Masaccio and Masolino

If the above, as we have outlined it according to its meaning, represents the chronology of the episodes in the Life of Saint Peter cycle, then one is suddenly struck, in terms of the execution of the frescoes, by the precise, consecutive distribution of the scenes between the two artists as they worked together on the scaffold. We will attempt to define the nature of this collaboration by examining the extant scenes of the second register, the only one to provide evidence for their simultaneous involvement. A logical assumption is that the scaffold ran first along one side of the chapel and then on the other. On the same scaffold on the right side, Masolino and Masaccio worked next to each other, with Masolino executing *The Healing of the Crippled Man and the Raising of Tabitha* and *The Fall*, while Masaccio was responsible for executing *Saint Peter Baptizing the Neophytes* on the back wall to the right of the window. On the scaffold along the left side, the same operation was repeated in reverse, with Masaccio doing *The Expulsion* and *The Tribute Money* on the left wall, while Masolino executed the fresco of *Saint Peter Preaching* on the back wall to the left of the window.

Continuing to verify this method of alternation on the scaffold and the division of the spaces equally between the two artists, we were able to hypothesize also the unfolding of the work in the top register for the lunette scenes that were destroyed in the eighteenth century. We know from Longhi's identification that Masolino had painted the *Calling of Saints Peter and Andrew* on the left wall. According to early sources, the other scenes at this height were thought to have been painted also by Masolino. But the recovery of the underdrawing or *sinopie* for the two scenes done in the half-lunettes on either side of the window on the back wall has led to important new hypotheses. There appears to be no doubt regarding the perfect correspondence of the drawing in the right lunette with Masolino's graphic style, when compared with the frescoes he had done on the eve of starting the Brancacci Chapel project, namely the *The Legend of the Cross* restored by Procacci in 1943 in the Church of Sant'Agostino, Empoli.[84] The hand of Masolino and his presence is certain in this cycle. But when we observe the huddled figure of Saint Peter in the *sinopia* of the left lunette, the nature of the "handwriting" in suggesting form and designating volume seems to surpass the linear, flowing gesture associated with Masolino. Therefore, if this drawing was not done by Masolino, then clearly it must have been done by Masaccio.

Assuming that this is evidence for the initiation of the project by the artists working together, there could then have been at this level also an equal distribution of the spaces according to an alternation on the scaffold in the same manner as below. The conclusion from this would be that the *Shipwreck* on the right wall was painted by Masaccio. Our hypothesis, therefore, that Masaccio began immediately to work with Masolino on the chapel frescoes would better explain not only the nature of their collaboration but also the unified concept of the project from the very beginning. It is absolutely unfounded, in point of fact, to suggest that Masolino alone had conceived the components of all the scenes and then would have changed them because he was pushed to do so by Masaccio. The contrary is equally impossible to support, that Masaccio entered into the work of the chapel as a renderer of scenes already delineated by another artist. It is difficult to accept the idea that Masaccio simply colored in the compositions of Masolino, author of the entire project which had already been studied in detail and agreed upon by the client.[85] Furthermore, if Masaccio actually did come into the project only after the work had reached the middle register, then there would not be the same overall balance of work in the chapel that certainly was agreed upon by the two men. Rather, there would have been a more casual division of the sections that not even the ultimate continuation and conclusion of the work by Masaccio could have brought into a homologous relationship.

The relationships of the scenes in terms of volumes, perspective and rhythms are instead so well-balanced, from wall to wall and scene to scene, that it would be impossible not to think of planned collaboration. In verification of our hypothesis, this division of the scenes and spaces would have given to the entire chapel a perfect unity; the two artistic idioms alternating in such a context would not have been overly contrasted in juxtaposition with each other, either in the horizontal sequence of the scenes or in the vertical view from one register to the next. In this way, a very necessary unification was achieved without disorder or discord. Neither artist completed an entire wall alone on the second register. Instead, both inserted scenes interchangeably into a whole that received its optical homologousness from the clean colors and the clarity of expressions assembled within categories and movements in precise, alternating correspondences.

It is sufficient to exemplify this point by comparing the two most famous scenes completed while the two artists were working in tandem, *The Tribute Money* and *The Healing of the Crippled Man and the Raising of Tabitha*. In the very different "performances" of the scenes, the characters of the drama nonetheless move in scenic spaces whose basic outlines bespeak an obvious similarity and identical manner of generation. As it appears from the plans, the same perspective order was adopted, and both "stages" were conceived as if they had first been tied together visually, then separated and placed facing each other on the walls. The fundamental worth of such a deliberate, studied balance can immediately be felt, not as an accidental occurrence but rather as an intentional design from the start. These alternations of the scenic spaces were necessary for the purpose of collaboration because the chapel is not viewed in terms of separate areas and registers, other than in direct confrontation with individual scenes. The initial impact is that of the whole, therefore it should and could not give instant evidence of the hands of two different artists. Another important homologizing element, other than the chromatic clarity, was that of the system of painted pilasters dividing the scenes in each register. This constituted "architecture within architecture," opening out the spaces and the levels to the actions of the figures.

Objections to the hypothesis of immediate collaboration might be made on the basis that Vasari had attributed all the frescoes of the top register to Masolino. But Vasari, who was a very attentive observer, does not manifest the same exactitude in his descriptions of the scenes on the top level as he does in those for the lower registers. It should be noted that, on the basis of an oral tradition known to him, not objective documentation, he only concedes Masaccio's intervention in the chapel "at the time of the death of Masolino da Panicale, who had begun it."[86] It is logical to suppose, then, that Vasari would not have preoccupied himself with distinguishing and reading what was taken for granted as Masolino's work, and instead would have concentrated greater attention on Masaccio's work in the registers below. Proof of Vasari's neglect of the area he considered "Masolinian" is the fact that he omitted any description of the scene in the back wall lunette of Peter as the Universal Pastor (*Feed My Lambs, Feed My Sheep*). As for the two scenes we have hypothesized as having been done by Masaccio in the top register, *The Repentance of Peter* which Vasari mentions may only have depicted the lone figure of the saint, from which little could have been gathered to indicate signs of innovation.[87] As for the *Shipwreck* on the right wall, perhaps it did not depart entirely from accepted current iconography as proved and sanctioned by custom many times over. Only the most careful examination, not conditioned by the "historical" information which Vasari possessed, could have led to the recognition of a different hand from that of Masolino in these scenes.

The project for the decoration of the Brancacci Chapel must have been formulated in advance, therefore, according to the reconstruction plan provided above. Upon close inspection, the division of the work was stipulated as an evenly shared involvement in the entire decoration. Masolino was to do eight scenes plus the vault with the *Evangelists*; Masaccio was to do the other eight scenes plus the scene of *The Crucifixion of Saint Peter* above the altar. This expected balance was not achieved, since the project was never completed as a collaboration between the two men. In fact, at the time when Masolino was to begin painting in the bottom register, he left for a long stay in Hungary, with Masaccio remaining to finish the work by himself. With the bottom register still incomplete, Masaccio then stopped his work in the chapel to go to Rome with Masolino upon his return from Hungary. In Rome, the two artists worked together on another collaborative project, the altarpiece for the Church of Santa Maria Maggiore (corpus by Masolino, Museum of Capodimonte, Naples; wing by Masaccio, National Gallery, London; wing by Masolino, Philadelphia Museum, Johnson Collection). Here, however, it was not necessary to merge the two artistic idioms visually, as it was in the Brancacci Chapel frescoes. Instead, the work was divided between the inside and the outside of the triptych, each of which could be handled independently of the other. Unfortunately, this new equal and amicable division of labor never saw its collaborative completion either. This time it was Masolino who concluded the work, having been left with the unfinished exterior as the result of Masaccio's untimely death, just short of his twenty-seventh birthday if records are correct.

Returning to the scenes in the Saint Peter cycle, we would like to emphasize the exact correlation of the pictorial representations with the "historical" sources, the New Testament Gospels and the Acts of the Apostles, as well as ancient stories about Saint Peter in *The Golden Legend*. Peter and his brother Andrew, both fishermen in Galilee, were called to be apostles of Jesus who made them "fishers of men." At first, Peter accompanied Christ during his ministry, then he became the leader of the apostles in the missionary work of spreading the gospel. Finally, he went to Rome, where he founded the first Christian community. He was martyred by crucifixion (upside down) under the Roman emperor Nero in A.D. 64.

Peter's physical appearance, which was established typologically and remained constant in the iconography, makes him quite recognizable among his fellow apostles in the Life of Saint Peter cycle. His general description is that of a middle-aged man, stocky in build, with gray curly hair and a short curly beard. He is shown either as balding at the temples or tonsured, and he has strongly-defined facial features. Throughout, he is dressed in a blue tunic over which he wears a yellow cloak. Both Masaccio and Masolino (and later Filippino Lippi as well) made explicit reference to this already consolidated image of Peter, but they did not adopt exactly the same facial matrix. Each instead created his own version using a different technique of execution.

Masaccio rendered Peter's powerful head with wide swaths of color, giving him a wavy mass of hair in the earlier scenes of his life in the second register and depicting him with the traditional tonsure in the scenes near the end of his life in the first register. In *The Tribute Money*, Masaccio used a *terra verde* base for the flesh color which often shows through in areas. For the figure of Peter at the far right of the painting, he used broad areas of color and showed him with untidy puffs of hair. In the central grouping, on the left where Peter listens intently to Christ's command, his face is handled with a more controlled gesture and more elaborate brushwork. Peter's pose here is nearly frontal, and he conveys to the spectator the appearance and gravity of a philosopher figure on the order of Plato. He has the look of a thinker, a mature man and a senator; his hair is almost white and his eyebrows even have a few white hairs. The typological invention of the head of Peter which recurs in this cycle has been related to portraits of philosophers from Antiquity. Yet, while he has the imposing head of a thinker, his temperament is conveyed as brusque and impetuous by the wavy mass of curls and the short, heavy neck inserted between broad shoulders—evidence for the physical energy of a man compelled by life. This robust build recalls the powerful physiognomy of a Hercules, as represented not only on ancient sarcophagi but also on the reverse of Roman coins with which Masolino showed his familiarity at the Palazzo Orsini.[88] In *Peter Baptizing the Neophytes*, the saint's thick neck is thrown into relief by the strong "light" coming from the chapel window at the left, while his profile is also intensified volumetrically with the half-light to great sculptural effect.

In *The Raising of the Son of Theophilus*, the saint in the act of performing the miracle shows for the first time the tonsure that initiated the religious tradition. As told in *The Golden Legend*, at the time of his arrest for preaching in Antioch, his captors had cut the hair from the top of his head as a sign of contempt for his Christian faith.[89] Masaccio recorded the fact here and in succeeding scenes, where Peter is shown with a "triple tonsure" of three concentric circles diminishing in size toward the crown of the head. The visual reference is to the *triregno* or tiara, the "triple crown" worn by the pope on solemn occasions, and both the papal tiara and Peter's three-ringed tonsure symbolize the imperial, royal and religious empowerment of the head of the Church of Rome.[90] While the presence of the triple tonsure must be inferred from the length of the hair along the temples, due to the frontal views of his head in the scenes of *Peter in the Chair* and *Peter Healing with His Shadow*, it is clearly evident in the nearly full profile view in *The Distribution of Goods*, where it acquires positive value by sacred definition.

Masolino, on the other hand, used a more controlled graphic approach to his Peter, with the curls constructed by a minutely detailed drawing technique. Likewise, the skin and features, and therefore the expression, of the face were rendered with infinitesimally small brushstrokes that create volume by a nearly *sfumato* effect of smoothly graduated tonal shadings. Filippino, in his scenes in the bottom register, all chronologically near the end of Peter's life, also depicts the saint as a mature man. But while his Peter has white hair, it is defined as a heavy mass without a tonsure in both scenes of *Dispute with Simon Magus and the Crucifixion* and in *Saint Peter Being Visited by Saint Paul in Prison*. Only in *Peter Liberated from Prison* on the right entrance pilaster does Filippino depict the triple tonsure.

The Cleaning

In 1980, prior to the recent work in the Brancacci Chapel, the restorer Cesare Brandi wrote the following description:

> This famous chapel is likely to disappoint those who imagine it from color reproductions which tend to lighten the somber tone of the frescoes. And whether this tone is due in part to the fire more than to time can be argued from the fact that, in tonality, Filippino's frescoes don't differ at all from those of Masolino and Masaccio, whereas they ought to be much more highly colored, as seen in the Strozzi Chapel of the Church of Santa Maria Novella in Florence and, especially, in the Carafa Chapel of the Church of Santa Maria sopra Minerva in Rome, completed shortly after the Brancacci Chapel. It should be said, however, that the frescoes in Florence and Rome have been cleaned, while the Brancacci Chapel has had no restoration intervention on the pictorial surfaces, since they are fortunately in good condition. But the discovery of a little section on the right, up high, at the edges of the canopy, which had remained hidden and protected by plaster, provides a totally different scale and is closer to Masolino's tonal values in the Church of San Clemente in Rome. Yet it is doubtful that, in any future cleaning, as hoped for as it is feared, it would be possible to retrieve this sort of scale for all of the frescoes. Experience shows that the parts of a painting that remain hidden for centuries have a state of preservation different from those in sight, and not only because of subsequent interventions or superimpositions. On the other hand, even Masaccio's panel paintings have a rather low, dark, even smoky tonality, similar to what is seen now in the Brancacci Chapel.[91]

The recent recovery of large protected areas of painting from behind the altar brought further essential clarification of the extraordinary limpidity of the original colors. From the time of our first cleaning tests, we were assured of a total recuperation of the colors in the unprotected areas that had been "darkened" not by the fire but by alteration due to materials applied to them in the interventions subsequent to 1771, and due to the accumulation of soot from candles and of dirt. In fact, the whole cycle had been "varnished" more than once with a mixture or *beverone*[92] made up of organic substances, mainly proteins such as egg yolks mixed with egg whites, milk or milk protein.[93] In his *Manuale del restauratore* (*Restorer's Guide*) published in 1866, Ulisse Forni outlined the following method: "The painted surface of the intonaco is given a coat of casein [milk protein] thinned with water and applied with a soft, flat brush; once this is dry, a second coat of the same distemper is applied crosswise over the first" (p. 38).

This technique was widely practiced, especially between 1700 and 1800, to brighten and consolidate color pigments during restoration, perhaps after the execution of a "light" cleaning with dry bread crumbs or after a more energetic one with potash, alcohol or acetic acid. After the fire and the removal of the soot, the Brancacci Chapel had reopened to the public in 1782, but at the end of the century, a general restoration of the chapel was done, and "egg varnish" was used at that time following an undoubtedly laborious cleaning during which potash may have been used, perhaps even applied hot, although no mention is made of this in any document. It is known, however, that by this means "all the grease and smokiness promptly gave way without damaging the colors."[94]

Filippino Lippo and Masaccio, The Raising of the Son of Theophilus and Saint Peter in the Chair, *detail, in raking light*

In 1840, Giovanni Rosini visited the chapel and deemed the frescoes to be in excellent condition,[95] but a little over twenty years later Cavalcaselle (1864) found that they had deteriorated in many areas. Concerning the *Expulsion*, Cavalcaselle recalled that the fresco stood out against the blue background formed by the sky, but that the color had "lost much of its original vigor, especially in the figure of the angel which had darkened more than the others." For *The Tribute Money*, he noted that the sky was "a somber color as dark as it was heavy. A few pieces of clothing, and especially Saint Peter's, have lost their originally lively colors."[96] The clothing referred to is that of Peter in the central grouping near Christ, which has effectively and irremediably lost the original brightness of its yellow ocher color due to the effects of the heat from the fire, which turned the pigment reddish brown. Judging from Cavalcaselle's descriptions, it appears that the rest of the colors had been lowered in tone by the application of the "varnish" which must have already created a darkish film over the frescoes.[97]

The last restoration done by Filippo Fiscali in 1904, as already discussed, ended up being a simple dusting which did not include any cleaning with bread crumbs, since this was deemed incorrect.[98] This dusting project took only two months, meaning that the restorer surely did not remove the protein concoction, which would have required a completely different operation known to be one of the most arduous tasks for a restorer. Forni wrote: "The major damage that can be encountered in a fresco is when it has been covered with any type of varnish, be it glue, or resin melted in fixed or volatile oils; these are partially but never totally removed, and therefore always hinder a good restoration." As mentioned earlier in this chapter, Filippo Fiscali was constantly being checked on by an inspection team and by the Regional Office, which specifically limited his work to a "light dusting," which is why visitors to the chapel immediately afterwards described the entire cycle as still dark.

Around 1939, Carlo Gamba expressed the opinion that *The Tribute Money* on the side wall was rather well preserved in its entirety but *Saint Peter Baptizing the Neophytes* on the back wall was not. There, he noted, "the figures are quite ruined, maybe because of prior damage from the fire."[99]

It should be borne in mind that the concoction on the frescoes remained there for almost two hundred years; it became darkened by dirt and by soot from the smoke of oil lamps and candles which completely altered the true chromatic reality of the entire cycle. So many artists of our century were thus inspired by a "falsehood"—a painting style defined as austere, rough and nearly barren in its simplicity, when compared to the radiance of Gothic painting or the saturated tones of the Flemish artists.[100] Masaccio was looked upon as the essential artist by metaphysical painters and by painters concerned with "plastic values" (*valori plastici*). No one in the twentieth century had ever spoken of Masaccio in the same terms of color and light used for Fra Angelico. The somber tone of the Brancacci Chapel was considered a characteristic trait of Masaccio's work which was seen as tragic and severe.

Was it justified then to remove these dark tonalities from these frescoes? The recent cleaning[101] was decided upon because the entire cycle was in poor condition and had suffered over the years, and certainly not because of a fixation with big discoveries or out of the desire for a spectacular result, as seems to be the case elsewhere at the present time. The *beverone* certainly was not the "golden tone" of those varnishes so favored in the nineteenth century and deliberately applied to many paintings. Nor was it the egg white (glair) used by the artist to give greater density to the surface so that in aging, a sheen or glaze would be conferred to the color. That "glazed" aspect is actually an integral part of the work, which many restorers today erroneously eliminate, scraping it off with surgeon's scalpels because its gray veil is very difficult to remove and can only be done mechanically. Nor was this a case where that alteration or overlay called "patina" ought to be maintained because, as Brandi wrote, "preservation and ultimate integration made it an intrinsic part in respect to that potential unity of the work of art which is the goal of the restoration."[102]

To the contrary, the *beverone* resulted in a negative action that caused the complete obscuration of the work, "a 'negative secondary act' that 'must be' erased by 'a third act' which was our correct and critical act of restoration; [whereas a true] 'patina' is instead a primary connotation of the work and part of its existence in time, its truly positive 'time-life,' and therefore it cannot be erased or separated from it; this is a 'positive secondary act,' that is, one which is not an artificial occurrence, but rather part of the natural history of the immediate existence of a work, the very texture which conveys its expressive value."[103] But in the case of the Brancacci Chapel, it was an issue of an arbitrary addition which disfigured, perverted and obscured the appearance of the original work. It had not been preserving, but rather it had been attacking it with dirt and mold for a long time.

The draftsmen and engravers who copied the scenes in the Brancacci Chapel between 1700 and 1800 interpreted the shapes created by the "bloom" of the deteriorating organic, degradable substances as actual formal elements. The Lasinios and D'Agincourt, in their nineteenth-century engravings, rendered the areas invaded by salts and stained by dampness as trees and shrubs along the hillsides. Even earlier, Piroli (c. 1795) noted details that were important for reference during the cleaning. In working after the scene of *Saint Peter in the Chair*, this attentive painter did not copy into his drawing the mysterious figure in red in the group of four men at the far right, because it had disappeared under a layer of plaster. This figure was discovered and recuperated in the recent restoration from under heavy overpainting in an excessive compensation for a lost piece of intonaco. In the Lasinio engraving, the man in red appears in the company of another figure that no longer exists, and which was probably removed in Filippo Fiscali's cleaning in 1904. In his copy after the scene of *The Raising of the Son of Theophilus*, Piroli indicated a large, deep shadow cast by the roof projection of the building on the left, which is difficult to accept as an addition or invention of that artist. Perhaps it was an adaptation made in a prior restorative intervention that was subsequently eliminated, since it is not found again in the prints of engravers postdating his. In Piroli's *Tribute Money*, which little resembles Masaccio in style, the four apostles on the right in the central grouping are without haloes, obviously not distinguishable at the time even in outline.

The recent restoration made it possible to follow up on the research of Ugo Procacci,[104] and the dismantling of the altar resulted in the discovery of most of the original window jambs decorated with stylized leafy scrollwork and two medallion heads, as well as the fragments of a scene still on the back wall above the altar and below the windowsill. These large sections of painting, well preserved because they were covered up for such a long time, constituted a "specimen" of great importance for the cleaning process as a basis of comparison, at least initially, since the "true" frescoes were completely hidden under the dark layer of filth. In fact, the first attempts to discover and liberate the original "fabric" or context from the *beverone* were done, in direct rapport with and reconciled to these fragments, on the immediately adjacent frescoes of *The Baptizing of the Neophytes* by Masaccio and *Saint Peter Preaching* by Masolino. It was important to see if the "veiled" colors would even respond in the same way—that is, with the same tones as those found to be so bright and clear in the "protected" fragments. As in an archaeological excavation where the research advances slowly through thinly stratified layers of the earth, so evolved our first cognitive moment of the original fresco fabric. Testing here and there on all the scenes, we sought to arrive gradually, identifying the various pigments and the different techniques of the three artists in order to accomplish those equilibrations necessary to a correct and well-balanced "restitution" of the work.

The *Raising of the Son of Theophilus and Saint Peter in the Chair* concerned us a great deal initially because it had been painted by two different artists at different times. In fact, it was fifty to sixty years after Masaccio completed his work that Filippino made his repair of two large lacunae in this scene. This was quite well done in that Filippino undertook to "interpret" Masaccio's work in a discerning way so that the repairs could not be seen. He was certainly the first Masaccio "scholar" and, "filled with the spirit" of this master, Filippino was able to pick up in an extraordinary way the threads of the work left unfinished. From our first testings of this painting, however, it was apparent to us that Masaccio's painting was actually more luministic in approach. In his modeling, the forms were thrown into relief by "staining" of the highlights with a strong white intensity. Filippino, on the other hand, worked in much lower relief, constructing his volumes via contour lines rendered with the point of the brush and color gradations applied in dense, even brushstrokes without strong contrast. The question might arise as to why Filippino did not attempt to illuminate his figures in the same manner as Masaccio. Probably, Masaccio's strong highlights were no longer visible in the modeling of the forms; the smoke from the candles and oil lamps and the accumulation of dust had already lowered the luminous values of the original surface.

The immediate realization of these differing chromatic realities came from a comparison of two heads—one of the Carmelite in profile by Masaccio in the right-hand group around Peter and the other of the man on the right in the central group by Filippino, constituting a kind of double-headed "Janus." This is actually where the cleaning system was instituted, growing out of the fear of causing two dark patches in the middle of Masaccio's scene. We were required to discover and create a method of carrying out a gradual overall cleaning which would allow us to become familiar with the work, layer by layer, until we reached the desired effect.[105] Instead of proceeding by "plugs" or small squares, arriving immediately at the final surface, we began by removing a thin layer of the *beverone* from the entire scene and then repeated this procedure again and again until the final result was achieved. By being able to "see" the whole fresco in a temporary state and contemplate the whole, then move on to "adjustments" and balancings, there was a favorable possibility of keeping "under control" aspects of the work that might otherwise have eluded our recognition.

While the final goal of our work on this scene was certainly not to leave Masaccio more "veiled" to harmonize with Filippino, or to force the latter to be more luminous, certain balancings seemed appropriate. For example, in the background, an effort was made to preserve all those "patinas" and that "sense of time" that attenuated the brillance of the colors there. If the marble-paneled wall framing the foreground figures, the buildings and the landscape with the plants would all have been made brighter than they now appear, they would come forward and overpower the array of figures established in the foreground. These figures are in accurate relationship, in spite of their chromatic diversity, because they were carefully oriented within their perspective planes. The resulting scene is therefore balanced and each "level" situated in the proper position with relation to the viewer.

After our initial attempt to become acquainted with the individual techniques of Masaccio and Filippino and their coexistence within the same scene, our work then turned to the first two scenes that had only been briefly tested, Masaccio's *Baptizing* and Masolino's *Preaching* on the back wall. The major revelation in the cleaning of the *Preaching* was undoubtedly the recovery of the wooded mountain that linked up visually with the one in the *Tribute Money* across the ruined corner pilaster. Masolino, it was discovered little by little, revealed an insurpassable painting technique. The pictorial surface was achieved with an invisible woven texture and a fineness of bisque porcelain. On the other hand, in Masaccio's *Baptizing*, it quickly became clear how important the "restitution" of light and color values were in the restoration process. Here, a quite unexpected landscape was recovered—if one recalls that this scene had suffered the most damage from efflorescence of salts, staining from humidity and deterioration of the overpainting (the stream had been completely repainted). An unusually strong painterly surface, practically "summary" in comparison with Masolino's "bisque" finish, was recovered, along with the modeling of draperies in complementary colors (instead of light and dark tones of the same color) and other proto-Mannerist color uses. Also striking here is the refined and intense anatomy of the three nudes (the kneeling nude in "cameo" profile has the sculptural power of the *Belvedere Torso* before its existence was ever discovered) and, behind the shivering neophyte, the complementary-color modeling of the cloak of the man at the far right, foreshadowing the manneristic color use in the Sistine Chapel. The two scenes are articulated with the same balance—Peter in the left foreground making a gesture with his arm, behind him two onlookers and at the right the crowd against a mountainous background and the sky. The cleaning moved forward here with the careful reading of these receding planes, here removing and there compensating, and even taking away completely in the case of areas of overpainting, such as the stream in the *Baptizing*.

Constituting an element of concern with regard to the "equilibrium" in certain areas were the color changes wrought by the heat of the fire—that is, where the ferrous yellow and *terra verde* pigments had turned reddish brown. This was an irreversible condition that remained in the same state at the conclusion of our restoration. Saint Peter's robe in the *Tribute Money*, for example, has lost most of its brightness. While it belongs to the foreground, its location in the overall space risks being "altered" because it constitutes an area lower in tone and more similar to that of the background.

Many of the original refinements that were added *a secco* (over the dry intonaco) were removed completely during previous restorations, where drastic means had been employed in cleaning the frescoes. Baldinucci wrote in 1681 that such cleanings "risked washing away the 'tonings,' half-tints and retouchings that were the final rendering constituting a good part of their preparation."[106] Evidence for the careless "washings" of past centuries can be seen in areas where the blues were applied *a secco*,[107] especially in the skies where some small residues of the original color have been found preserved in the linear depressions left from the measuring strings, for example in the sky of *The Raising of Tabitha*. The azurite was preserved in more substantial quantities on the robes of Christ and Peter, but where it was found missing, the patinas were maintained and preserved because they still constituted in and of themselves an "idea" of the blue color. This was done for Peter's robe at the right where he is giving the coin to the tax collector in *The Tribute Money*, and also for his robe in *The Distribution of Goods*.

In *The Expulsion*, the background sky ought to resemble in intensity the sky of *The Tribute Money*, where the original azurite has been preserved. The grayish sky now seen behind Adam and Eve is in fact the preparatory undercoat, which appears in other scenes as well. But even here, traces of the azurite pigment were discovered preserved by the glue used for gilding the rays that stream from the gate of the Garden of Eden, hitting Adam's back. Despite the overall gray tone, the background shows unusual brightness where it surrounds and defines the outlines of the two figures.

The blue sky in the *Tribute Money* is striated with clouds that are white on top and dark underneath, touched by sunlight and foreshortened. The mountains recede into the distance in size and gradations of brightness, with the highlighting the most intense on the houses and rows of shrubs on the nearest mountainside. The amazing new appearance of the lake after restoration acquired enormous significance in the measuring of spatial distance, as did the redefinition of all the haloes, including the four missing ones that had been hidden under dirt. All their existing original fragments emerged in a clear pattern of elliptical-perspective definition, and what remained of their gold leaf was reconstituted with a gold color selection considered essential to define the exact location of the figures in space. In addition, underneath the

Masaccio, The Tribute Money, *detail, during restoration*

Masaccio, The Expulsion, *detail, during restoration*

incorrect alterations that had been done at the far right, we recovered the *sinopia* from which we were able to "reconstruct" the entrance bridge to the city. An extremely important recovery was the landscape reappearing between the right edge of the tax collector's house and the corner pilaster, demonstrating that the mountains continued the horizon line of the adjacent scene of *Saint Peter Preaching*, which we took as proof for the unity of the scenic plan. Also significant was the recovery in *The Tribute Money* of the technique of repeated use of white to play up the lighting and formal definition of volumes. This is clearly seen in the head of Christ which, although patterned on an iconographic model used by Masolino, was rendered in a painterly technique completely different from his.

Of great importance in the scene of *Peter Healing with His Shadow* was the recovery, from behind the Baroque altar, of the church structure and the marvelous optical exercise discussed earlier regarding the deviation from the vertical of the window jamb. Even Peter's shadow reappeared, reestablishing the rhythm of his step, along with the Corinthian column marking the end of the street at the intersection in the way still used in Florence today.

Clarifications and certainties emerged from the cleaning with regard to the architectural background in *The Raising of the Son of Theophilus*. For reasons of both technique and the succession of the *giornate*, the entire background is absolutely attributed to Masaccio, including the vases and trees along the wall. We also confirmed that the head of the Carmelite in the group at the left edge of the fresco was originally painted by Masaccio and that the features were restored by Filippino. An inspection in raking light clearly shows the intervention by Filippino overlaying the surface. This is the single portrait remaining undamaged from the time of the *damnatio memoriae*, in which the people portrayed by Masaccio from the Brancacci circle were obliterated. That this was an ongoing practice is shown by a later *damnatio* involving the features of one of the persons portrayed in this scene by Filippino, on which there is still evidence of deliberate scratching. (Interestingly, in his restoration of the friar's portrait, Filippino gave the figure a new habit but failed to paint in its feet.) Particularly noted was Masaccio's treatment of the roof sections in this scene. In comparison, Masolino's roofs on the houses in *The Raising of the Tabitha* stand outside the material solidity of Masaccio's style, not only in the kind of tiles but also in painterly descriptiveness and the color of the whole.

Important recoveries were made in the right half of the *Theophilus* fresco depicting *Saint Peter in the Chair*. Between the standing group at the far right and the seated Saint Peter, there is a blue strip whose reason for existence has now been clarified. In an inspection done by infrared reflectography, it was possible to see that this was the arm of one of the figures on the right—specifically that of the figure identified as Masaccio—with the hand reaching out to touch Saint Peter. This had been hidden in a corrective intervention which can perhaps be attributed to Filippino. This gesture repeats the one traditionally made by pilgrims to Rome in touching the foot of the ancient bronze statue of Peter, and this could be evidence for the accuracy of Vasari's record of an early trip by the painter to Rome. Quite extraordinary in their definition after the cleaning, the portraits in this group have been identified from the left as Masolino, Masaccio looking outward, Alberti in profile, Brunelleschi and, finally, the previously hidden fifth and unidentified man in red.

There are many other discoveries and ramifications of the recent restoration. In the *Distribution of the Goods of the Church*, the *giornata* including the pink robe and the feet of Saint John and the hands of Ananias was discovered to be an intervention by Filippino that could definitely be attributed to him not only on the basis of style but also by the identicality of the feet with those in *Saint Peter Liberated from Prison*, painted entirely by Filippino. The problem of the leaves added to Adam and Eve in *The Fall* and *The Expulsion* was resolved by their elimination, since they bore no historical significance. They had been executed sometime after 1652, and their prior nonexistence is recorded in both a Michelangelesque drawing and a description of Masaccio's "nudes" by Pietro da Cortona in his *Trattato di pittura*. The clearer reading of the pictorial texture rendered possible by the cleaning has allowed us to demonstrate the substantial differences between the two equally outstanding painters, Masolino and Masaccio. It has also allowed us to distinguish even more clearly the manner in which Filippino interwove his colorations.

There were some notable technical discoveries, with the list of principle ones including the new reading of the *giornate* and their order of succession, the significance of the recovered window jamb decoration, and the reading of the network of incised lines to guide the architectural perspective and string indentations to measure spaces that had been made in the intonaco. Also very important were the remains of azurite pigment found in the marking-line indentations left by the measuring strings in the sky of *The Raising of Tabitha*, showing that it was originally bright blue and not milky gray. As for the technique used to transfer the drawings, there are some signs of pouncing with chalk dust in the decorations by Masolino, as well as incised lines marking the contours of the forms. Possibly there is pouncing dust present also on one of Masolino's figures in *The Raising of Tabitha*, as seen in an infrared reflectographic examination showing a different underlying pattern on the tunic of the man in green in the loggia with Tabitha.

These are the main innovations and the new terms set for judging the work which came to light during the cleaning; these are more fully described and illustrated in the catalogue of the individual scenes.

OPPOSITE:
Masaccio, The Raising of the Son of Theophilus and Saint Peter in the Chair, *detail*

The Pictorial Restoration

Masolino, The Healing of the Crippled Man and the Raising of Tabitha, *detail*

If "concoctions" were mainly used to brighten the colors, the "retouchings" were necessary to integrate missing areas, to reinforce faded colors and to hide abrasions. Here, many areas had been heavily overpainted which, with the dirt deposits on top, completely hid parts of the fresco painting even from the most experienced eye, a good example of which is the case of the man dressed in red located at the far right side of *The Raising of the Son of Theophilus and Saint Peter in the Chair*. After this area was cleaned, however, the original figure discovered underneath the repainting was more than we could have hoped for, as so often happens with important paintings which have passed under the hands of restorers. Very often, as emphasized even by Forni in the last century, "a less deteriorated painting than it first appeared to be is found underneath the restoration, because the incompetent restorer has a difficult time staying inside the limits of the missing parts; instead he strays beyond them, daubing all around so that his ineptitude does not betray itself, although the new doesn't betray or imitate the old."[108]

At the end of our cleaning operation, with the recovery of a "new" painting, free and clear of any overlay whatsoever, we still had an equally difficult problem of what to do about the small and large areas of loss that had emerged over the whole cycle. Given our goal of achieving a reintegrated pictorial context at the conclusion of the restoration, we did not intervene in those "tonings" and "adjustments" of the type still often used by artists today to rebalance a painting. This balance is frequently destroyed in the cleaning phase during current restorations, thereby repeating the same errors made in the recent and distant past. The point has been made in defense of the inviolability of the work of art since the time of Baldinucci, who wrote that "excellent pictures must not be retouched, by whomever it may be, because it will be very difficult, more or less, sooner or later, not to recognize the restoration, as slight as it might be, and the truth is, a painting which is not genuine will be greatly discredited."[109] In the Brancacci frescoes, it was only a matter of eliminating the "negativity" of the losses in the chromatic context by reconnections, which are now carried out by chromatic selection and chromatic abstraction using methods and principles revived by us and much elaborated upon in the Florentine "school" of restoration since the time of the recuperation of Cimabue's *Crucifix*.[110] Using the method of chromatic selection, all of those figural integrations made in the chapel frescoes at the time of the restoration after the 1771 fire were redone. We considered these not to have been pure invention and therefore accorded them their full historical weight as careful, faithful interpretations of the lost intonacos, assisted by the underlying *sinopie* wherever present. After all, "there is no ancient or even just old repainting where its documentary value is not presumed, by consequence, to bear witness to the lost original either as a pure and simple attempt at preservation or at least as a reproduction."[111]

One example of this was the repair made for the loss of part of the clothing and the body of the woman holding a baby in her arms in the *Distribution of Goods and the Death of Ananias*. The reintegration of this figure appears already to have been done by the time of Lasinio's engraving and Cavalcaselle's Notebook drawing.[112] Other missing sections that were repaired earlier are: the left temple portico in *The Healing of the Crippled Man and the Raising of Tabitha*, the lower part of the group of kneeling figures on the far right in *The Raising of the Son of Theophilus and Saint Peter in the Chair*, part of the stonework of the building at the left in *Saint Peter Healing with his Shadow* and the top part of *The Expulsion*.

In the particular case of Masolino's *The Fall*, it was possible for us to improve formally on the eighteenth-century restoration by a better conformity with the underdrawing rediscovered under the intonaco of that renovation. This resulted in a better definition of the branches and leaves on the tree in the upper right-hand corner where the loss of the painted surface had occurred. Similarly, in *The Tribute Money*, we carefully reworked and redeveloped the section in the immediate area of the low wall at the far right from the precise indications of the *sinopia*, also found under the intonaco of the restoration. In particular, the linear perspective arrangement, which had been poorly interpreted and redrafted in the previous restoration, was readjusted according to its original precise definition. Moreover, the haloes in this scene, which had been lost over time partly due to drastic cleanings done in the past, were also recovered and redefined through chromatic selection. This was done using the rediscovered graphic definitions of the elliptical forms that were essential to the spatial arrangement of the figures in Masaccio's painting and as primary elements for the comprehension of the forms and their perspective construction. In those areas where formal delineations were lacking, we proceeded according to the method of chromatic abstraction, in which an optical reconnection with the surrounding areas was made to "reduce" the negative effect of the loss in the original surface. This was opposed to a fully "neutral" approach that always seems "empirical" and "defective" and ultimately results in a no less arbitrary or completely imaginary intervention.[113]

[1] L. Pandimiglio, "Felice di Michele vir clarissimus e una consorteria: i Brancacci di Firenze," *Quaderni del restauro*, 3, 1987, pp. 12ff.

[2] ". . . quam Pierus Piuvichesis quondam eius pater fieri reliquia in dicta ecclesia," A.S.F., *Notarile Antecosimiano*, M352 (1370–71), c. 116r.

[3] Accounts for 1382–1401, dated March 28, 1387: "Pietanze a quegli frati que chavarono la volta sotto la chappella de' Branchacci" and "achi portoe e chi mura per tutto quello tempo" (A.S.F., *Conventi soppressi*, 113, 82, c. 95r). In seventeenth-century accounts, the chapel's foundation date is given as 1390 (A.S.F., *Conventi soppressi*, 113, 7, p. 114 and 13, p. 44). See Pandimiglio, "Felice di Michele," p. 13; and A. Molho, "The Brancacci Chapel: Studies in Its Iconography and History," *Journal of the Warburg and Courtauld Institutes*, 40, 1977, pp. 72–73, which mentions and uses the three documents. For Antonio as founder of the chapel, see P. Meller, "La Cappella Brancacci: Problemi ritrattistici e iconografici," *Acropoli*, 1961, p. 198.

[4] There was an Antonio di Piero di Piuvichese in the Santo Spirito branch of the Brancacci family, but he died between 1383 and 1389. Another Antonio from the Santa Maria Novella branch, born in 1402 and documented up to 1469, may be the one indicated by Vasari.

[5] Milanesi, using information from L. Passerini, published Felice's will (discussed in Molho,

"Brancacci Chapel," p. 86) and corrected Vasari's identification of Antonio as patron in G. Vasari, *Le vite de' più eccellenti pittori, scultori ed architettori* (1568), ed G. Milanesi, Florence, 1878–1881, 2 of 9 vols., p. 296.

[6] The Catasto records for the years immediately following the decoration of the chapel in the Carmelite church confirm his prestigious activities and involvement in business matters of notable and considerable dimensions (Pandimiglio, "Felice di Michele," pp. 56ff.).

[7] We concur with the probable chronology for the decoration established by L. Berti (*Masaccio*, Milan, 1964) as being from the end of 1424, when the collaboration of Masolino and Masaccio began, up to 1427 or 1428, when Masaccio left Florence for Rome with the fresco cycle still unfinished.

Procacci (*Masaccio*, Milan, 1951) believes instead that Masolino began the work alone on the now-destroyed top register in the first half of 1425. Then, after his stay in Hungary from September 1, 1425 to July 1427, he resumed work on the second register in collaboration with Masaccio. This would restrict the chronology of the cycle (except for the top register) to a single year, from the summer of 1427 to the summer of 1428. This thesis seems difficult to adhere to, mainly because it would mean a very rapid change in Masaccio's style from the scenes in the second register to those below. Another consideration is that, during this same time frame, Masaccio was occupied with other work, namely the *Annunciation* for the Church of San Niccolò and the *Trinity* (1428) in the Church of Santa Maria Novella, which wouldn't have allowed sufficient time to complete a cycle that demanded profound contemplation of every element. Rejecting this hypothesis, then, and considering again a contemporaneous collaboration between Masaccio and Masolino, a good part of the fresco cycle they worked on together in the second register would have to date prior to Masolino's departure for Hungary in 1425. On the other hand, a consideration of the chronology asserted by Procacci does lead to some results. If Masolino left Florence in May 1428 (for which there is still no concrete evidence), the two worked together only on the second register (otherwise Masolino's hand would be present in the first). Then, Masaccio alone executed the remainder of the work attributed to him on the first register before departing for Rome at the end of the year.

[8] This happened probably in 1460, "the year in which the Society of Santa Maria del Popolo was founded, or the following year" (U. Procacci, "La Cappella Brancacci: vicende storiche," in "La Cappella Brancacci nella chiesa del Carmine a Firenze," *Quaderni del restauro*, 1, February 1984, p. 9). See also the following note.

[9] For the date of this intervention, see L. Berti and U. Baldini, *Filippino Lippi*, Florence, 1957, pp. 77 and 23. As a means of understanding fully the ethics of Filippino's intervention, it is important to emphasize also his bona fide restoration of the damage that had occurred to the figure of Saint John in Masaccio's *The Distribution of Goods*. There, as in the *Theophilus*, his work was done in total respect for all that could be saved of the original work of Masaccio (U. Baldini, "Restauro della Cappella Brancacci, primi risultati," *Critica d'Arte*, 9, 1986, p. 66).

The giving of the commission to Filippino is attributed to the Carmelite friars because of the impoverished circumstances of those Brancacci who still had some connection with the chapel. In a 1473 inventory of the church, the chapel was still referred to as the "chapel of the Brancacci or of Our Lady." A few decades later, in another inventory of November 6, 1501, it was referred to only as the "chapel of Our Lady" (J. Mesnil, "Per la storia della Cappella Brancacci," *Rivista d'Arte*, 8, 1912, p. 35; and Procacci, "Capella Brancacci," 9ff.). For the possible involvement in the commission to Filippino of the Society of Santa Maria del Popolo, see Molho, "Brancacci Chapel," p. 83. Recently, L. Pandimiglio revived the hypothesis of an initiative by Cardinal Tommaso Brancacci in favor of the intervention by Filippino ("Felice di Michele," p. 112), as proposed earlier by H. Brockhaus ("Die Brancacci-Kapelle in Florenz," *Mitteilungen des Kunsthistorisches Institutes in Florenz*, 3, 1930, p. 181) and P. Meller ("Cappella Brancacci," pp. 197ff.). Perhaps the commission played to political ends in the repainting of *Theophilus* with different faces in place of the destroyed portraits of the "outlaw consorts" of his father. In this way, he would have confirmed the "renunciation" pronounced by Giuliano de' Medici on the exiles in 1435. Having lost its power and wealth by this time, of course, the Brancacci family would no longer have been able to assure its patronage, which was nevertheless prolonged in a progressively attenuated form up until the middle of the sixteenth century. The *Register of Chapels and Tombs* of the Carmelite church for 1689 records the chapel as free of patronage due to the extinction of the family, or its dispersal around the world from Paris to the Indies, which happened around 1571.

[10] A.S.F., *Conventi soppressi*, 19, cited in Mesnil, "Per la storia," p. 35.

[11] Procacci, "Cappella Brancacci," p. 9. This earliest mention of an intervention by cleaning in the frescoes appears in an entry in *I Ragionamenti delle regole des disegno*, a manuscript by Alessandro Allori preserved in the Biblioteca Nazionale, Florence, which reads: "We took a look at the beautiful Chapel of Masaccio and that the brothers had had cleaned again to such a degree that it can be seen much better than before." A note in the margin ascribes the date "c. 1565."

[12] Records of Father Girolamo Castaldi, cited in Procacci, "Cappella Brancacci," p. 9. The work mentioned was done under the patronage of the Florentine patrician Raphael Guicciardini (P. Coccapani, *Descrizione delle feste . . . per la solenne translazione del corpo di Sant'Andrea Corsini*, Rome, 1675).

[13] Oltinelli and Pietro da Cortona, *Trattato della Pittura e Scultura, uso e abuso loro composto . . . per offrirlo ai Signori Accademici del Disegno di Fiorenza e d'altre città christiane*, Florence, 1652. Oltinelli is identified here as a theologian and Pietro as a sculptor.

[14] Pointed out by U. Baldini, "Le figure de Adamo e Eva formate affatto ignude in una cappella di una principale chiesa di Fiorenze," *Critica d'Arte*, 53, no. 16, 1988, p. 76.

[15] A document of 1676, cited by K. Lankheit (*Florentinische Barockplastik. Die Kunst am hofe der letzen Medici 1670–1743*, Munich, 1962, p. 254, doc. 114) and E. L. Goldberg (*Patterns in Late Medici Art Patronage*, Princeton, 1938, p. 229), reveals how Cosimo III would not permit the sculptor Ercole Ferrata to work from a nude model. During his reign in 1721, the "nude and shameless" statues of Adam and Eve by Bandinelli were taken "in the dead of the night" from the Cathedral where they had been since their origin in 1551 (H. Acton, *Gli ultimi Medici*, Turin, 1962, p. 178). Even the nude statues in the Uffizi troubled the conscience of Cosimo, who, in this same year, decided to place a moral ban on Michelangelo, charging Giovanni Battista Foggini, as reported by Baldinucci (*Zibaldone Baldinucciano*, ed. B. Santi, Florence, 1981, 2, p. 478) "to cast in bronze, according to his good taste, the bits of cloth that now cover, where necessary, the famous statues of *Dusk*, *Morning* and *Dawn* by the hand of Michelangelo, found with others in the Chapel of the Princes in our Basilica of San Lorenzo." Wisdom was exercised with regard to the "reversibility" of the intervention, as pointed out by Baldinucci, which mitigates to some extent this insult to artistic integrity: "These draperies are, in their final state, completely similar to the few others found there by the hand of Michelangelo himself. And they are accommodated with prudence so that, although one cannot see how, they can be removed and replaced again with little damage to these statues." But, considering that a church official of the time actually wanted to put pants on a crucifix, anything was possible in those years.

[16] Procacci, "Cappella Brancacci," p. 10, citing the memoirs of Father Benedetto Ricci, who reported the recollections of the elderly fathers who witnessed the event.

[17] The objection to Ferroni could well have been on the part of the Corsini family, who perhaps did not look favorably upon on the presence of this new arrival in their "religious territory."

[18] In his quest for an object of patronage, Ferroni acquired the Chapel of San Giuliano in the Church of the Annunziata in Florence, which he remodeled and decorated without impediments of any kind. He changed the name to the Chapel of San Giuseppe (Saint Joseph) and installed *The Death of St. Joseph*, painted on canvas by Carl Loth, over the fresco of *Saint Julian* (c.1454–55) by Andrea del Castagno (not brought to light again until 1857). For the renovation, he employed Foggini, the same architect who had done the Corsini Chapel in Santa Maria del Carmine.

[19] Ms. Riccardiano 2141, Qu. IV.XXXIX, c. 229v, cited in Procacci, "La Cappella Brancacci," p.10.

[20] G. Bottari, Preface to Borghini, *Il Riposo*, 2nd ed., 1730.

[21] Records of Father Pietro Paolo Manetti for May 1, 1736, date of the termination of all the work (A.S.F, *Conventi soppressi*, 113, vol. 29, signed K, c. 17), cited in Procacci, "Cappella Brancacci," p. 10. In his commentary for the 1758 edition of Vasari's *Vite* (1, p. 228), Bottari described the paintings as "fresh," in contrast to what he had written in 1730.

[22] Mesnil, "Per la storia," pp. 34ff.

[23] G. Richa, *Notizie istoriche delle chiese fiorentine divise ne' suoi quartieri*, Florence, 1754–62, 10 of 10 vols. (1762), p. 40.

[24] The ceiling of the new semicircular domed vault was installed at a higher level than the preceding Gothic groin vault which resulted in its complete destruction. Even so, there were some who thought it might be possible to recover the Masolino decoration from the ceiling (U. Procacci, "L'incendio della chiesa del Carmine del 1771: *La Sagra* di Masaccio; gli affreschi della

cappella di San Giovanni," *Rivista d'Arte*, 14, 1932, p. 192).
25 Mesnil, "Per la storia," pp. 34ff.
26 Procacci, "L'incendio," p. 192.
27 U. Baldini, "Nuovi affreschi nella Cappella Brancacci, Masaccio e Masolino," *Critica d'Arte*, 49, no. 1, April–June 1984, p. 70; and O. Casazza, "Il ciclo delle Storie di San Pietro e la 'Historia Salutis': Nuova lettura della Cappella Brancacci," *Critica d'Arte*, 51, no. 9, April–June 1986, p. 69.
28 "This chapel lacked the altar and step of marble to accompany all the rest; and Brother Andrea Spezzini not long afterward remedied this. So that, when this chapel was furnished with its lamps, candlesticks, flower urns and altar frontal, all of silver, candles, flowers, veil, etc., it did not make an unworthy appearance; we poor brothers were able to be satisfied" (cited in Mesnil, "Per la storia," pp. 34ff.).
29 All documents here are taken from the transcriptions in U. Procacci, "Cappella Brancacci," pp. 12ff. See Notes 30–35 immediately following.
30 From the contemporaneous records of Father Ranieri Chiti.
31 Reported in the *Gazetta Toscana*, a newspaper of the time, and in nearly the same wording in the pamphlet, *Relazione del grand'incendio seguito nella chiesa de' RR. Padri dei Carmine nella notte del dì 29 gennaio.*
32 *Relazione distinta dello spaventevole incendio della chiesa dei RR.PP. del Carmine di Firenze seguito la notte precedente al dì 29 gennaio 1771 colla distruzione quasi totale della medesima* (pamphlet).
33 *Trenodia ad imitazione di quella del profeta Geremia fatto in occasione dell'orribile incendio della chiesa dei padri del Carmine di Firenze sequito la notte precedente al dì 29 gennaio 1771 colla versione della medesima in versi toscani e con alcune brevi istoriche annotazioni* (pamphlet).
34 *Descrizione istorica del sacro tempio del Carmine della città di Firenze come esisteva avanti l'incendio de' 29 febbraio* [sic] *1771 e della costruzione della nuova chiesa aperta per la prima volta la mattina del dì 15 settembre 1782*, Florence, 1782
35 *Ristretto di notizie antiche e moderne della chiesa di Santa Maria del Carmine di Firenze*, Florence, 1782.
36 O. Casazza, "La grande gabbia architettonica di Masaccio," *Critica d'Arte*, 16, 1988, p. 96.
37 Procacci, "Cappella Brancacci," pp. 12ff.
38 V. Follini, *Firenze antica e moderna*, Florence, 1802, 8, p. 94.
39 On May 30, 1780, Cangini had written to the marquis Brancacci, titular heir to the descendancy of the chapel and a resident of Paris, soliciting his help with the restoration of the serious damage caused by the fire. On July 8, Brancacci responded by officially renouncing the patronage of the chapel, since his family had lived in Paris for such a long time (his letter was even signed in the French mode, "De Brancas") and no longer had any interest in being connected with Florence (Procacci, "L'incendio," pp. 157–60). See also, especially for the Riccardi family, G. De Juliis, "La Cappella Riccardi in San Pancrazio a Firenze," *Commentari*, 1–4, 1978, pp. 137ff.
40 A. S. F., Carte Riccardi, F. 144, c. 214r. Then as today, the lower chapel (burial vault) was entered via a narrow stone stair, near the back wall and level with the floor, of a small room directly behind the chapter room near the stairs that lead to the convent.
41 See entry on Meucci ceiling fresco.
42 Among the projects immediately carried out in the chapel, according to the records, were: the renovation of the reliquary containing the remains of Blessed Angelino Mazzinghi, which was badly damaged in the fire; the creation of a new canopy for the altar panel of *The Madonna del Popolo*, miraculously saved because it had been moved to the convent a short time before the fire; and the installation of a marble railing at the chapel entrance.
43 Cited by De Juliis ("Cappella Riccardi," p. 142), the Latin inscription, dated 1782, records the transfer of the patronage of the chapel, decorated with the famous frescoes of Masolino and Masaccio, from the Brancacci family to the marquis Gabriello Riccardi, subdeacon of the Diocese of Florence, who acquired it in honor of the Madonna del Popolo and Blessed Angelino Mazzinghi of the Carmelite Order: "HOC ANTIQUA GENTIS BRANCACCIAE / SACELLUM / PICTIS. A. MASOLINO ET MASACCIO / PARIETIBUS CELEBERRIMUM / VETERIS INCENDIO TEMPLI DEFORMATUM / GABRIEL MARCHIO RICCARDIUS / METROPOLIT ECCL FLORENT / CANONICUS SUBDESCANUS / A. PATRONIS LIBERE RENUNTIATUM / PLENIS CAENOBITARUM SUFFRAGIIS / IURE PATRONATUS ACQUISITO / IN HONOR B.M.V. A. POPULO NUNCUPATAE / ET B. ANGELI MAZZINGHI CARMELIT / RESTITUIT AUXIT ORNAVIT. / SIBIQUE ET SUIS VOLENTIBUS / REQUIETORIUM POSUIT / ANN. MDCCLXXXII.

Also cited by De Juliis is a summary of the work carried out for Subdeacon Riccardi (A.S.F., Carte Riccardi, F. 144, c. 214r-v) as follows: "He had all the Pictures refinished and reconditioned, he had the royal vault redone, and above it, the floor with the Railing, and marble steps, as well as a completely new Altar, Steps, Ciborium, Tomb wherein lies the Body of the Blessed Angelino Mazzinghi, the stair, all in various types of marble arranged in attractive symmetry, and having considered this, he had made at his own expense the Canopy gilded on the inside and carved on the outside, and goldleafed where the Head of the Christ Child was done in relief on the Blessed Virgin of Carmel, called "La Morina" [the Moorish Madonna] which had nearly always been located over the Ciborium of the Altar, which he had decorated, and enriched with the sixteen Bronze Candlesticks, eight of them at the top of the two steps, and on the level with the Altartable with the Coat of Arms at the foot, these were all of differently proportioned heights; and finally, all was done at the expense of the above-mentioned Subdeacon, including the side Marbles which were repaired and renovated where necessary, because they had been detached by the force of the fire and badly stained from the substances (*mestura*) which had been melted."
44 Procacci, "L'incendio," p. 159, note 1.
45 Originally a half-length image of Christ in benediction between two angels, his body had been covered up to the neck with mock gold leaf (A. Paolucci, *Capolavori e restauri*, exhib. cat., Florence, 1986, p. 425).
46 Paolucci, *Capolavori*, p. 425, who also writes concerning the recent removal of this overpainting.
47 Archivio Soprintendenza alle Gallerie, Florence, Commission for the Preservation of Works of Art, 1864, file 2, ins. 1.
48 Archivio Accademia BB.AA., Florence, 1834, file 23, ins. 24 (document discovered by Gabriella Incerpi).
49 Archivio Soprintendenza alle Gallerie, Commission for the Preservation of Works of Art, 1864, file 2, ins. 1 and 1866, file B, posit. 3, ins. 4.
50 Letter of June 10, 1904, written to the prefect of Florence to call a meeting of the Commission for the Preservation of Monuments because at that time the need for restoration had arisen again.
51 This report dated September 22, 1860, was sent to Paolo Feroni, Director of the Royal Sculpture Gallery and signed by Emilio Burci, Ulisse Forni and reporter Carlo Pino, who proposed for the rehabilitation of the frescoes "to give a light, lively tint, varying its tone and color here and there, so that it is not visually offensive . . . and finally to clean the whole work carefully, using cotton swabs and soft brushes dipped in milk or in another simple, glutinous liquid, as best suits the place, and thereby to enliven and once again give consistency to the colored surface, which has flaked in many areas and lost its original shine."
52 Taking his cue from Filippo Panizzi who also wrote a history of Italian painting, "obtaining it not from other people's books, but only from the direct observation of paintings," Cavalcaselle made sketches of nearly every painting in the Chapel and complete, finished drawings after some, with comments and annotations to refresh his memory.
53 As mentioned, these observations originated with Calvalcaselle as a result of his close, firsthand, analytical rereading of the walls of the Brancacci Chapel and the fidelity of the splendid drawings he did after them in his Notebook. There, each tiny detail assumes meaning as a notation from memory which is often extremely valuable, in contrast to the lithographs and chromolithographs which illustrate his English and Italian texts. These are only reproductions in reduced size done by various draftsmen after the original engravings of Carlo and Giovanni Paolo Lasinio (see Appendix) and printed by Thompson. Published for the first time in the English edition of 1864, two of these reproductions for *The Raising of the Son of Theophilus and Saint Peter in the Chair* and *The Dispute with Simon Magus and the Crucifixion of Saint Peter* were cut from the English volume and used by Cavalcaselle to make notes in preparation for the Italian edition. Whatever constituted a new and different reading for the chapel was marked in ink on these reproductions and, for the most part, faithfully recorded in the volume covering the frescoes published in 1883. We do not have either the drawings or the annotated engravings with his new firsthand readings for *The Fall*, the *Expulsion*, *The Tribute Money*, *Saint Peter Preaching*, or the *Baptizing* (see O. Casazza and P. Cassinelli Lazzeri, *La Cappella Brancacci: conservazione e restauro nei documenti della grafica antica*, Modena, 1989).
54 *Arte e Storia*, August 30–September 10, 1890, p. 175. Concerning the request, work had still

not begun in December 1891, even though it had been officially approved.
[55] Completion of the repairs was reported in a letter of February 26, 1897, from the Regional Office for the Preservation of Monuments to the Ministry. In a letter of June 25, 1895 from the Regional Office to the Commune of Florence, a request had been made "to fix the suspended lamp which illuminates the Chapel, rendering it movable with an appropriate apparatus so as to avoid, in lighting it, the use of a ladder which, slipping from one's grasp and falling, could knock dangerously against one of the walls—as it happened recently—thereby causing damage." The mechanism was installed in March, 1896.
[56] This claim may have been true, but there are also records of altar candles being blown out instead of snuffed.
[57] Reported in *Arte e Storia*, January 25, 1903, p. 3.
[58] "The grandiose size and projection of the altar canopy clashes in its forms with the severe simplicity of the surroundings, and the bright color of the marble truly damages the tranquil harmony of the frescoes. But these marble decorations are not only backed against the wall; in their most essential and projectings parts, they are very solidly built into the wall itself, thereby touching up against the precious frescoes of the three great Florentine masters. No delicacy, no scrupulous care in the execution of the masonry work would avoid the danger for the intonaco covered with the beautiful frescoes due to hammer blows and scalpels which might make it buckle, lift up and fall. It would certainly be a vain effort to try to find someone who would dare to take on this responsibility in front of the civilized world. It would be easy to find a way to attenuate the harsh effect of the color, giving the marble a more calm and harmonious patina. And such a method could also be applied to the marble bases of the pilasters which support the chapel arch and to the railing.

The existing altar could also undergo substantial modifications, since it is already totally isolated from the walls, and therefore the reasons invoked in other proposals to eliminate it do not hold water. The altar could be reduced to the table, and to the lower first step, by removing the wide upper step, which is high and loaded with Baroque decorations, and with it a wooden box above it containing the bone of a Saint could also be removed and situated elsewhere."
[59] The minister approved the proposal and in a letter of August 13, 1903, gave direct responsibility for arranging the cleaning of the frescoes to Arturo Faldi, a deputy member of the Superior Council of Fine Arts in the Florence office. The controversy did not end there. E. Romualdo Pantini, president of the Committee for the Masaccio Centenary, expressed his views in a Florence newspaper favoring "reopening the Gothic window from which Masaccio drew the overall harmony of the arrangement and the chiaroscuro." He also deplored "the main altar's enormous marble canopy, the large window out of place, the flourishes in the eighteenth-century decoration of the round ceiling, some worn-out gold molding which has come loose, the dust that rises and falls with the vibrations of the fresco and the deteriorating scenes on either side of the Byzantine Madonna." As for the skylight built the year before on the outside of the chapel wall "to prevent the rain from pelting down onto the terrace from which light enters the chapel," he recommended that this ought to be followed up by demolishing the terrace (following a view expressed by the engineer Bellincioni who had studied the causes of deterioration), because it retained water that doesn't drain off, and the reconstructing of the stair below it in another area, as had been approved by the Ministry ("Nella Cappella Brancacci, la festa intima," *Il Marzocco*, October 25, 1903).
[60] Reported in letter of February 6, 1904, from Carmelite prior, Alberto Bertieri, to the director of the Regional Office for the Preservation of the Monuments of Tuscany.
[61] Letter of June 7, 1904, to the director of the Regional Office for the Preservation of Monuments of Florence stamped "urgent and confidential."
[62] Letter of June 25, 1904, from the prefect of Florence to the chief director of architecture of the Regional Office for the Preservation of the Monuments of Tuscany.
[63] Letter of July 30, 1904. For the use of bread crumbs in cleaning frescoes, see the section in this chapter on the cleaning.
[64] Statement dated November 12, 1904, signed E. Gelli, T. Conti, R. Mazzanti and A. Socini.
[65] Letter of November 29, 1904 from the Technical Office of the Commune to the Head of the Regional Office for the Preservation of Monuments with a request for inspection of the work.
[66] The inspection of the chapel by the Commission for the Preservation of Monuments and Excavations of the Province of Florence is Item 1 in the minutes of the meeting of December 6, 1904.
[67] The report also states: "Having seen the excellent result obtained by the re-cleaning of these frescoes, the Commission expresses its strongest desire for similar cleaning work to be done on the famous frescoes by Ghirlandaio in the choir of the Church of Santa Maria Novella and on the frescoes, also by Ghirlandaio, in the Sassetti Chapel of the Church of Santa Trinità which are in deplorable condition."
[68] Article in *La Nazione*, May 11, 1908, in which the proponent was Alessandro Chiappelli.
[69] Deliberation made by the Commune Council made into an executive order with a letter dated April 11, 1908 from the prefect.
[70] This is depicted in two photographs published in the *Bollettino d'Arte*, 1917, p. 290. The photographs show still *in situ* the sculpted "angels" adorning the pediment of the altar.
[71] Discussed in a letter from the head of the Army Corps of Engineers dated May 28, 1918, to the Regional Office for the Preservation of Monuments.
[72] Letter from Arduino Colasanti, general director of the Ministry, to Alessandro Chiappelli, reported in *Il Marzocco*, May 20, 1928.
[73] Letter of February 6, 1929, from Giovanni Poggi, director of Medieval and Modern Art in Tuscany, to the Office of Fine Arts of the Commune.
[74] Mentioned in "Le opere del Comune nel primo decennio dell' E.F.," *Firenze*, 1, no. 9–10, Sept.–Oct. 1932, p. 12.
[75] See U. Procacci, "Relazione dei lavori eseguiti nella chiesa del Carmine di Firenze per la ricerca di antichi affreschi," *Bollettino d'Arte del Ministero della Pubblica Istruzione*, 27, 1933–34, p. 327.
[76] Letter of November 11, 1946 from the Carmelite prior, Martiniano Della, to the mayor and the director of Monuments.
[77] The readings were taken by the Chemistry Laboratory of the Opificio delle Pietre Dure (O.P.D.) and by restorers Mauro Matteini and Arcangiolo Moles. This inaugurated the plan for the restoration, which got under way in 1983.
[78] See p. 286.
[79] The rediscovered colors (which have nothing in common with the "obscurations" of the present general condition) show us the great value the frescoes would have had in their original state in the linking of light and form. More than a century after their execution, an attentive Vasari—who had very good perceptions in this sense—ended his biography of Masaccio with a list of the "most celebrated sculptors and painters who have since worked and studied in this chapel and become excellent and illustrious." The list begins with Fra Giovanni da Fiesole, an artist who, at first, seems to be the antithesis of Masaccio and a conservative bastion of the old "Gothic style," but he was born nevertheless out of the Brancacci frescoes.
[80] See Baldini in the previous chapter, and also Baldini, "Nuovi affreschi."
[81] Vasari wrote that *The Repentance* (where Saint Peter is crying over his sin of denial") came after the *Calling*, meaning to the right. He also linked the *Shipwreck* to the *Raising of Tabitha* in the register immediately below it, writing, "He made the stormy shipwreck of the Apostles here, and when Saint Peter liberated Petronilla, his daughter, from harm."
[82] R. Longhi, "Fatti di Masolino e Masaccio," *Critica d'Arte*, 3–4, July–Dec. 1940, p. 146. The painting published by Longhi is now in the Matteini Collection, Florence.
[83] Scholars have often inferred symbolic relationships between the Life of Saint Peter cycle and the life and activities of Felice Brancacci. Its commercial-maritime significance is mentioned by L. Berti (*L'opera completa di Masaccio*, Milan, 1968, p. 92ff.), Brockhaus ("Die Brancacci-Kapelle") and F. Antal (*Florentine Painting and its Social Background*, London, 1948). Reference to the conflict between Florence and Milan and to papal arbitration is suggested by P. Meller ("Cappella Brancacci"), and others see, in the unusual configuration of the *Tribute Money*, an allusion to taxation, since the Catasto or income declaration was instituted in Florence in 1427 to relieve the fiscal problems of the war effort. C. De Tolnay ("Note sur l'iconographie des fresques de la Chapelle Brancacci" in "Studi in onore di Giusta Nicco Fasola," *Arte Lombarda*, 10, 1965, p. 69ff.), noting the incongruity of the scenes of Adam and Eve in the cycle, proposed that two other episodes from Genesis, *Adam and Eve at Work* and *The Sacrifice of Cain and Abel*, had been planned for the areas where Filippino painted the scenes of Peter in prison, and other scenes from Genesis would have been on the front of the chapel, recalling a similar configuration by Jacopo della Quercia for the portal of the Church of San Petronio, Bologna." A recent hypothesis formulated by Pandimiglio ("Felice di Michele") and summarized by R. Zorzi emphasizes the political importance of the iconography for Felice and his circle. Felice could not have been unaware of the fact that the narration of the Saint Peter cycle reaffirmed papal supremacy in the Church and sanctified the antiquity of the Carmelite Order, whose

presence was so strongly represented physiognomically in Masaccio's *Raising of the Son of Theophilus*. While these are all religious themes, they are nonetheless relevant in terms of Felice's "pro-papal" political stance.

[84] See M. Salmi, *Masaccio*, Milan, 1947, p. 84; U. Baldini, *Seconda mostra di affreschi staccati*, Florence, 1958, p. 37; and U. Procacci, *Sinopie e affreschi*, Milan, 1960, pp. 61 and 227.

[85] Alberti wrote later, in relation to a custom and norm established since the time of Cennini: "And when we have to paint an *istoria* [a visually expressive, meaningful scene], most of us will first think about the manner and the order which would be the most beautiful, and we will make our concepts and models of the whole scene and each of its parts, firstly, and we will call in friends to advise us about it" (L. B. Alberti, *Della pittura* [Florence, 1436], trans. and ed. L. Mallé, Florence, 1950, p. 112).

[86] Vasari, *Vite*, 1878–81, 2, p. 294. Also in the first edition of 1550, he expressed himself in the same way, but with more embellishment: "In the meantime, the death of Masolino came about; and since the Brancacci Chapel remained imperfect, Masaccio was called to Florence by his very dear friend, Filippo di Ser Brunellescho, and, because of him, was employed to finish said chapel."

[87] Masolino's ability also to create dramatic figures is exemplified in the crippled man portrayed in the Tabitha scene. In the past, this figure was attributed by some to Masaccio, and, of course, Cavalcaselle even attributed the whole Chapel to Masaccio.

[88] See P. Bocci Pacini, "Umanesimo in Masolino," *Gli Uffizi. Studi e Ricerche*, n. 5, 1988, p. 22.

[89] "Then, what had been done to offend the first among the apostles became a sign of honor for the whole clergy. The tonsure of the hair came to signify the purity of life because impurities of the head collect in the hair; the abandonment of all exterior beauty, because hair is ornamental; the renunciation of worldly goods because, nothing must come between the priest and God, but their embrace must be tight and the vision of Divine Glory must have no veil. Thus the tonsure is circular because the circle has no beginning nor end, just as God has no beginning nor end for the priests who are his ministers; and moreover, the circle has no corners, which means that the priests cannot have anything vile in their life, because refuse gathers in corners. The circle is moreover the most beautiful of all shapes as God made the celestial creatures in this way: and beauty must decorate the mind and the words of those who dedicate themselves to God. Finally, this is the simplest of figures because, as Saint Augustine says, no other figure is formed by a single line, and the simplicity of doves has to live within the heart of every minister of God" (*The Golden Legend*, p. 193).

[90] A. Parronchi ("Torna Masaccio in luce e colore," *Arte e Vacanze*, 2, no. 8, Florence, 1989, pp. 17–18) also sees the hair falling in triple layers from the crown as a prefiguration of the papal tiara.

[91] C. Brandi, *Disegno della pittura italiana*, Turin, 1980, p. 176.

[92] G. Secco Suardo, *Manuale ragionato per la parte meccanica dell'arte del ristauratore dei dipinti*, Milan, 1866, p. 303.

[93] The "varnish" was identified in chemico-physical analyses performed by the Syremont of Milan, directed by Paolo Parrini.

[94] G. Piva, *L'arte del restauro*, Milan, 1972.

[95] G. Rosini, *Storia della pittura italiana esposta coi monumenti*, Pisa, 1840, 2, p. 263ff.

[96] J.A. Crowe and G.B. Cavalcaselle, *Storia della pittura in Italia*, Florence 1875–1909, vol. 2 of 11, 1883.

[97] For Cavalcaselle's observations, see each of the entries on the individual scenes.

[98] Piva advised: "After having dusted the painting with a soft brush, gently rub it with firm bread crumbs (from the preceding day), taking great care and removing any bits that may remain attached to the painting with a scraper" (*L'arte del restauro*, p. 207).

[99] C. Gamba, "Masaccio," *Emporium*, April, 1939.

[100] G. Fiocco, "Dodici stazioni dell'arte: Masaccio, o la conquista dello spazio," *Domus*, 134, 1939, pp. 81–82.

[101] In the cleaning, the many layers of protein mixture applied after the fire of 1771 were removed in a solid state, having been transformed into a gelatin using a chemically reactive resin method developed at the Syremont under the direction of Paolo Parrini.

[102] C. Brandi, *Teoria del restauro*, Rome, 1963.

[103] U. Baldini, *Teoria del restauro e unità di metodologia*, 2, Florence, 1981.

[104] U. Procacci, "Relazione dei lavori eseguiti nella chiesa del Carmine di Firenze per la ricerca di antichi affreschi," *Bollettino d'Arte*, 27, 1933–1934, p. 327.

[105] The cleaning system was developed by Paolo Parrini.

[106] F. Baldinucci, *Vocabolario toscano dell'arte del disegno*, Florence, 1681.

[107] The azurite was appled with a binder of thin glue and egg yolks (C. Cennini, *Il libro dell'arte* [Florence, early 15th century], ed. F. Brunello, pref. L. Magagnato, Vicenza, 1971, p. 93).

[108] Forni, *Manuale*, p. 75.

[109] Baldinucci, *Vocabolario*, s.v. "Rifiore."

[110] U. Baldini, "Il restauro del Crocifisso di Cimabue," *Atti del Convegno sul restauro delle opere d'arte* (1976), Florence, 1981, p. 67 ff.; Baldini, *Teoria del restauro*, 2 vols., Florence, 1978 and 1981; O. Casazza, *Il restauro pittorico nell'unità di metodologia*, Florence, 1981; U. Baldini, *Metodo e ricerca, operatività e ricerca nel restauro*, Florence, 1982; and U. Baldini and O. Casazza, *The Crucifix by Cimabue*, Milan, 1983 (exhib. cat. for The Metropolitan Museum of Art in New York).

[111] A. Paolucci, "Considerazioni sulle indagini rivolte per il progetto Piero della Francesca," in *Un progetto per Piero della Francesca*, Florence, 1989, pp. 75–77.

[112] Casazza and Lazzeri, "Cappella Brancacci," p. 33.

[113] Brandi, *Teoria del restauro*, 46ff.

APPENDIXES

ENGRAVINGS BY GIOVANNI PAOLO AND CARLO LASINIO

G. P. and C. Lasinio, The Tribute Money, Saint Peter Preaching *and* The Baptizing of the Neophytes, *engravings, Florence, Department of Prints and Drawings, Uffizi Gallery*

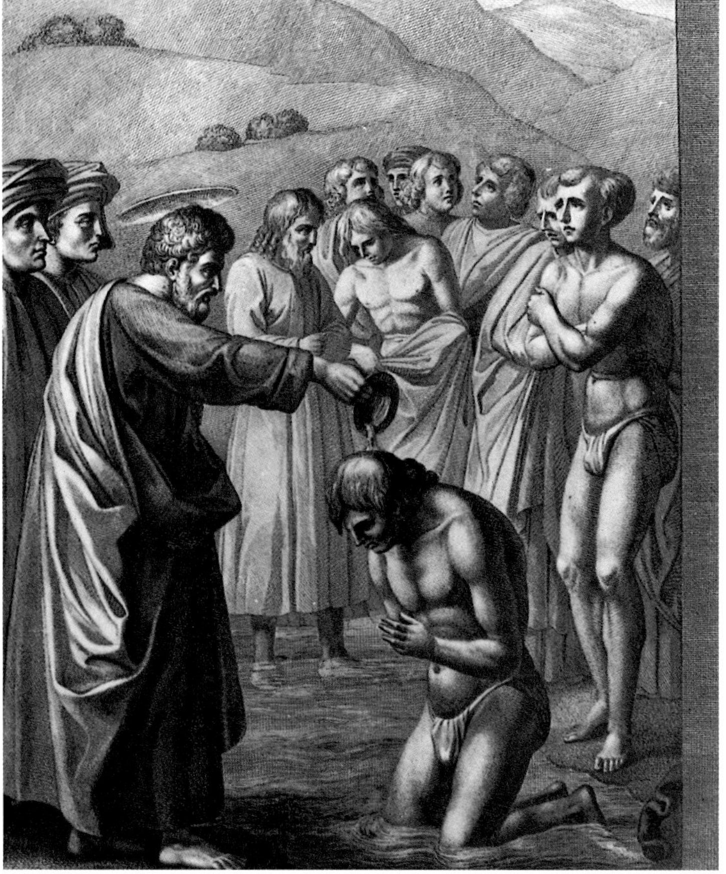

DRAWINGS FROM THE NOTEBOOK OF GIOVANNI B. CAVALCASELLE

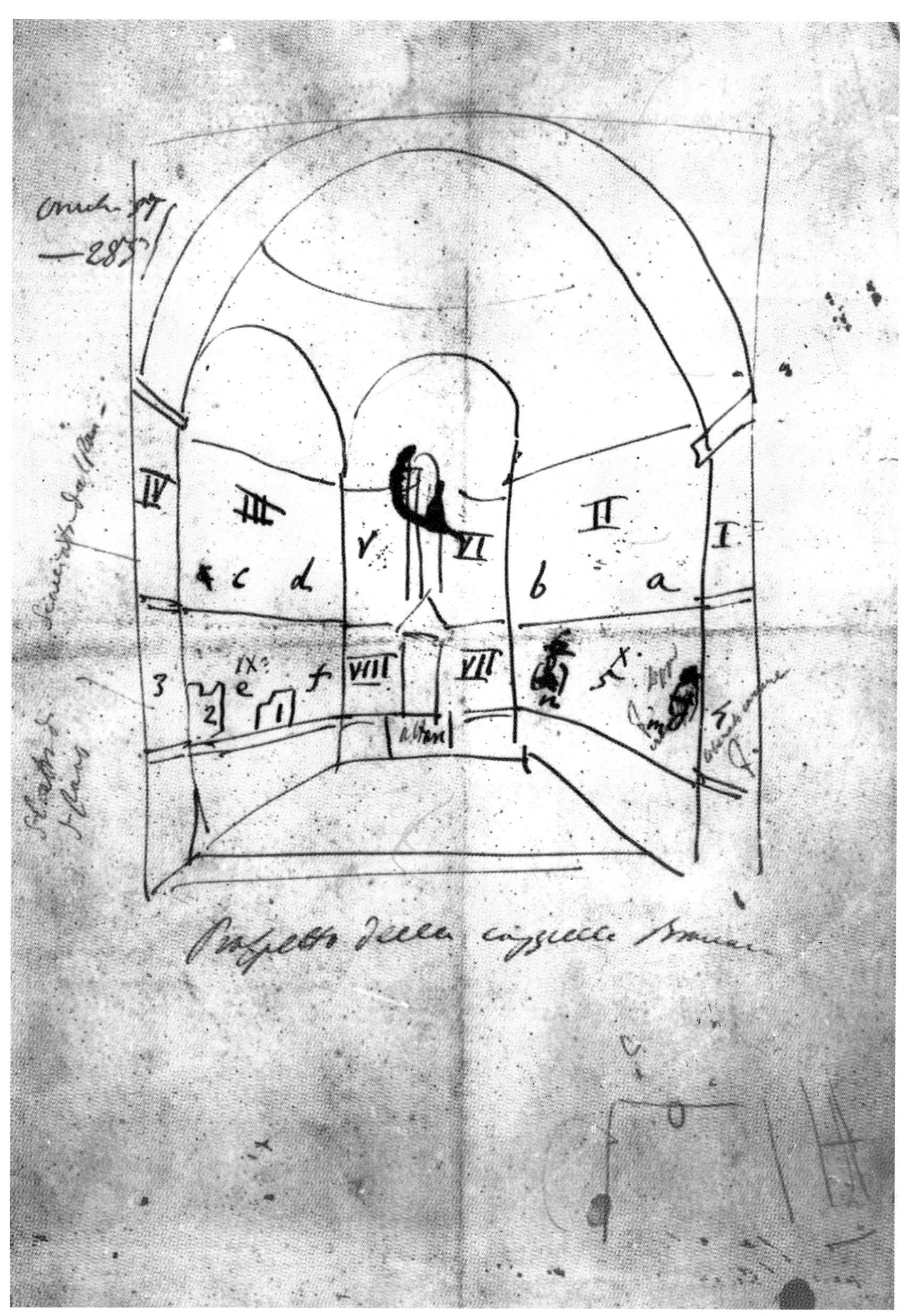

View of the Brancacci Chapel, from the Notebook of G. B. Cavalcaselle, Venice, Biblioteca Marciana

The Healing of the Crippled Man and the Raising of Tabitha,
from the Notebook of G. B. Cavalcaselle, Venice, Biblioteca Marciana

The Distribution of Goods and the Death of Ananias,
from the Notebook of G. B. Cavalcaselle, Venice, Biblioteca Marciana

Saint Peter Healing with His Shadow,
from the Notebook of G. B. Cavalcaselle, Venice, Biblioteca Marciana

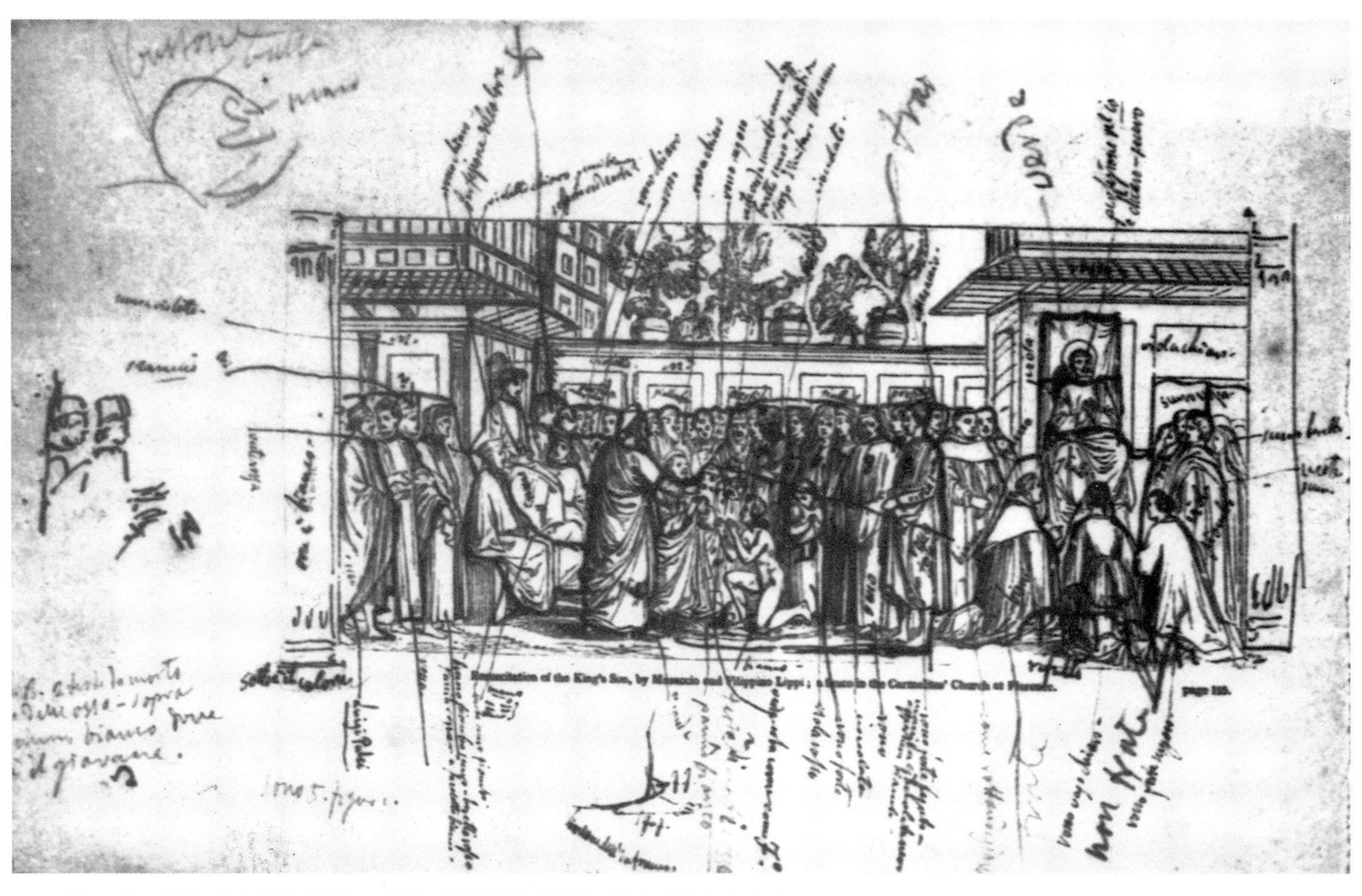

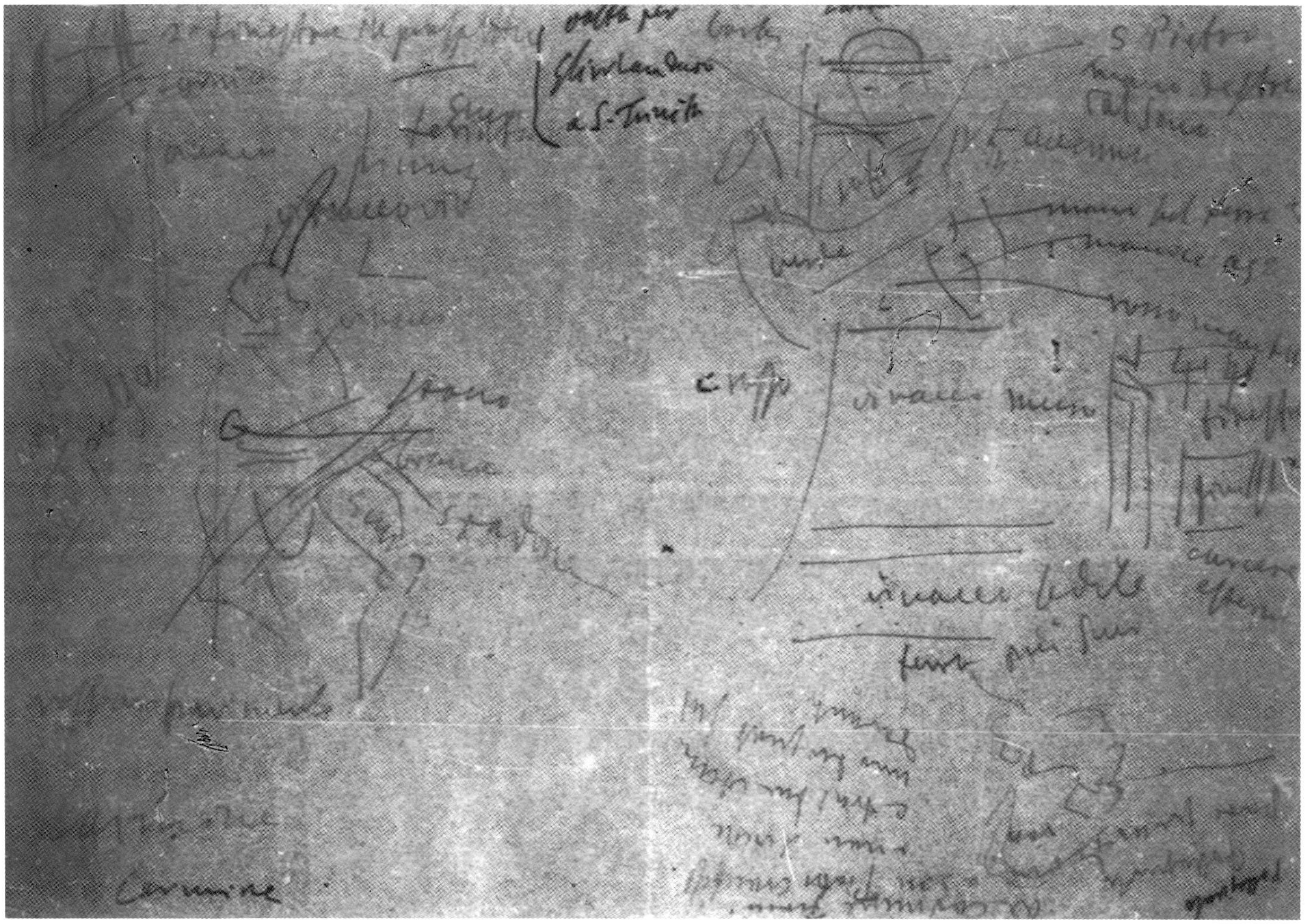

OPPOSITE AND BELOW:

The Raising of the Son of Theophilus and Saint Peter in the Chair,

from the Notebook of G. B. Cavalcaselle, Venice, Biblioteca Marciana

Saint Peter Visited in Prison by Saint Paul,
from the Notebook of G. B. Cavalcaselle,
Venice, Biblioteca Marciana

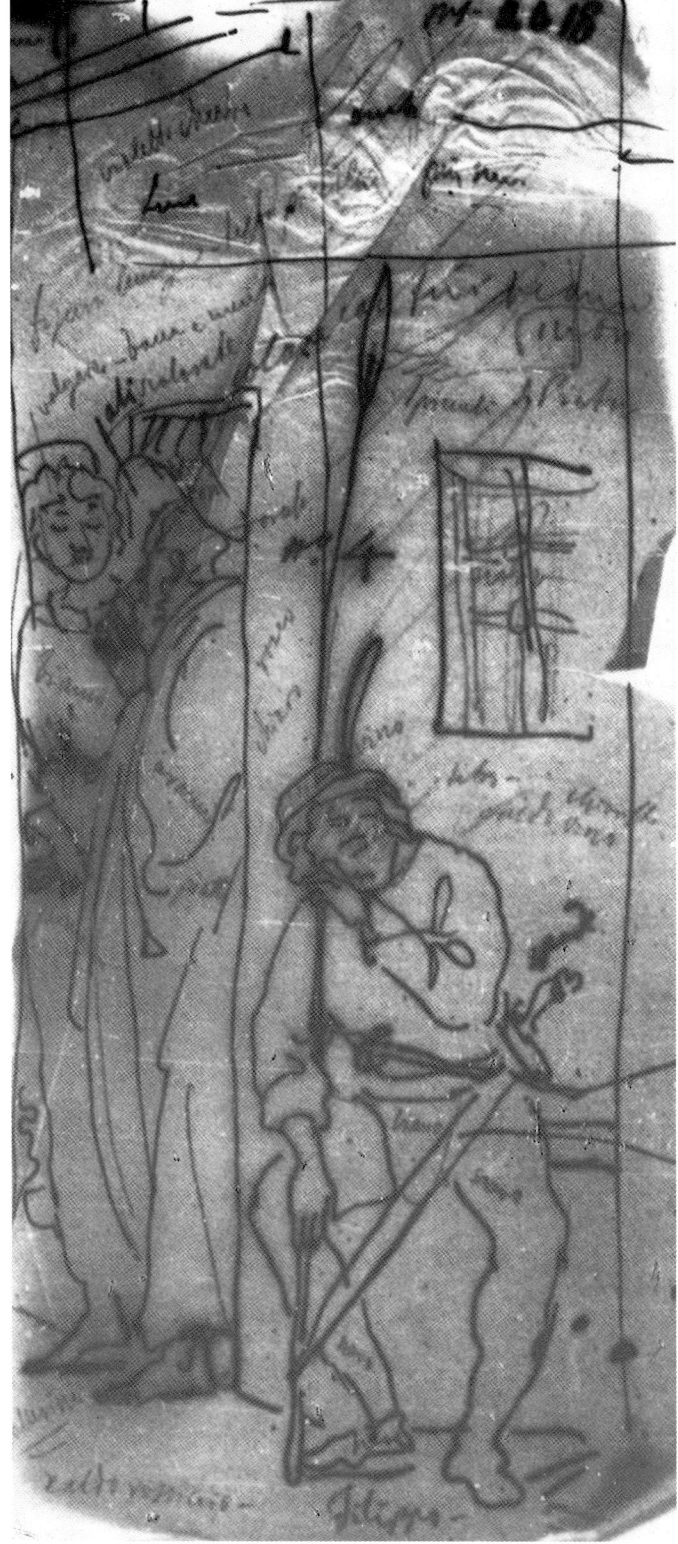

Saint Peter Liberated from Prison,
from the Notebook of G. B. Cavalcaselle,
Venice, Biblioteca Marciana

The Dispute with Simon Magus and the Crucifixion of Saint Peter,
from the Notebook of G. B. Cavalcaselle, Venice, Biblioteca Marciana

DIAGRAMS OF THE *GIORNATE* IN THE FRESCOES OF THE BRANCACCI CHAPEL

The continuous line in black delineates and delimits the giornate *or sections of fresh plaster (intonaco) applied little by little in the course of the execution of the scenes. The arrows indicate the direction of the overlaying of each section with the previously executed sections. The numbers in red indicate a possible chronological sequence for the entire work.*

Masolino, Adam and Eve: The Fall, *diagram of the* giornate

Masaccio, Adam and Eve: The Expulsion,
diagram of the giornate

Masaccio, The Tribute Money, *diagram of the* giornate

3
22
6
7
4
3
25
24
8
10
9
5
26
11

Masolino, Saint Peter Preaching, *diagram of the* giornate

Masaccio, The Baptizing of the Neophytes, *diagram of the* giornate

Masolino, The Healing of the Crippled Man and the Raising of Tabitha, *diagram of the* giornate

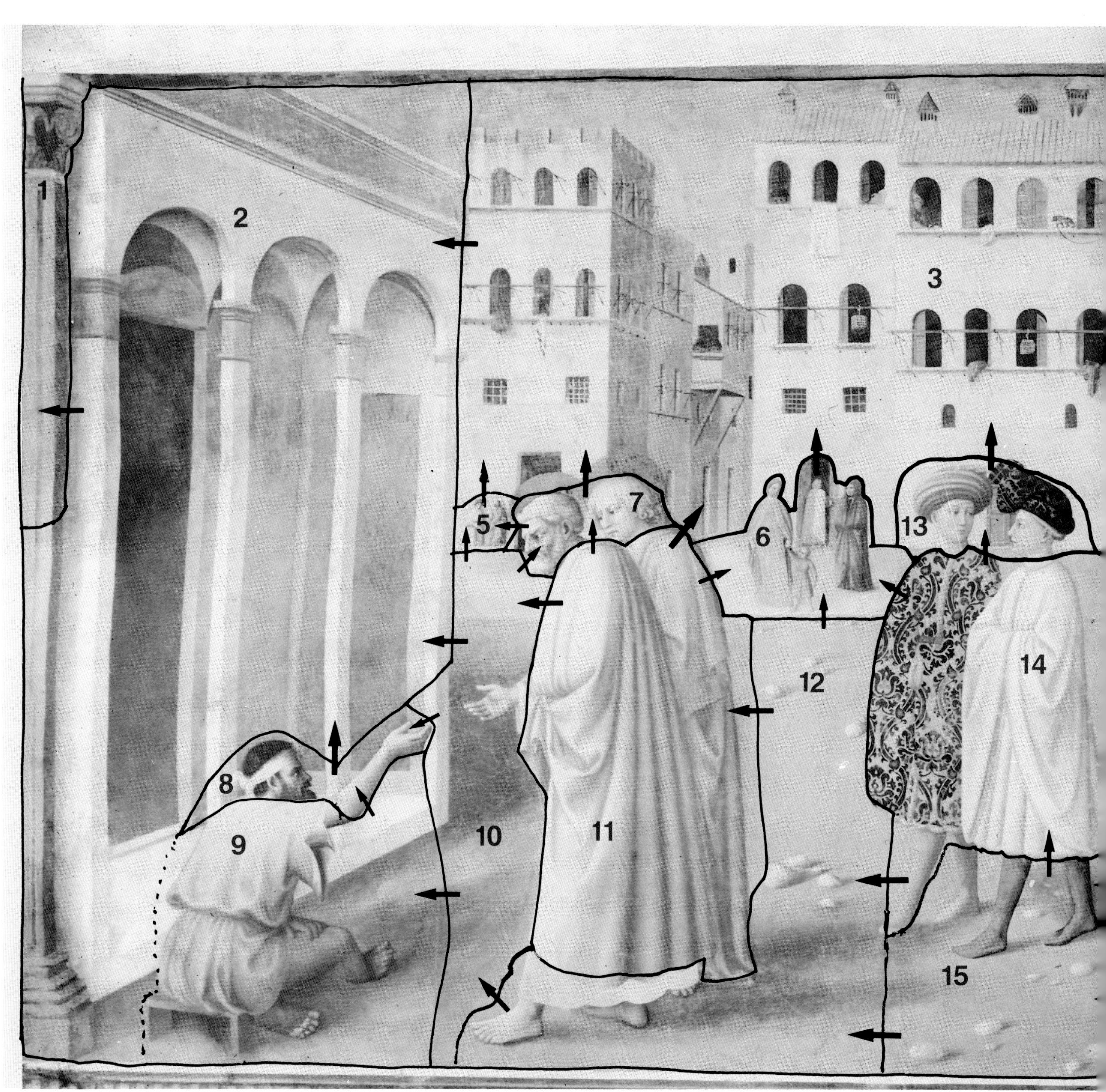

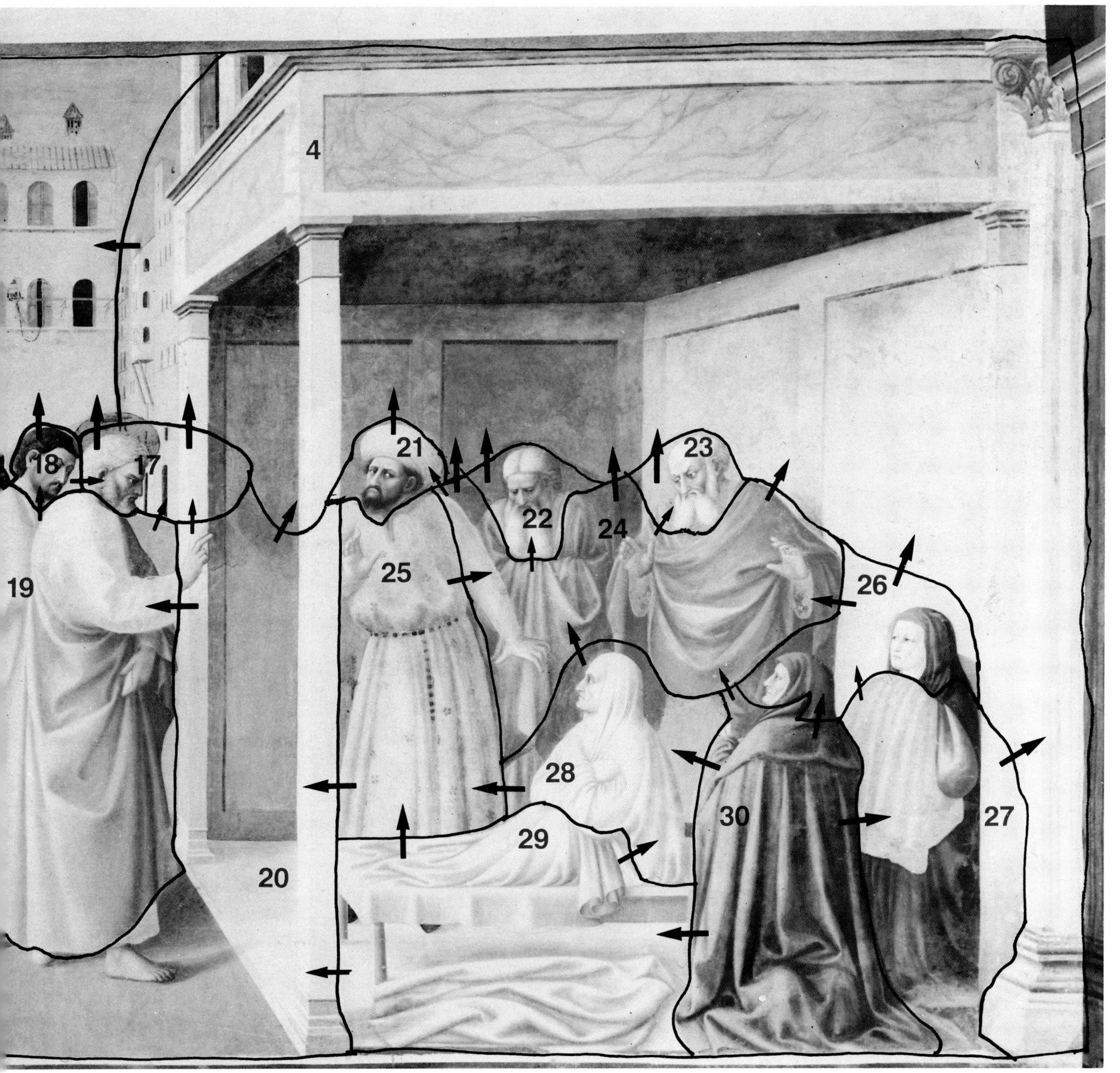
4
18
17
21
23
22
24
19
25
26
28
30
27
29
20

Masaccio,
The Distribution of Goods
and the Death of Ananias,
diagram of the giornate

Masaccio, Saint Peter Healing with His Shadow, *diagram of the* giornate

Masaccio and Filippino Lippi,
The Raising of the Son of Theophilus and Saint Peter in the Chair,
diagram of the giornate

3
4
9
10
2
11
12
19
47
48
49
17
16
18
15
51
50
21
20
14
13

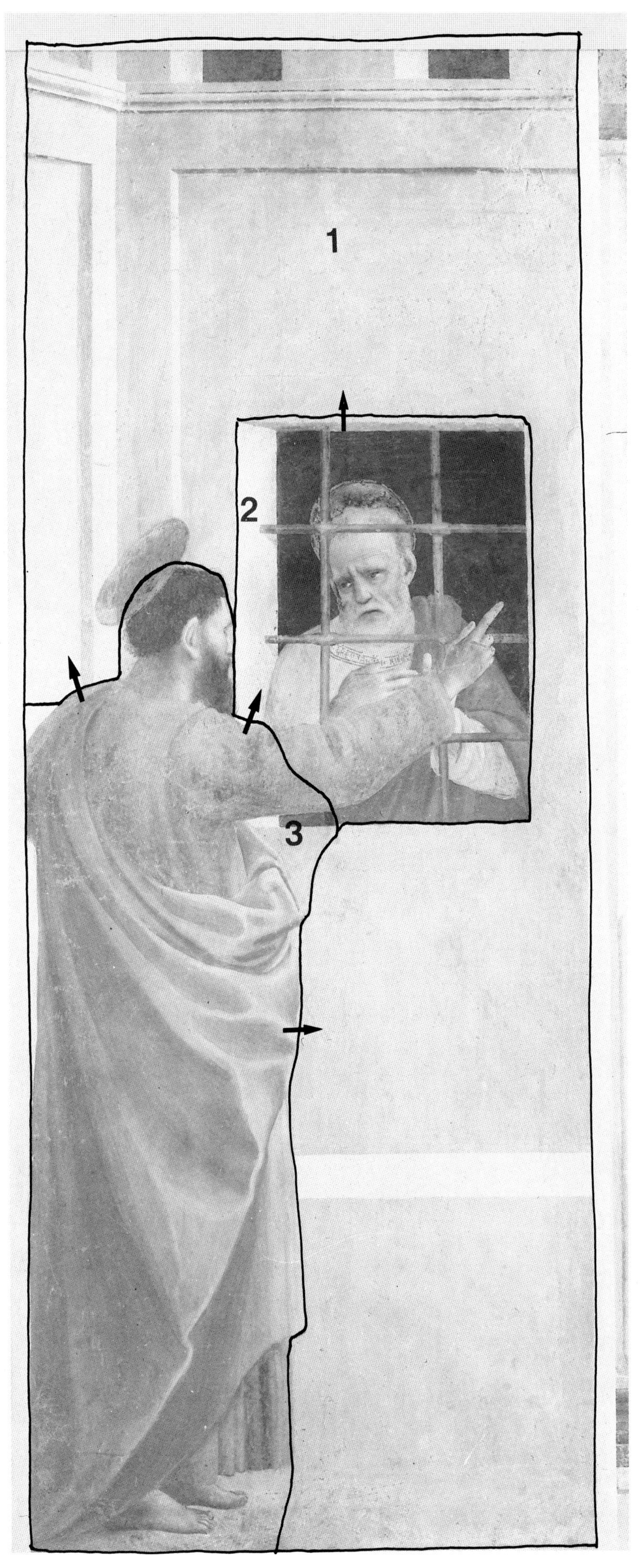

Filippino Lippi, Saint Peter Visited in Prison by Saint Paul, *diagram of the* giornate

Filippino Lippi, Saint Peter Liberated from Prison, *diagram of the* giornate

Filippino Lippi, The Dispute with Simon Magus and the Crucifixion of Saint Peter, *diagram of the* giornate

3
6
7
30
34
40
41
27
31
33
37
38
39
26
35
32
28
25
24
36
29
42

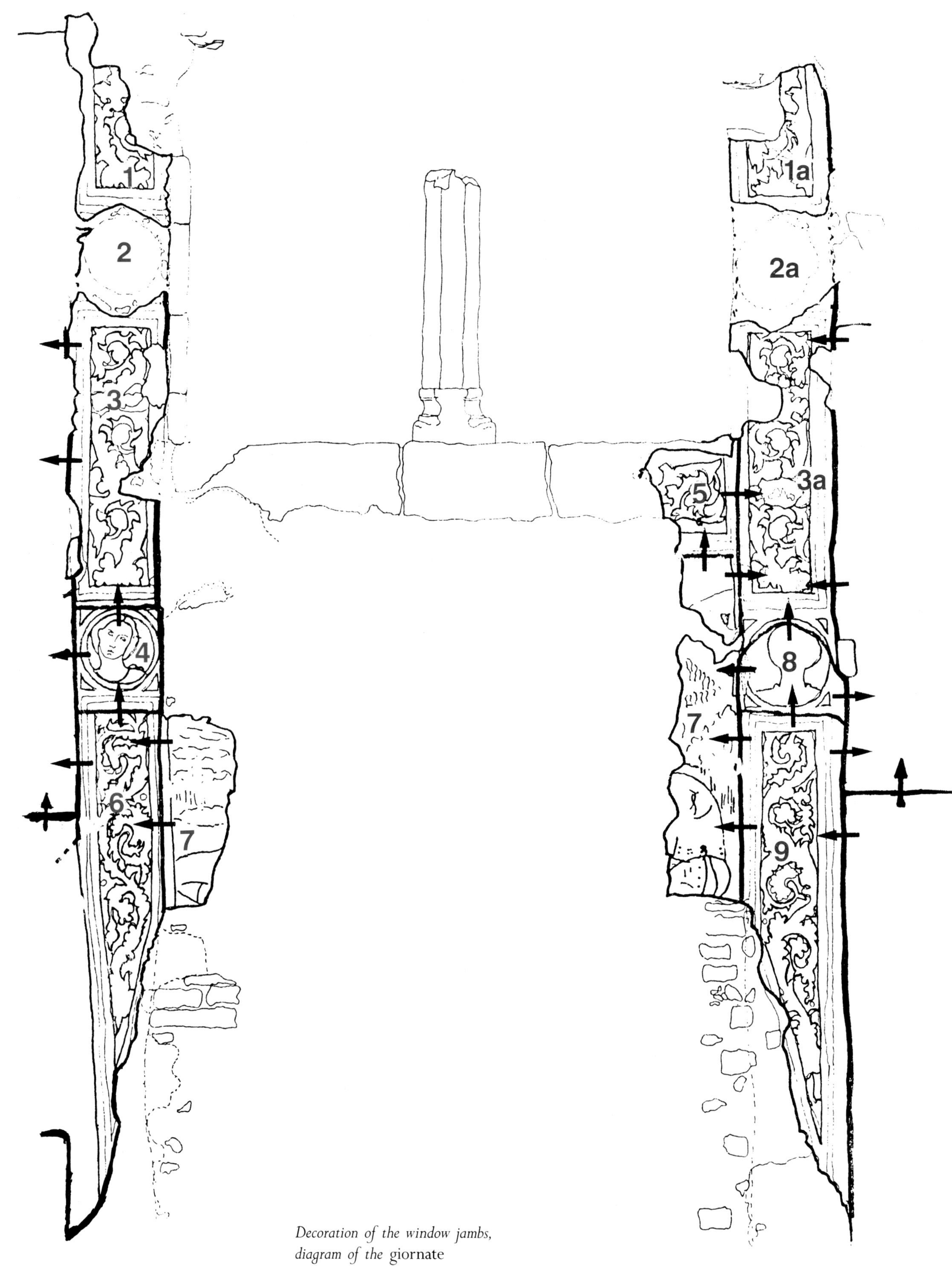

Decoration of the window jambs, diagram of the giornate

BIBLIOGRAPHY

13th century, second half

Voragine, Jacobus de, *The Golden Legend*, trans. by G. Ryan and H. Ripperger (1941), reprint New York, 1969.

15th century, first decade

Cennini, Cennino, *Il libro dell'arte*, ed. by F. Brunello, pref. by L. Magagnato, Vicenza, 1971. [*The Craftsman's Handbook*, trans. by D. V. Thompson, Jr., New York, 1954.]

1436

Alberti, L. B., *Della Pittura*, ed. by L. Mallé, Florence, 1950. [*On Painting*, trans. by John R. Spencer, New Haven, rev. ed. 1966.]

1451–1464

Filarete, A. (Antonio Averlino), *Trattato di Architettura*.

15th century, second half

Manetti, A., *Vite di XIV uomini singhulary in Firenze dal MCCCC innanzi*, ed. by G. Milanesi, Florence, 1887.

1481

Landino, C., *Commento a Dante*, 1st edition, Florence.

1510

Albertini, F., *Memoriale di molte statue e pitture . . . di Florentia*, Florence.

1550

Vasari, G., *Le vite de' più eccellenti architetti, pittori et scultori italiani*, Florence.

1568

Vasari, G., *Le vite de' più eccellenti pittori, scultori ed architettori*, 3 vols., Florence. (See 1848 and 1878.)

1584

Borghini, R., *Il Riposo*, Florence, 2nd ed., 1730.

Lomazzo, G. P., *Trattato dell'arte della pittura*, Milan.

1591

Bocchi, F., *Bellezze della città di Firenze*, facsimile reprint by M. G. Cinelli, Florence, 1677.

1662

Monti, F. and G. Tancredi, *Masaccio*, Rome.

1675

Coccapani, P., *Descrizione delle feste. . .per la solenne traslazione del corpo di Sant'Andrea Corsini*, Rome.

1681

Baldinucci, F., *Vocabolario toscano dell'arte del disegno*, Florence.

1681–1728

Baldinucci, F., *Notizie de' professori del disegno da Cimabue in qua*, 4 vols., Florence.

1689

Antinori, G., *Ristretto delle cose più notabili della città di Firenze*, Florence.

1699

De Seine, F., *Nouveau voyage en Italie*, 2, Lyon.

1745

Carlieri, C. M., *Ristretto delle cose più notabili della città di Firenze*, Florence.

1754–1762

Richa, G., *Notizie istoriche delle chiese fiorentine divise ne' suoi quartieri*, Florence, 10, 1762.

1765

Guida per osservare con metodo le cose notabili della città di Firenze, Florence.

1766

Lastri, M., *L'osservatore fiorentino sugli edifici della sua patria*, Florence, (other editions 1775, 1791, 1836).

Richard, Abbot, *Description historique et critique de l'Italie*, 3, Dijon.

1767

Riccardi, G., *Ristretto delle cose più notabili della città di Firenze*, Florence.

1769–1791

Reynolds, J., *Discourses Delivered at the Royal Academy*, London.

1770

Patch, T., *Selections from the Works of Masaccio. . . .*, 3, Florence; and *The Life of Masaccio*, Florence.

1778

Cambiagi, G., *L'Antiquario fiorentino, ossia guida per osservare con metodo le cose notabili della città di Firenze*, Florence.

1782

Pelli, G., "Elogio di Tommaso, o Maso detto Masaccio," in *Elogi degli uomini illustri toscani*, 2, Lucca.

1790

Fineschi, V., *Il Forestiere istruito in S. Maria Novella*, Florence.

Follini, V., *Firenze antica e moderna*, 8, Florence.

1795–1796

Lanzi, L., *Storia pittorica dell'Italia del Risorgimento delle belle arti fin presso la fine del XVII secolo*, Bassano.

1809

Dall'Armi, G., *Le pitture di Masaccio esistenti in Roma nella Basilica di S. Clemente*, Rome.

1812

Lasinio, G. P. and C., *Peintures de Masaccio, Masolino . . . .*, Florence.

1818

Pitture a fresco esistenti in alcune chiese fiorentine, 1818–1832, drawn by G. P. Lasinio and engraved by C. Lasinio.

1823

Séroux D'Agincourt, J. B., *Histoire de l'art par les monuments*, 3, Paris.

1827–1831

Rumohr, C. F., *Italienische Forschungen*, Berlin-Stettino, 2 of 3 vols., pp. 243–51 (ed. by J. von Schlosser, Frankfort, 1920, pp. 376–81).

1830

Nibby, A., *Itinerario di Roma*, 1, Rome.

1832

Masselli, G. *Note alle Opere di G. Vasari*, 1, Florence.

Valéry, M., *Voyages historiques et littéraires en Italie*, 3, Paris.

1834

Gherardi-Dragomanni, F., *Memorie della Terra di S. Giovanni nel Valdarno superiore*, Florence.

1838–1840

Gaye, G., *Carteggio inedito di artisti nei secoli XIV, XV, XVI*, 1 (1838) and 2 (1840), Florence.

1840

Rosini, G., *Storia della pittura italiana esposta coi monumenti*, 2, Pisa, pp. 263ff.

1845

Jameson, A. M., *Memoirs of the Early Italian Painters etc.*, London.

1846

Missirini, M., *Masaccio* (Lecture), Florence.

1847

Kugler, F. D., *Handbuch der Geschichte der Malerei*, Berlin, 1, pp. 304ff.

1848

Milanesi C., G. Milanesi, C. Pini, P. V. Marchese, "Sulle pitture della Cappella Brancacci etc.," in G. Vasari, *Le vite de' più eccellenti pittori, scultori ed architettori* (1568), Florence, 3, pp. 165–91 and 255ff.

Reumont, A., "Kapelle Brancacci: Masaccio und Filippino," *Das Kunstblatt*, p. 117.

Rosini, G., *Sulle pitture de Masaccio nella Cappella Brancacci, etc.*, Pisa.

1850

Breton, E., *Notice sur Tommaso Guidi dit Masaccio*, Saint-Germain-en-Laye.

1855

Burckhardt, J., *Der Cicerone*, Basel (Italian ed., Florence, 1952).

Springer, A. H., *Handbuch der Kunstgeschichte* (Stuttgart), Italian ed. by C. Ricci, Bergamo, 1913, p. 105ff.

1856

Fantozzi, F., *Nuova guida di Firenze*, Florence.

Selvatico, P., *Storia estetico-critica delle arti del disegno*, Venice, pp. 333ff.

1860

Milanesi, G., "Le vite de alcuni artefici fiorentini scritte da G. Vasari etc.," *Giornale storico degli Archivi toscani*, Florence, 4, pp. 194–96 (new ed. Siena, 1873).

1861

Interno della Chiesa di S. Maria Novella dopo i restauri fatti nel 1861, Florence. (Anonymous)

Intorno ai lavori di S. Maria Novella di Firenze, Florence. (Anonymous)

Rio, A. F., *De l'art chrétien*, Paris.

1863

Amari, M., *I diplomi arabi del R. Arch. fiorentino*, Florence.

1864–1871

Crowe, J. A. and G. B. Cavalcaselle, *A New History of Painting in Italy from the Second to the Sixteenth Century*, London. (Italian ed. *Storia della pittura in Italia*, 11 vols., Florence 1875–1909: 2, 1883).

1866

Forni, U. *Manuale del restauratore*, Florence.

Secco Suardo, G., *Manuale ragionato per la parte meccanica dell'arte del ristauratore dei dipinti*, Milan.

1868

Layard, A. H., *The Brancacci Chapel*, London.

1869

Santi Mattei, P., *Ragionamento intorno alla antica chiesa del Carmine di Firenze*, Florence.

Zahn, A., "Masolini und Masaccio," *Jahrbücher für Kunstwissenschaft*, pp. 155–71.

1870

Lübke, W., "Masolino und Masaccio," *Jahrbücher für Kunstwissenschaft*, pp. 280–86.

Reumont, A., "Die Kapelle der h. Katharina in S. Clement zu Rom," *Jahrbücher für Kunstwissenschaft*, pp. 75–79.

1876

Delaborde, H., "Des oeuvres et de la manière de Masaccio," *Gazette des Beaux-Arts*, pp. 369–84.

Thaussing, M., "Masaccio und Masolino in der Brancacci Kapelle," *Zeitschrift für bildende Kunst*, pp. 225–38.

1877

Pini, C. and G. Milanesi, *La scrittura di artisti italiani*, 1, s. 1, n. 14.

Symonds, J. A., *Renaissance in Italy*, London.

1878

Vasari, G., *Le vite de' più eccellente pittori scultori ed architettori* (1568), ed. by G. Milanesi, Florence, 1878–81. (Reprint Florence, 1971.)

1880

Woermann, K., "Masaccio und Masolino," *Grenzboten*, 39, p. 324.

1881

Catellacci, D., "Diario di Felice Brancacci ambasciatore con Carlo Federighi al Cairo," *Archivio Storico Italiano*, pp. 157–58.

1882

Woltmann, A. and K. Woermann, *Geschichte der Malerei: die Malerei der Renaissance*, 2, Leipzig.

1883

Lermolieff, I. (G. Morelli), *Kunstkritische Studien über italienische Malerei*, Leipzig.

1885

Richter, J. P., *Notes on Vasari*, London.

1887

Lübke, W., *Essai d'histoire de l'art*, 2, Paris.

Tanfani-Centofanti, L., *Donatello in Pisa*, Pisa.

1888

Müntz, E., *Les collections des Médicis au XV siècle*, Paris.

1889

Cole, T., "Masaccio," *The Century Magazine*, September, p. 659.

Müntz, E., *Histoire de l'art pendant la Renaissance*, 1, Paris, (review by O. Maruti in *Archivio Storico dell'Arte*, 1890, p. 147).

Stillman, W. J., "Masaccio," *The Century Magazine*, September, pp. 653–59.

Wickhoff, F., "Die Fresken der Katharinen Kapelle in S. Clemente zu Rom," *Zeitschrift für bildende Kunst*, pp. 301–10, (review by C. De Fabriczy in *Archivio Storico dell'Arte*, 1889, pp. 381–83).

1890

Meyer, J., "Filippino Lippi," *Jahrbuch der königlich preussischen Kunstsammlungen*, 11, pp. 3ff.

1891

Marrai, B., "Gli affreschi della Cappella Brancacci al Carmine," *Arte e Storia*, April 10, pp. 59–60.

1893–1894

Catalogue of the Exhibition of Early Italian Art in the New Gallery, London.

1894

Cocchi, A., *Notizie storiche intorno antiche immagini di nostra Donna etc.*, Florence.

Müntz, E., "Les plateaux d'accouchés etc.," in *Fondation Eugène Piot*, Paris, pp. 203–32.

1895–1899

Schmarsow, A., *Masaccio-Studien*, 5 vols., Leipzig.

1896

Berenson, B., *Florentine Painters of the Renaissance*, New York (2nd ed. 1900).

Justi, L., *Die italienische Malerei des XV. Jahrhunderts*, Berlin (s.d.)

1897

Philippi, A., *Die Kunst der Renaissance in Italien*, 1, Leipzig.

1898

Tanfani-Centofanti, L., *Notizie di artisti tratte da documenti pisani*, Pisa.

1900

Bode, W., "Donatello als Architekt und Decorator," *Jahrbuch der königlich preussischen Kunstsammlungen*, p. 28.

Filangeri di Candida, A., "La Pinacoteca Nazionale di Napoli," *Napoli nobilissima*, March, p. 34.

Filangeri di Candida, A., "Un quadro acquistato dalla Galleria del Museo Nazionale di Napoli," *L'Arte*, p. 74.

Knudtzon, F., *En Brochure om Masaccio*, Copenhagen, 1901.

Marrai, B., "Il tabernacolo col gruppo del Verrocchio in Orsanmichele," *L'Arte*, pp. 346–52.

Weisbach, W., "Der Meister des Carrandschen Triptychous," *Jahrbuch der königlich preussischen Kunstsammlungen*, p. 37.

1901–1940

Venturi, A., *Storia dell'arte italiana*, Milan, 7/1 of 25 vols., 1909, pp. 86 and 113–26.

1902

Bayersdorfer, A., "Masaccio und Filippino, Fresken in der Brancacci Kapelle," *Leben und Schriften aus seinem Nachlass*, pp. 56–58.

Berenson, B., *The Study and Criticism of Italian Art*, London.

De Fabriczy, C., "Ancora del tabernacolo col gruppo del Verrocchio in Orsanmichele," *L'Arte*, pp. 46–48 and 336–40.

Kreutz, M. K., *Masaccio*, Berlin.

Layard, A. H., *The Italian Schools of Painting etc.*, 1, London.

Supino, J. B. and B. Marrai, "Ancora del tabernacolo col gruppo del Verrocchio in Orsanmichele," *L'Arte*, pp. 185–89.

Wood Brown, J., *The Dominican Church of S. M. Novella*, Edinburgh.

1903

Carnesecchi, C., "Messer Felice Brancacci," *Miscellanea d'Arte*, pp. 38–40.

D'Ancona, P., "La tavola di Masaccio ora nella R. Galleria de Belle Arti," *Miscellanea d'Arte*, pp. 174–77.

Del Badia, J., "Tommaso . . . detto Masaccio e Giovanni suo fratello," *Rassegna Nazionale*.

Marrai, B., "Il tabernacolo col gruppo del Verrocchio in Orsanmichele," *Rivista d'Arte*, pp. 36–38.

Poggi, G., "La tavola di Masaccio per il Carmine di Pisa," *Miscellanea d'Arte*, October-November, pp. 182–88.

1904

Mackowsky, H., "Filippino Lippi," in *Das Museum*, 8, p. 40 and 9, p. 24.

Magherini-Graziani, G., *Masaccio: Ricordo delle onoranze rese in S. Giovanni Valdarno nel dì 25 ottobre 1903*, Florence.

Marasse, M., "Masaccio und S. Clemente in Rom," *Die Kunst-Halle*, pp. 257, 273 and 290.

Pantini, R., "La cappella della Passione in S. Clemente a Roma," *Emporium*, pp. 31–52.

1905

Chiappelli, A., *Pagine d'antica arte fiorentina*, Florence.

Konody, G. P., *Filippino Lippi*, London.

Leonardi, V., "Affreschi dimenticati del tempo di Martino V," *Atti del Congresso internazionale di Sc. Stor.*, Rome, pp. 286–308.

Poggi, G., "Masolino e la Compagnia della Croce a Empoli," *Rivista d'Arte*, 3, pp. 46ff.

Reymond, M., "L'architecture des peintres aux premières années de la Renaissance," *Revue de l'Art ancien et moderne*, pp. 41–42 and 48–50.

Sortais, G., "Masaccio et la Chapelle Brancacci," *Etudes*, 42, bk. 104, pp. 343–71.

Supino, J. B., *Les deux Lippi*, Florence.

1906

Mesnil, J., "Notes dur Filippino Lippi," *Rivista d'Arte*, 3, pp. 100ff.

Milanesi, G., *Nuove annotazioni e commenti a "Le Opere de Giorgio Vasari,"* Florence, 2, pp. 287ff.

Schubring, P., "Notizie di Berlino," *L'Arte*, p. 384.

Suida, W., "L'altare di Masaccio, già nel Carmine a Pisa," *L'Arte*, pp. 125–27.

1907

Berenson, B., "La scoperta di un dipinto di Masaccio," *Rassegna d'Arte*, p. 139.

1908

Berenson, B., "La Madonna pisana di Masaccio," *Rassegna d'Arte*, pp. 81–85.

Kraus, F. X., *Geschichte der Christlichen Kunst*, Freiburg, pp. 180–84.

Patini, R., "Masaccio," *The Connoisseur*, pp. 25–28 and 87–90.

Peratè, A., in *Histoire de l'art*, Paris, pp. 597–600.

Toesca, P., *Masolino da Panicale*, Bergamo.

von Hadeln, D. F., "Andrea di Giusto und das dritte Predellen Stück von pisanischen Altarwerk des Masaccio," *Monatshefte für Kunstwissenschaft*, pp. 785–89.

1909

Berenson, B., *The Florentine Painters of the Renaissance with an Index to Their Works*, New York, 3rd edition.

Muther, R., *Geschichte der Malerei*, 1, Leipzig.

Poggi, G., "Note su Filippino Lippi," *Rivista d'Arte*, 6, pp. 305ff.

1911

De Rinaldis, A., *Pinoteca del Museo Nazionale di Napoli*, Naples.

Fry, R., "Exhibition of Old Masters at the Grafton Galleries," *Burlington Magazine*, November, p. 71.

Mesnil, J., *L'art au Nord et au Sud des Alpes à l'époque de la Renaissance*, Brussels.

Venturi, A., *Storia dell'Arte Italiana*, Milan, 7/1, pp. 643ff.

1912

Kurt, W., *Die Darstellung des nachten Menschen in dem Quattrocento von Florenz*, Berlin.

Mesnil, J., "Per la storia della Cappella Brancacci," *Rivista d'Arte*, 7, p. 34 and 8, pp. 34–40.

Woermann, K., *Von Apelles zu Böcklin und weiter*, Esslingen, pp. 41–48.

1913

Kern, G. J., "Das Dreifaltigkeits Fresko von S. Maria Novella," *Jahrbuch der königlich preussischen Kunstsammlungen*, pp. 36–58.

Mesnil, J., "La fresque de la Trinité etc.," *Bulletin de l'Art ancien et moderne*, pp. 223–24.

1914

Mesnil, J., "Masaccio et la théorie de la perspective," *Revue de l'Art ancien et moderne*, pp. 145–46.

1920

Gamba, C., "Il Palazzo e la raccolta Horne a Firenze," *Dedalo*, 1, p. 177.

Wieleitner, H., "Zur Erfindung der verschiedenen Distanzkonstruktionen in der malerischen Perspektive," *Repertorium für Kunstwissenschaft*, p. 253.

1921

Bode, W., *Beschreibendes Verzeichnis der Gemälde im Kaiser-Friedrich Museum*, Berlin and Leipzig.

Giglioli, O. H., *Masaccio*, Florence.

1922

Escher, K., *Malerei der Renaissance in Italien*, 1, Berlin.

1923

Bode, W., *Die Kunst der Frührenaissance in Italien*, Berlin, pp. 34–35.

Schubring, P., *Cassoni*, Leipzig.

1923–1924

Schmarsow, A., "Masolino oder Masaccio in Neapel?" *Repertorium für Kunstwissenschaft*, pp. 289–93.

1924

Popovitch, S., "Conception of Space in Old Masters," *Burlington Magazine*, p. 227.

Somaré, E., *Masaccio*, Milan.

1925

Chiappelli, A., "Masaccio e Filippino," *Arte del Rinascimento*, pp. 370ff.

Schmarsow, A., "Neue Beiträge zu Masolino und Masaccio," *Belvedere*, pp. 145–47.

1926

Beenken, H., "Masaccio," *Belvedere*, pp. 167–78.

Chiappelli, A., "Un capolavoro antico sotto nuova luce," *Il Marzocco*, June 20.

Mesnil, J., "Masaccio and the Antique," *Burlington Magazine*, 48, pp. 91–98.

1927

Dvořák, M., *Geschichte der italienischen Kunst im Zeitalter der Renaissance*, Munich, 1, pp. 47–62.

Longhi, R., *Piero della Francesca*, Rome.

Mesnil, J., *Masaccio et les débuts de la Renaissance*, L'Aja.

Salmi, M., "Gli affreschi di Castiglione Olona," *Dedalo*, 8, pp. 227ff.

1928

Gamba, C., "L'influsso di Masaccio nel Quattrocento," *Il Marzocco*, April 8.

Mesnil, J., "Die Kunstlehre der Frührenaissance im Werke Masaccios," in *Vorträge 1925–1926, Bibliothek Warburg*, Leipzig, pp. 122–46.

Schmarsow, A., *Masolino und Masaccio*, Leipzig.

Tarchiani, N., "La fortuna di Masaccio," *Il Marzocco*, April 22.

Van Marle, R., *The Development of the Italian Schools of Painting*, The Hague, 10, pp. 251–307.

1929

Bacchi, G. et al., "Per Masaccio nel V Centenario della sua morte," *Rivista Storica Carmelitana*, July–September.

Berenson, B., "Un nuovo Masaccio," *Dedalo*, pp. 331–36.

Giglioli, O. H., "Masaccio (saggio de bibliografia ragionata)," *Bolletino del R. Istituto di Arch. e Storia dell'Arte*, 3, pp. 55–101.

Gronau, G., s.v. "Filippino Lippi," in U. Thieme and F. Becker, *Allgemeines Lexikon der bildenden Künstler*, 23, Leipzig.

Mengin, U., *Les deux Lippi*, Paris.

Mesnil, J. "Masolino ou Masaccio?" *Gazette des Beaux-Arts*, pp. 206–9.

Pittaluga, M., "Masaccio e L. B. Alberti," *Rassegna italiana*, pp. 779–90.

Pittaluga, M., "Rinascimento italiano," *L'Arte*, pp. 90–93.

Pittaluga, M., Review of J. Mesnil, *Masaccio et les débuts de la Renaissance*, *Belvedere*, pp. 240ff.

Sacher, H., *Die Ausdruckskraft der Farbe bei Filippino*, Strassburg.

Salmi, M., "L'autoritratto di Masaccio nella Cappella Brancacci," *Rivista Storica Carmelitana*, pp. 99ff.

1929–1930

Beenken, H., "Zum Werke des Masaccio, II: Die Altarbilder für S. Maria Maggior in Florenz," *Zeitschrift für bildende Kunst*, pp. 156–65 and 112–19.

Stechow, W., "Zum Masaccio-Masolino Problem," *Zeitschrift für bildende Kunst*, 63, pp. 125–27.

1930

Berenson, B., "A New Masaccio," *Art in America*, pp. 45–53.

Brockhaus, H., "Die Brancacci-Kapelle in Florenz," *Mitteilungen des Kunsthistorisches Institutes in Florenz*, 3, pp. 160–82.

Giglioli, O. H., s.v. "Masaccio," in U. Thieme and F. Becker, *Allegemeines Lexikon der bildenden Künstler*, Leipzig, 24, pp. 193–95.

Kleinschmidt, B., *Die Heilige Anna*, Dusseldorf.

Pittaluga, M., "La critica e i valori romantici di Masaccio," *L'Arte*, pp. 139–64.

Schmarsow, A., "Zur Masolino-Masaccio Forschung," *Zeitschrift für bildende Kunst*, 64, April, pp. 1–3.

Venturi, L., "A Madonna by Masaccio," *Burlington Magazine*, 57, pp. 21–27.

Venturi, L., "Contributi a Masolino, Lorenzo Salimbeni e Iacopo Bellini," *L'Arte*, p. 165.

1931

Lindberg, H., *To the Problem of Masolino and Masaccio*, Stockholm.

Venturi, L., *Pitture italiane in America*, Milan.

1932

Beenken, H., "Masaccio und Masolinos Fresken von San Clemente in Rom," *Belvedere*, pp. 7–13.

Berenson, B., *Italian Pictures of the Renaissance*, Oxford.

Bodmer, H., "Der Spätstil des Filippino Lippi," *Pantheon*, 9, pp. 126ff. and 10, pp. 353ff.

Colasanti, A., "Masaccio," *Leonardo*, pp. 436ff.

Mesnil, J., "Vues nouvelles sur l'art de Masaccio," *Revue de l'Art ancien et moderne*, 62, pp. 145–62.

Procacci, U., "L'incendio della chiesa del Carmine del 1771: *La Sagra* di Masaccio; gli affreschi della cappella di San Giovanni," *Rivista d'Arte*, 14, pp. 141–232.

Procacci, U., "Documenti e ricerche sopra Masaccio e la sua famiglia," *Rivista d'Arte*, pp. 489–503.

Salmi, M., *Masaccio*, Rome.

Trenkler, F. "Beiträge zur Masaccio-Forschung," *Wiener Jahrbuch für Kunstgeschichte*, pp. 7–16.

1933

Brizio, A. M., Reviews of M. Salmi, J. Mesnil and H. Beenken, *L'Arte*, pp. 147–49.

Oertel, R., "Die Frühwerke des Masaccio," *Marburger Jahrbuch für Kunstwissenschaft* (Marburger/Lahn), 7, pp. 191–289.

1933–1934

Procacci, U., "Relazione dei lavori eseguiti nella chiesa del Carmine de Firenze per la ricerca di antichi affreschi," *Bollettino d'Art del Ministero della Pubblica Istruzione*, 27, pp. 327–34.

1934

Ciaranfi, A. M., s.v. "Filippino Lippi," *Enciclopedia Italiana*, 21.

Gamba, C., Review of M. Salmi, *Masaccio* (1932), *Pan*, 2, November, pp. 470–72.

Oertel, R., "Masaccio und die Geschichte der Freskotechnik," *Jahrbuch der preussischen Kunstsammlungen*, 55, pp. 229–40.

Salmi, M., *Masaccio*, Paris.

Toesca, P., s.v. "Masaccio," *Enciclopedia Italiana*, 22.

Kennedy, R. Wedgwood, Review of M. Salmi, *Masaccio* (1932), *Art Bulletin*, pp. 396–97.

1935

Pittaluga, M., *Masaccio*, Florence.

Procacci, U., "Documenti e ricerche sopra Masaccio e la sua famiglia," *Rivista d'Arte*, pp. 91ff.

Scharf, A., *Filippino Lippi*, Vienna.

Wasserman, G., *Masaccio und Masolino*, Strassburg.

1936

Meiss, M., "The Madonna of Humilty," *Art Bulletin*, 18, p. 435.

1937

Cecchelli, C., *Iconografia dei Papi*, Rome.

Morassi, A., "Die Fresken des Masolino in Baptisterium vom Castiglione Olona," *Pantheon*, 19, pp. 72ff.

1938

Goldberg, E. L., *Patterns in Late Medici Art Patronage*, Princeton.

Neilson, K. B., *Filippino Lippi*, Cambridge, Mass.

1939

Bargellini, P., *Città di pittori*, Florence.

Fiocco, G., "Dodici stazioni dell'arte: Masaccio, o la conquista dello spazio," *Domus*, February, no. 134, pp. 81–82.

Gamba, C., "Masaccio," *Emporium*, April, pp. 173–88.

1940

Longhi, R., "Fatti di Masolino e di Masaccio," *Critica d'Arte*, 3–4, pp. 145–91.

Oertel, R., "Wandmalerei und Zeichnung in Italien," *Mitteilungen des Kunsthistorisches Institutes in Florenz*, pp. 217ff.

1940–1954

Paatz, W. and E., *Die Kirchen von Florenz*, 6 vols., Frankfurt.

1941

Hamann, R., "Masaccio und Filippino Lippi," in *Festschrift für Wilhelm Waetzoldt. . . .*, Berlin, pp. 81ff.

1942

Longhi, R., in *Umanità e germanesimo*, Florence.

1943

Lavagnino, E., "Dicesi è morto a Roma," *Emporium*, pp. 97ff.

Salmi, M., *Civiltà fiorentina del primo Rinascimento*, Florence.

1944

Gengaro, M. L., *Umanesimo e Rinascimento*, Turin.

Toesca, P., *Masolino a Castiglione Olona*, Milan.

1945

Toesca, E. Berti, "Per *La Sagra* di Masaccio," *Arti Figurative*, 3, pp. 148–50.

Fiocco, G., *Pittura toscana del Quattrocento*, Novara, pp. xii–xv.

1946

Proccaci, U., in *Mostra d'opere d'arte restaurate*, Florence, pp. 45–46.

1947

Pittaluga, M., in *Dizionario Letterario Bompiani*, Milan, 4, pp. 571–72.

Salmi, M., *Masaccio*, Milan, 2nd edition.

1948

Antal, F., *Florentine Painting and Its Social Background*, London.

Steinbart, K., *Masaccio*, Vienna.

1949

Ragghianti, C. L., Notes to *Le Vite* by G. Vasari, Milan, pp. 325–27.

1950

Longhi, R., "Recupero di un Masaccio," *Paragone*, 5, pp. 3–5.

Longhi, R., "Gli affreschi del Carmine, Masaccio e Dante," *Paragone*, 9, pp. 3–7.

Pittaluga, M., Review of M. Salmi, *Masaccio* (1948, 2nd ed.), *Rivista d'Arte*, 26, pp. 229ff.

Scharf, A., *Filippino Lippi*, Vienna.

1951

Clark, K., "An Early Quattrocento Triptych from Santa Maria Maggiore, Rome," *Burlington Magazine*, pp. 339–47.

Davies, M., *The Earlier Italian Schools*, National Gallery Catalogues, London.

Galetti, U. and E. Camesasca, s.v. "Cernusco," *Enciclopedia della Pittura Italiana*.

Procacci, U., *Masaccio*, Milan, (2nd ed. 1952).

1952

Longhi, R., "Presenza di Masaccio nel trittico della Neve," *Paragone*, 25, pp. 8–16.

Meiss, M., "London's New Masaccio," *Art News*, 51, pp. 24–25.

Paatz, W. and E., *Die Kirchen von Florenz*, Frankfort, 3, pp. 201ff.

Pope-Hennessy, J., "The Santa Maria Maggiore Altarpiece," *Burlington Magazine*, p. 31.

Ragghianti, C. L., Review of U. Procacci, *Masaccio* (1951), *Sele-Arte*, 2.

Salmi, M., "Gli scomparti della pala di S. Maria Maggiore acquistati dalla National Gallery," *Commentari*, pp. 14–21.

Salmi, M., s.v. "Masaccio," *Enciclopedia Cattolica*, Vatican, 8, pp. 266–71.

Salvini, R., *Catalogo della Galleria degli Uffizi*, Florence.

1953

Grassi, L., *Tutta la pittura di Gentile da Fabriano*, Milan.

Procacci, U., "Sulla cronologia delle opere di Masaccio e di Masolino tra il 1425 e il 1428," *Rivista d'Arte*, pp. 3–55.

1954

Baldini, U., "Masaccio," *Catalogo della Mostra di Quattro Maestri del Primo Rinascimento*, Florence, pp. 11–17.

Baldini, U., "Restauri dei dipinti fiorentini in occasione della Mostra di quattro maestri del Rinascimento," *Bollettino d'Arte*, pp. 221–40.

1955

Argan, G. C., "Le peinture en Italie centrale—Masaccio," in Lassaigne, J. and G. C. Argan, *De Van Eyck à Botticelli*, Geneva, pp. 83–97.

Carrà, C., "Masaccio," in *Il Cinquecento* (Libera Cattedra di Storia della Civiltà fiorentina), Florence, pp. 209–16.

1956

Hauser, A., *Storia sociale dell'arte*, Italian trans., 2, Turin.

Procacci, U., "Il Vasari e la conservazione degli affreschi della Cappella Brancacci al Carmine e della Trinità in S. Maria Novella," *Scritti in onore di L. Venturi*, pp. 211–22.

1957

Baldini, U. and L. Berti, *Prima mostra de affreschi staccati*, Florence.

Berti, L. and U. Baldini, *Filippino Lippi*, Florence.

Brandi, C., "Filippino e l'ultimo quattrocentista," *Saggi su Filippino Lippi*, Florence, pp. 35ff.

Brandi, C., "I cinque anni cruciali per la pittura fiorentina del '400," *Studi in onore di M. Marangoni*, Pisa, pp. 167–75.

Chastel, A., *L'Arte Italiana*, Italian trans., Florence.

Fiocco, G., "Incontro tra Filippino e Masaccio," in *Saggi su Filippino Lippi*, Florence, pp. 87ff.

Mariani, V., "L'Arte di Filippino Lippi," in *Saggi su Filippino Lippi*, Florence, pp. 73ff.

Salvini, R., "Botticelli e Filippino," in *Saggi su Filippino Lippi*, Florence, pp. 53ff.

1958

Baldini, U., in *Seconda mostra di affreschi staccati*, Florence.

De Tolnay, C., "Renaissance d'une fresque," *L'Oeil*, January, pp. 37–41.

Gamba, F., *Filippino Lippi nella storia della critica*, Florence. (Extensive bibliography.)

Procacci, U., *La tecnica degli antichi affreschi e il loro distacco e restauro*, Florence.

1959

Gori-Montanelli, L., *Architettura e paesaggio nella pittura toscana*, Florence.

Micheletti, E., *Masolino da Panicale*, Milan.

Offner, R., "Light on Masaccio's Classicism," in *Studies in the History of Art dedicated to W. Suida*, London, pp. 66–73.

Parronchi, A., "Le due tavole prospettiche del Brunelleschi," *Paragone*, 109, p. 3.

Salvini, R., *Pittura Italiana, il Quattrocento*, Milan, pp. 8–17.

1960

Antal, F., *La pittura fiorentina e il suo ambiente sociale nel Trecento e nel primo Quattrocento*, Italian trans., Turin.

Borsook, E., *The Mural Painters of Tuscany*, London.

Francastel, P., *Lo spazio figurativo dal Rinascimento al Cubismo*, Turin.

Procacci, U., *Sinopie e affreschi*, Milan.

Ragghianti, C. L., in *Critica d'Arte*, 37, pp. 28ff.

1961

Berenson, B., *I disegni dei pittori fiorentini*, Milan, s. 1, p. 272, n.1.

Berti, L. "Masaccio 1422," *Commentari*, pp. 84–107.

Borsook, E., "A note on Masaccio in Pisa," *Burlington Magazine*, pp. 212–15.

Davies, M., *The Earlier Italian School*, National Gallery Catalogues, London, 2nd ed.

Meller, P., "La Cappella Brancacci: problemi ritrattistici e iconografici," *Acropoli*, 3, pp. 186ff. and 4, pp. 273ff.

1961–1962

Brandi, C., "Masaccio," Course handout, University of Palermo.

1962

Acton, H., *Gli ultimi Medici*, Turin.

Baldini, U., s.v. "Masaccio," *Enciclopedia Universale dell'Arte*, Rome, pp. 866–77.

Baldini, U., s.v., "Masolino," *Enciclopedia Universale dell'Arte*, Rome, pp. 920–24.

Berti, L., "Masaccio a S. Giovenale di Cascia," *Acropoli*, pp. 149–65.

Carli, E., *L'arte nel Rinascimento*, Milan, pp. 119–21.

Chiarini, E., "Una citazione della *Sagra* di Masaccio nel Ghirlandaio," *Paragone*, 149, pp. 53–55 and figs. 54–56.

Gioseffi, D., "Domenico Veneziano l'esordio masaccesco e la tavola con i SS. Girolamo e Giovanni Battista della National Gallery di Londra, *Emporium*, February, pp. 51–72.

LaJos, V., *Masolino és Róma*, Budapest.

Lankheit, K., *Florentinische Barockplastik: die Kunst am Hofe der letzen Medici 1670–1743*, Munich.

1963

Berenson, B., *Italian Pictures of the Renaissance, Florentine School*, London.

Brandi, C., *Teoria del restauro*, Rome.

Carli, E., *Rinascimento fiorentino*, Novara.

Meiss, M., "Masaccio and the Early Renaissance: The Circular Plan," *Studies in Western Art* (Acts of the 20th International Congress of the History of Art), Princeton, 2, pp. 123–45.

Oertel, R., "Perspective and Imagination," *Studies in Western Art* (Acts of the 20th International Congress of the History of Art), Princeton, 2, pp. 146–59.

Schlegel, U., "Observations on Masaccio's Trinity Fresco in S. Maria Novella," *Art Bulletin*, March, pp. 19–33.

1964

Barocchi, P., *Catalogo della Mostra di disegni, manoscritti e documenti de Michelangelo*, Florence.

Berti, L., *Masaccio*, Milan.

Gioseffi, D., s.v. "Prospettiva," *Enciclopedia Universale dell'Arte*, 11, p. 142, Pl. 120.

Verzeichniss der Gemälde in Museum Dahlem, Berlin.

Meiss, M., "The Altered Program of the Santa

Maria Maggiore Altarpiece," in *Studien zur toskanischen Kunst, Festschrift für L. H. Heydenreich*, Munich.

Previtali, G., *La fortuna dei Primitivi*, Turin.

1965

Bologna, F., *Gli affreschi della Cappella Brancacci*, Milan.

De Tolnay, C., "Note sur l'iconographie des fresques de la Chapelle Brancacci," in "Studi in onore di Giusta Nicco Fasola," *Arte Lombarda*, 10, pp. 69ff.

Fresques de Florence, exhib. catalog, Brussels.

Murray, P., in *Apollo*.

Procacci, U., *Masaccio e la Cappella Brancacci*, Florence.

Shell, C., "Francesco d'Antonio e Masaccio," *Art Bulletin*, 47, pp. 465–69.

1966

Berti, L., "Donatello e Masaccio," *Antichità Viva*, 5, no. 3, pp. 3–12.

Bologna, F., *Masaccio*, Milan.

Boskovits, M., "Giotto Born Again," *Zeitschrift für Kunstgeschichte*, 29, no. 1, pp. 51–56.

Parronchi, A., *Masaccio*, Florence.

Parronchi, A., "Prospettiva in Donatello e Masaccio," *Rassegna della istruzione artistica*, 1, no. 2, pp. 29–42.

Parronchi, A., *Studi su la dolce prospettiva*, Milan.

Pope-Hennessy, J., *The Portrait in the Renaissance*, London.

Shearman, J., "Masaccio's Pisa Altarpiece: An Alternative Reconstruction," *Burlington Magazine*, 108, pp. 449–55.

Simson, O. V., "Über die Bedeutung im Masaccios Trinitätsfresco in S. Maria Novella," *Jahrbuch der Berliner Museen*, 8.

1967

Berti, L., *Masaccio*, English trans., State College, Pa.

Clark, K., *Il nudo*, Milan.

Salmi, M., *Civiltà fiorentina del primo Rinascimento*, Florence.

von Einem, H., *Masaccios Zinsgroschen*, Cologne.

1968

Argan, G. C., *Storie dell'Arte italiana*, 2, Florence.

Berti, L., *L'opera completa di Masaccio*, Milan.

Chiarini, M., *Masaccio e la pittura del Quattrocento in Toscana*, Milan.

Sellheim, R., "Die Madonna mit der Schahâda," in *Festschrift Werner Caskel*, Leyden, pp. 308–15.

1969

Boskovits, M., *Mariotto di Cristofano: Un contributo all'ambiente culturale di Masaccio giovane*, Milan.

Chastel, A., *Le Mithe de la Renaissance*, Geneva.

Del Bravo, C., *Masaccio, tutte le opere*, Florence.

Fremantle, R., "Masaccio e l'antico," *Critica d'Arte*, 103, pp. 39–56.

1970

Fremantle, R., "Masaccio e l'Angelico," *Antichità Viva*, 6, pp. 39–49.

1971

Beck, J. H., "Masaccio's Early Career as a Sculptor," *Art Bulletin*, 53, pp. 177–95.

Polzer, J., "The Anatomy of Masaccio's *Holy Trinity*," *Jahrbuch der Berliner Museen*, 13, pp. 18–59.

Previtali, G., s.v. "Masaccio," *Encyclopaedia Universalis*, Paris, p. 252.

Salmi, M., *Civiltà artistica della terra aretina*, Novara.

1972

Dempsey, C., "Masaccio's *Trinity*: Altarpiece or Tomb," *Art Bulletin*, 54, 3, pp. 279–81.

Il tesoro di Lorenzo il Magnifico, exhib. cat., Florence.

Piva, G., *L'arte del restauro*, Milan.

Vayer, L., "Porträtproblem in Masaccios Kunst," *Jahrbuch des Kunsthistorischen Institutes der Universität, Graz*, 7, pp. 29–49.

1973

Fremantle, R., "Some documents concerning Masaccio and his mother's second family," *Burlington Magazine*, pp. 516–18.

Longhi, R., *Da Cimabue a Morandi*, Vicenza.

Watkins, L. B., "Technical observation on the frescoes of the Brancacci Chapel," *Mitteilungen des Kunsthistorisches Institutes in Florenz*, pp. 68–74.

1974

Ragghianti, L. C., *Il Libro de' Disegni del Vasari*, Florence.

1975

Boskovits, M., *Pittura fiorentina alla vigilia del Rinascimento*, Florence.

von Kritter, A. D., *Studien zum Petruszyklus in der Brancacci-Kapelle*, Berlin.

Fremantle, R., *Florentine Painting from Giotto to Masaccio*, London.

Fremantle, R., "Some New Masolino Documents," *Burlington Magazine*, pp. 117ff. and 659ff.

Longhi, R., "'Fatti di Masolino e di Masaccio' e altri studi sul Quattrocento," in *Opere complete de Roberto Longhi*, 8/1, pp. 3–65.

Marcucci, M. and A. Parronchi, *Marcucci, imitazioni di Masaccio*, Florence.

1976

Micheletti, E. *Gentile da Fabriano*, Milan.

Procacci, U., "Nuove testimonianze su Masaccio," *Commentari*, 27, pp. 223–37.

Romby, G. C., *Descrizioni e rappresentazioni della città di Firenze nel XV secolo*, Florence.

1977

Molho, A., "The Brancacci Chapel: Studies in Its Iconography and History," *Journal of the Warburg and Courtauld Institutes*, 40, pp. 50–98.

Parronchi, A., "Una *Nostra Donna* del Brunelleschi," *La Nazione*, January 15, 1977 (reprinted in *L'albero*, 58, 1977, pp. 28–30).

Ragghianti, C. L., *Filippo Brunelleschi, un uomo un universo*, Florence.

Wellver, W., "Narrative Method and Narrative Form in Masaccio's *Tribute Money*," *Art Quarterly*, pp. 40–58.

Wittkower, R., *Dall'antichità al Novecento*, Turin.

1978

Amaducci, B., *La Cappella Brancacci e l'opera di Masaccio*, Florence.

Baldini, U., *Teoria del restauro e unità di metodologio*, 2 vols., Florence, (1, 1978; 2, 1981).

Beck, J. H., *Masaccio: The Documents*, (The Harvard University Center for Italian Renaissance Studies, Villa I Tatti), Locust Valley, New York.

Beck, J. H., "Una prospettiva . . . di mano di Masaccio," in *Studies in Late Medieval and Renaissance Painting in Honor of Millard Meiss*, New York, pp. 48–53.

De Juliis, J., "La Cappella Riccardi in S. Pancrazio a Firenze," *Commentari*, 1–4, pp. 137ff.

Del Bravo, C., "Nicchia con crocefisso e statue," in *Essays Presented to Myron P. Gilmore*, Florence, 2, pp. 131–32.

Fremantle, R., "Note sulla parentela di Mariotto di Cristofano con la famiglia di Masaccio," *Antichità Viva*, 3, pp. 52–53.

Lorenzo Ghiberti, "materia e ragionamenti," exhib. cat., Florence.

Petrioli Tofani, A. M., *Masaccio*, Florence.

Wakayama, Eiko M. L., "Lettura iconografica egli affreschi della Cappella Brancacci: analisi dei gesti e della composizione," *Commentari*, 1–4, pp. 72–80.

1979

Cinelli, B. and F. Mazzocca, *Fortuna visiva di Masaccio nella grafica e nella fotografia*, exhib. cat., San Giovanni Valdarno and Florence.

Gli Uffizi, catalogo generale, Florence.

Procacci, U., "Masaccio e la sua famiglia negli antichi documenti," in *La Storia del Valdarno*, 2, no. 24, September 1981, pp. 553ff.

Shapley, F., *Catalogue of the Italian Paintings*, National Gallery, 1, Washington, D.C.

1980

Barocchi, P., *Palazzo Vecchio: committenza e collezionismo medicei*, exhib. cat., Florence.

Borsook, E., *The Mural Painters of Tuscany*, Oxford, 2nd ed.

Brandi, C., *Disegno della pittura italiana*, Turin.

Cole, B., *Masaccio and the Art of Early Renaissance Florence*, Bloomington, Ind.

Goffen, R., "Masaccio's *Trinity* and the Letter to the Hebrews," *Memorie domenicane*, 11, pp. 489–504.

Procacci, U., *Masaccio*, Florence.

Romanini, A., "Arnolfo e gli 'Arnolfo' apocrifi," in *Roma Anno 1300*, Atti del 24th Congresso Internazionale di Storia dell'Arte Medieval, Rome, May 19–24 (pub. 1983, pp. 27ff.)

Wohl, H., *Domenico Veneziano*, Oxford and New York.

1981

Berti, L., "*La Trinità* di Masaccio," in *Santa Maria Novella*, Florence, pp. 127–32.

Casazza, O., *Il restauro pittorico nell'unità di metodologia*, Florence.

Procacci, U., "Masaccio e la sua famiglia negli antichi documenti," *La storia del Valdarno*, 2, no. 24, pp. 553ff.

Watkins, L. B., *The Brancacci Chapel Frescoes: Meaning and Use* (1976), Ann Arbor.

Zibaldone Baldinucciano, ed. by B. Santi, Florence.

1982

Baldini, U., *Metodo e ricerca, operatività e ricerca nel restauro*, Florence.

Berti, L., "Diario dagli Uffizi: il disegno di Masaccio," *Nuova Antologia*, 117, pp. 252–70.

1983

Baldini, U., and O. Casazza, *The Crucifix by Cimabue*, Milan.

Langedijk, K., *The Portraits of the Medici*, 2, Florence.

Volpe, C., "Il lungo percorso del 'dipingere dolcissimo e tanto unito,'" *Storia dell'Arte italiana*, Turin, 5, p. 255, note.

1984

Una mostra di Masaccio in casa di Masaccio, exhib. cat., San Giovanni Valdarno and Florence.

Baldini, U., "Nuovi affreschi nella Cappella Brancacci, Masaccio e Masolino," *Critica d'Arte*, 49, no. 1, pp. 65–72.

Micheletti, E. et al., *Masaccio e l'Angelico, due capolavori della Diocesi di Fiesole*, exhib. cat., Fiesole.

L'opera ritrovata, exhib. cat., Florence.

Procacci, U., "La Cappella Brancacci, vicende storiche," in "La Cappella Brancacci," *Quaderni del restauro*, 1, pp. 9ff.

Procacci, U. and U. Baldini, "La Cappella Brancacci nella chiesa del Carmine a Firenze," *Quaderni del restauro*, 1, pp. 9–12 and 20.

1985

Collareta, M., in *Omaggio a Donatello*, exhib. cat., Florence.

Himmelmann, N., "Nudità ideale," *Memoria dell'Antico*, 2, pp. 191–278.

Paolucci, A., *Il Museo della Collegiate di S. Andrea in Empoli*, Florence.

Sisi, C., *Michelangelo e i maestri del Quattrocento*, Florence.

1986

Adorno, P., *L'arte italiana*, 2, Florence.

Baldini, U., "Restauro della Cappella Brancacci, primi risultati," *Critica d'Arte*, 51, no. 9, pp. 65–68.

Beck, S., *Masaccio: i documenti*, San Giovanni Valdarno, Florence.

Berti, L., "L'ambiente artistico fiorentino," *Art e Dossier*, 3, "Donatello," pp. 8–17.

Borsook, E., and F. Superbi Gioffredi, *Tecnica e stile: esempi di pittura murale del Rinascimento italiano*, Florence.

Casazza, O., "Il ciclo delle Storie di San Pietro e la 'Historia Salutis': nuova lettura della Cappella Brancacci," *Critica d'Arte*, 51, no. 9, pp. 69–84.

Casazza, O., "Settecento nella Cappella Brancacci," *Critica d'Arte*, 51, no. 11, pp. 66 and 68–72.

Dallaj, A., *Masolino da Panicale, le storie di Maria e del Battista a Castiglione Olona*, Milan.

Jacobsen, W. "Die Konstruktion der Perspektive bei Masaccio und Masolino in der Brancacci Kapelle," *Marburger Jahrbuch für Kunstwissenschaft*, 21, pp. 73ff.

Paolucci, A., in *Capolavori e restauri*, exhib. cat., Florence, p. 425.

Pope-Hennessy, J., *La scultura italiana del Rinascimento: Saggi*, Turin.

1987

Baldini, U., "Prime risultanze per il restauro," *Quaderni del restauro*, 3, pp. 21ff.

Bocci Pacini, P., "Nota archeologica sulla nascita di Venere," *Gli Uffizi, studi e ricerche*, no. 4, p. 22.

Boskovits, M., "Il percorso di Masolino: precisazioni sulla cronologia e sul catalogo," *Arte Cristiana*, 718, pp. 45ff.

Briganti, G., "E Masaccio torna a brillare," *La Repubblica*, January 2.

Colle, E., *Masaccio*, Montepulciano.

Frosinini, C., "Alcune precisazioni su Mariotto di Cristofano," *Rivista d'Arte*, pp. 443ff.

Guarducci, M., "Un Arnolfo di meno: Riflessioni sulla statua bronzea di S. Pietro nella Basilica Vaticana," *Xenia*, 14, pp. 111–18.

Pandimiglio, L., "Felice di Michele *vir clarissimus* e una consorteria: i Brancacci di Firenze," *Quaderni del restauro*, 3.

Petrucci, F., "La pittura a Firenze nel Quattrocento," in *La pittura in Italia: il Quattrocento*, Milan, 1, pp. 272–301.

Pisani, R. Proto, *Masolino a Empoli*, Empoli.

Tazartes, M., "La pittura a Pisa e a Lucca nel Quattrocento," in *La pittura in Italia: il Quattrocento*, Milan, 1, pp. 305–14.

Wakayama, Eiko M. L., "Masolino o non Masolino. . . . ," *Arte Cristiana*, 719, pp. 125–36.

1987–1988

Gurrieri, F., and R. Cecchi, "Masolino da Panicale e la chiesa di Villa a Castiglione Olona," *Rivista d'Arte*, 43, pp. 93ff.

1988

Baldini, U., in *I pittori della Brancacci agli Uffizi*, Florence.

Baldini, U., "Le figure di Adamo e Eva formate affatto ignude in una cappella di una principale chiesa di Fiorenza," *Critica d'Arte*, 53, no. 16, pp. 72–77.

Berti, L., *Masaccio*, Florence.

Bocci Pacini, P., "Umanesimo in Masolino," *Gli Uffizi, studi e ricerche*, no. 5, p. 22.

Briganti, G., "Masaccio oltre il Medioevo" (interview by Stefano Malatesta), in "Masaccio e Piero," *La Repubblica*, supplement to no. 239, November 2, pp. 4–26.

Caneva, C. "L'ultimo della Brancacci," *Gli Uffizi, studi e ricerche*, no. 5, pp. 85ff.

Caneva, C. and B. Pacciani, in *Masaccio restituito*, Reggello.

Casazza, O., "La grande gabbia architettonica di Masaccio," *Critica d'Arte*, 53, no. 16, pp. 78–97.

Guarducci, M., "Riflessioni sulla statua bronzea di S. Pietro nella Basilica Vaticana," *Xenia*, 18, pp. 57ff.

Settis, S., A. La Regina and G. Agosti Farinella, *La colonna Traiana*, Turin.

Verdon, T., "La Sant'Anna Metterza: riflessioni, domande, ipotesi," *Gli Uffizi, studi e ricerche*, no. 5, pp. 33–58.

1989

Baldini, U., "Dalla scoperta di San Giovenale a quella della Brancacci," *Gli Uffizi, studi e ricerche*, no. 5, pp. 16–18.

Baldini, U., "Del *Tributo* e altro di Masaccio," *Critica d'Arte*, 54, no. 20, pp. 29–38.

Berti, L. and R. Foggi, *Masaccio*, Florence.

Bologna, F., "Nota," *La Nazione*, December 7.

Casazza, O., "Al di là dell'immagine," *Gli Uffizi, studi e ricerche*, no. 5, pp. 93ff.

Casazza, O., "La documentazione grafica della Cappella Brancacci," in O. Casazza and P. Cassinelli Lazzeri, *La Cappella Brancacci, conservazione e restauro nei documenti della grafica antica*, Modena.

Casazza, O. and P. Cassinelli Lazzeri, *La Cappella Brancacci, conservazione e restauro nei documenti della grafica antica*, Modena.

Cresti, C., "Cappella Brancacci, una proposta: di quell'altare farne un paravento," *La Nazione*, November 15.

Cuccini, G., *Arnolfo di Cambio*, Perugia.

Giuliano, A., *I cammei, dalla Collezione Medicea del Museo Archeologico di Firenze*, Rome.

Lorber, M., in *Critica d'Arte*, 14, p. 43.

Mori, G., Review of L. Berti, *Masaccio* (1988), *Art e Dossier*, March.

Nardi, G., "Cappella Brancacci: la storicizzazione, restauri e valori," *La Nazione*, November 23.

Nardi, G., "Cappella Brancacci: una storia fiorentina," *La Nazione*, November 12.

Natali, A., Review of L. Berti, *Masaccio* (1988), *Giornale dell'Arte*, no. 64, February.

Paolucci, A., "Cappella Brancacci, è gia deciso," *La Nazione*, November 15.

Paolucci, A., "Considerazioni sulle indagini svolte per il progetto Piero," in *Un progetto per Piero della Francesca*, Florence, pp. 75–78.

Parronchi, A., "Cappella Brancacci: no all'altare," *La Nazione*, November 12.

Parronchi, A., "Torna Masaccio tra luce e colore," *Arte e Vacanze*, Florence, 2, no. 8, pp. 17–18.

Rossi, P. A., "Cappella Brancacci, una proposta: facciamola vedere 'vuota,'" *La Nazione*, November 23.

Rossi, P. A., "Lettura del *Tributo* di Masaccio," *Critica d'Arte*, 54, no. 20, pp. 39–42.

Zeri, F., "Cappella Brancacci: è un vero scandalo," *La Nazione*, November 15.

1990

Casazza, O., *Masaccio e la Cappella Brancacci*, Florence.

INDEX

Numbers in *italic* refer to pages on which illustrations appear.

E

F

G

H

I

J

K

L

M

Q

R

S